Cenk Özbay is Associate Professor of Gender Studies and Sociology in the Faculty of Arts and Social Sciences at Sabanci University. He holds a PhD in Sociology from the University of Southern California. His research interests are gender and sexualities, masculinity studies, urban sociology, work and labour, neoliberalism and mobilities. In addition to his many publications in English and Turkish, he is a co-editor of *Yeni Istanbul Calismalari* (2014) and *The Making of Neoliberal Turkey* (2016).

'*Queering Sexualities in Turkey* is a pioneering study of heterosexually-identified young men with rural family origins who engage in compensated sex with middle-class gay clients in Istanbul. It richly melds compelling ethnography, in-depth interviews, and theory within a cultural and political-economy framework. Richly rewarding his readers with a powerful intersectional analysis through thick description and theoretical depth, Cenk Özbay shows how a closely studied case illuminates broader theoretical questions central to understanding the key roles of class, the body and heteronormativity in shaping embodied masculinities and sexualities. Engaging, original, beautifully written, and distinct for its global orientation, *Queering Sexualities in Turkey* is a must-read for gender and sexuality scholars, and an invaluable teaching resource in a wide range of disciplines.'

Gul Ozyegin, Professor of Sociology and Gender, Sexuality and Women's Studies at the College of William and Mary, Virginia and editor of *Gender and Sexuality in Muslim Cultures*

'Grounded in careful observation and richly theorised, Cenk Özbay's *Queering Sexualities in Turkey* stretches and deepens our understanding of the shifting dynamics of gender relations, sexual identity and sex work in neoliberal contexts.'

Michael A. Messner, Professor of Sociology and Gender Studies at the University of Southern California and co-author of *Some Men: Feminist Allies and the Movement to End Violence Against Women*

'Cenk Özbay's innovative and inspiring study provides queer studies scholarship with a much-needed critical focus on the regional operations of class, gender and sexuality. Benefitting from a cross-disciplinary and transnational range of academic literature, Özbay's analyses prove to be a powerful intervention to existing debates on globalisation of sexualities, and the geopolitics of knowledge production in Queer Studies.'

Cuneyt Cakirlar, Lecturer in Communications, Culture and Media Studies at Nottingham Trent University

QUEERING SEXUALITIES IN TURKEY

Gay Men, Male Prostitutes and the City

CENK ÖZBAY

I.B. TAURIS
LONDON · NEW YORK

Published in 2017 by
I.B.Tauris & Co. Ltd
London • New York
www.ibtauris.com

Copyright © 2017 Cenk Özbay

The right of Cenk Özbay to be identified as the author of this work has been asserted by the author in accordance with the Copyright, Designs and Patents Act 1988.

All rights reserved. Except for brief quotations in a review, this book, or any part thereof, may not be reproduced, stored in or introduced into a retrieval system, or transmitted, in any form or by any means, electronic, mechanical, photocopying, recording or otherwise, without the prior written permission of the publisher.

Every attempt has been made to gain permission for the use of the images in this book. Any omissions will be rectified in future editions.

References to websites were correct at the time of writing.

Library of Modern Turkey 20

ISBN: 978 1 78453 317 5
eISBN: 978 1 78672 198 3
ePDF: 978 1 78673 198 2

A full CIP record for this book is available from the British Library
A full CIP record is available from the Library of Congress

Library of Congress Catalog Card Number: available

Typeset in Garamond Three by OKS Prepress Services, Chennai, India
Printed and bound by CPI Group (UK) Ltd, Croydon, CR0 4YY

To Alper

CONTENTS

List of Photographs   viii
Acknowledgements   ix

Introduction: Queering Sexualities in Turkey   1

1. Sexuality, Masculinity and Male Sex Work   30
2. Rent Boys and the Contours of Exaggerated Masculinity   57
3. Rent Boys' Intimacies in Neoliberal Times   84
4. Queer in the Spatial, Temporal and Social Margins   105
5. Contemporary Male Sex Work   125

Conclusion: Perverse Mobilities and Deviant Careers   145

Notes   157
Bibliography   179
Index   191

LIST OF PHOTOGRAPHS

Photograph 1. A poster that hung in public spaces and some college campuses in the summer of 2015, states, 'If you see someone who is doing the ugly business of the Lot Tribe [the people of Sodom and Gomorrah], kill the actor and the subject.' The Islamic Defence, apparently an online organisation, summons the reader to kill the homosexuals. Source: Cenk Özbay   22

Photograph 2. Three consecutive gay pride parades in Istanbul: Crowded and exuberant in 2014; the police intervening with water cannons and tear gas in 2015; and the government banning the whole pride parade with extreme sanctions, while queers responded by 'not gathering but dispersing around' in 2016. Source: kaosgl.org   148

ACKNOWLEDGEMENTS

Queering Sexualities in Turkey is the outcome of sporadic engagement with research and meditation about queer sexualities, masculinities, gay identity and male sex work in Istanbul, Turkey, between the years of 2003 and 2015. Given this longer-than-usual genealogy, there are many people who helped and contributed in different contexts to the formation of this book.

While I was trying to find my own way of doing original sociological research, Gul Ozyegin, during a dinner in late 2002, encouraged me to take a closer look and eventually design a study on male sex work practices for my master's degree at Bogazici University. She was also on the committee when I defended my thesis and presented the initial findings of my research on male sex work in August 2005. Since then she has always been there to help and encourage me in any possible way, and therefore I owe this book to her unfailing support.

At the Department of Sociology at Boğaziçi University, Nukhet Sirman was my thesis supervisor and a great inspiration. I have learnt an enormous amount from her about thinking, writing and teaching as an interpretive social scientist. The late Ferhunde Ozbay, another source of motivation and passion for social research, was also on my thesis committee. She was always wholeheartedly encouraging and meticulously critical toward me. Ayfer Bartu Candan met me for the first time while I was talking about male prostitution in 2003 and since then she has been an indispensable mentor, colleague, and friend.

While I was doing my doctoral studies at the University of Southern California, my PhD advisor, Mike Messner, patiently listened to what

I told him about male sex workers and read the pieces I wrote, although rent boys and the lives of Turkish queers were not the immediate topic that I was working on under his supervision. I have learnt intricate ways of studying men and masculinities through a critical lens and the curious methods of being a pro-feminist scholar from him. I owe him huge thanks for being such a great mentor and role model for all his students, including me.

Macarena Gomez Barris has always been an influential model for me and some sections of this book benefited greatly from her brilliant ideas, questions, and suggestions. Deniz Celikel, Kerem Bozok, Muge Leyla Yildiz, Evren Savci, Yesim Yasin, Maral Erol, Joy Lam, Glenda Flores, Engin Volkan, Sinan Birdal, James Thing, Nancy Lutkehaus, Sharon Hays, Tim Biblarz, Ed Ransford, Nina Eliasoph, Lynn Casper, Jack Halberstam, Pierrette Hondagneu-Sotelo, Ken Plummer, Peter Aggleton, Richard Parker, Don Barrett, Cuneyt Cakirlar, Serkan Delice, Serdar Soydan, Semih Sokmen, Yesim Arat, Aysecan Terzioglu, Dilek Unalan, Duygu Salman and Arzu Tektas provided support on the vague line between friendship, information and thought exchange, editing and guidance of sorts. I am deeply grateful to all of these great people as well as the anonymous reviewers of the manuscript.

Sercan Tas, Sinan Can Erdal and Gokce Selim Atici worked with me as research assistants for different research projects between 2013 and 2016. Their smart and practical contributions to those other projects gave me time to better focus on this one, and my conversations with them enriched my perceptions of gender and sexualities among the next generation. My students in 'Men, Masculinities, Sexualities' and the 'Sociology of Sex Work' classes at Bogazici University also helped me to configure the concepts and arguments that shaped this book.

At I.B.Tauris, I have benefited from Maria Marsh and Sophie Rudland's editorship as well as their support, advice and tranquility. Chana Kraus-Friedberg has always been a brilliant copyeditor and she has done a great job with the manuscript. I am deeply grateful to them.

Taner Ceylan's hyperrealist paintings, and especially his 'Karanfil Hasan' (2006), have very much affected and stimulated me. It is an indescribable honour and happiness to have his painting on the cover of my book, and I would like to thank him for the permission to use it.

I am significantly indebted to my numerous informants, respondents, interlocutors and friends, 'rent boys' and gay men from different walks of life, who talked to me in person, on the phone or via the internet, for different phases of this research. I did everything possible to hide their identities to protect the privacy they generously shared with me. As a scholar of sexuality studies, I am well aware that we are only able to talk about sexualities because our precious interviewees open their most personal and embodied experiences to us. This book could not have been imagined without my informants' contribution and collaboration. Final responsibility for this work is my own.

I owe heartfelt thanks to my sister Nur Özbay Okay and my brother-in-law Ali Okay for their unfading, passionate support, which I feel every moment in my life.

Finally, my partner Alper Tumbal has always been there to share life, make it worthy and meaningful, and talk to me in the language we two have created. I cannot express my profound devotion, love and gratitude to him with words. I therefore humbly dedicate this book to him.

Kadikoy, Istanbul

INTRODUCTION

QUEERING SEXUALITIES IN TURKEY

> I found out that sexual relations can be tedious and unrewarding. These are categories and divisions in the homosexual world. The queer gets together with the queer and everybody does everything. One sucks first, and then reverse roles. How can this bring any satisfaction? What we are really looking for is our opposite. The beauty of our relationships then was that we met our opposites.
> Reinaldo Arenas, *Before Night Falls: A Memoir*, translated by Dolores M. Koch (London, 1994), p. 106

> Gay culture is utterly triumphant and completely visible. But it seems very much a body culture; not at all a bookish culture.
> Edmund White, *The Flâneur: A Stroll Through the Paradoxes of Paris* (New York, 2001), p. 79

Umit is a handsome man in his late thirties, although he looks younger. He is a good friend of mine and also one of the key informants of this book. On the day I am describing, he took me to a place near Taksim Square, the notorious city centre. The area we visited has been gentrified over the last few years. Most derelict buildings (previously owned by Armenians and Greeks) have been demolished and rebuilt alongside the larger urban renewal projects which converted a neighbouring residential district into a hotel zone with exquisite cafés and restaurants. Here, in contrast, there are apartment buildings consisting of small, cosy units owned or managed by entrepreneurs or small-scale real estate agencies. Most of these units are rented on a daily basis for modest rates. During our visit in November 2015, a minimally furnished unit with two bedrooms is rented for 100–120 liras ($35–40) for weekend nights and for 80–90 liras ($25–30) for weekday nights.

We went into one of these apartments, where Umit was invited to a party. Three young gay men in their early-to-mid twenties rented the apartment on Friday and Saturday nights. They all lived in pretentious gated communities in the western suburbs of Istanbul, almost 50 km from the urban core and far from where queer nightlife and non-heteronormative entertainment are concentrated. They told me that they came and rented an apartment here almost every weekend in order to relax and to be near gay bars and dance clubs, as well as sexual opportunities that proximity might trigger. They used the bedrooms in the apartment for intimate sexual purposes and the small living room for socialising and conversation before and after sex.

On the Saturday afternoon when we visited the apartment, there were two other guests present, in addition to the three hosts. All five people seemed somewhat stoned, apparently suffering from more than just an ordinary hangover from clubbing the night before. Later, one of the hosts told me that a variety of drugs, including weed, G[1] and ecstasy (X), are regularly consumed in these apartments and that this one of the reasons people are willing to spend money on renting them for the weekend. Partying in this cultural context thus means alcohol, drugs, music, poorly lit surroundings and sex with anybody who happens to show up at the rented apartment, whether in groups of two or more.

None of these elements, which are standard among global queer youth when they party, surprised me. What did surprise me was the inclusion of rent boys as a part of the ongoing homosocial and homosexual fun. The gay hosts find rent boys from gay dating websites and mobile phone applications, invite them over to the apartments they are renting and have sex without further contact or emotional engagement, 'no strings attached.' One of them told me that 'everything is clean this way.[2] (You are) not dealing with the guy (rent boy) at (your own) home, not afraid of theft or violence or blackmail. He does not know where you actually live. If anything goes wrong, there are people around (to intervene). So you are not all alone with a guy that you don't actually know.'

When I asked him why the party-goers prefer rent boys over self-identified gay men who would seem to be safer partners, he told me, using the fading gay slang in Turkish, *Koli nakka, hatta koli nakaranta.* (There are not many cute [gay] guys to have sex with, there are not any at all.)

He then reiterated a widely shared belief of gay men I had spoken to, saying that gays were not exciting, not masculine and not sexy. He added, 'Although some rents look like menacing bandits who steal horses (*at hirsizi*) and act in weird ways, it is still better than dealing with self-indulgent and spoiled gays. They are all (like) women (*hepsi kadin*).'

Hepsi kadin, in this context, describes gay men as not just womanly, sentimental, soft, vain or extravagant; but also useless.

Later in the evening, the hosts of the party were gossiping about a rent boy with whom they had both had good sex the previous night. One host said, 'He sits here between (the two separate sex sessions with each) and talks about how his mobile phone was old. He complains that he could not afford a new one (It) means he implicitly asks us if we were willing to buy him a new one ... or paying him more than our deal in order to help finance his new phone. We pretended to listen and suggested that he work harder and save more.'

This is always a part of the game: The rent boy asks for more money than originally agreed, for the needs of his family or some other legitimate reason to which his customers would likely relate. However, the seasoned gays look the other way, send the rent boy away without annoying him, and then make fun of him and the encounter while simultaneously talking about and evaluating the sex itself.

The several hours I spent at this particular party, my conversations with the hosts and guests and my observations of their behaviour in the quasi-public space of the apartment illustrated a new cultural, social and spatial organisation of gay subculture in Istanbul. This whole *mise en scène* is significantly different from what I had been imagining over the last 15 years. The rent boys, sexual service providers on the same-sex commercial scene, are a part of – and participants in – the continuous transmogrification of modes of communication, embodied styles, codes of masculinity and de-territorialised sociabilities among queers in Istanbul. People change, values shift, urban spaces are reshaped and affective orientations are transmuted, but male sex work and queers' discordant reactions to it somehow persist. In Marc Padilla's words, 'The more things change, it would seem, the more they stay the same,' (2007: 6). *Queering Sexualities in Turkey* is about these changes.

****

This book is also about queer spaces, subjects, possibilities and incongruities in the Turkish context. As a keen undergraduate student, I attended a lesbian and gay activist meeting for the first time in October 1998. Back then, the internet was not in active use and it was extremely difficult for me to find the location of the meeting, which was supposed to be hidden. When I got there, there were approximately 20 men (no women) arriving and leaving at every moment, and it was the most crowded queer space I had ever been at. The following month, I went to a gay bar. It was almost hypnotic to be in a small place with a dozen gay men (again there were no women), whose existence I could not have even imagined two months before. Those were exciting days, both for me and for the flourishing queer activism in Turkey. Since then, I have always been an observer of, and a participant in, queer life in Istanbul, even while I was living in the USA for my doctoral studies.

I became intrigued by queer bodies that are involved in transactional sex and the illicit organisation of male sex work in the flourishing subculture of homosexuality in Istanbul in 2002, while I was involved in research on lesbians and bisexual women (Özbay and Soydan 2003). As part of that project, I attended public meetings, conducted interviews and observed night-time sociabilities in queer bars and dance clubs. I started to become more familiar with the dynamics of same-sex prostitution performed by a certain type of men who called themselves 'rent boys.'[3] I realised gradually that a number of gay men, including people I knew in my personal life, took part in male prostitution as customers, mostly in a clandestine manner.

As I explain in this book, it is never easy to convey the meaning of being gay in Turkey, which certainly has sex-negative culture: it is considered immoral, forbidden, despicable and sinful to talk about sexuality or the sexual/reproductive/genital parts of the body in public.[4] Sociological studies on eroticism and sexuality, almost non-existent in the country, are incontrovertibly a part of this sex-negative culture. In this sense, homosexuality is one of the most poisonous social taboos in the twenty-first century, even among the most modern, secular and well-educated classes of Turkish society. Life as an out gay individual without the support and communication channels of an entrenched gay community may come with at least one (often all) of the following burdens: laborious melancholia, unemployment, discrimination, disrespect, violence and forced loneliness. The unfettered nature of homophobia makes gay men more closeted and more likely to suffer low self-esteem or even paranoia. Male sex work, under these circumstances, turns into something about which society has no relevant imagination or terminology to express deep disapproval or hatred. It is an object that no one would dare to ponder or talk about, including gay men, who may purchase sexual services from rent boys only through secrecy and denial.

****

It was after midnight, an early Sunday morning. I was exhausted and the feel of the dance club I was in, SenGel, was not helping at all. The room was full of smoke and the sound of very loud Turkish pop-disco music, and I was squeezed among desiring and exuberant bodies incessantly dancing and gazing and cruising. While trying to find a tranquil place, however temporary, I bumped into Hasan, who was headed toward the same small chair at the same time but was kind enough to offer it to me. We shared the chair and started talking. He said he lived in a working-class migrant neighbourhood in the northern end of the city. He worked at a car repair shop and hung out at the rent boy clubs of Istanbul, such as SenGel and Bientot, on weekend nights about twice a month. Caramel-skinned, tall and toned, with a fierce expression, it seemed to me that Hasan would be popular among gay customers looking to pay for sex, and it turned out that this was true. He said it was *halal* (righteous according to Islamic law) money he got from transactional sex with men. 'Still,' he added, 'It comes and goes immediately. I don't make a real profit from it.'

After we talked a bit in a non-commercial, almost cordial fashion, he left. I assumed this would be our only interaction for the night and mentally recorded our conversation to write down in my notebook when I got back to my apartment. However, I saw him again later that night. He said he had found a man who was willing to pay him for oral sex at his hotel room nearby. The sexual and financial interaction (yielding a juicy $50) between them had concluded and he was back again looking for a second chance. When I asked if he were able to perform for a second time, he laughed and bragged about his bodily strength and physical qualities. He said he just needed a short time to 'recharge' his batteries and relax. He also said that he did ejaculate during sex but did not feel any pleasure, or satisfaction. That was the reason he could easily do it again with someone else.

Hasan is quite typical of the rent boy profile I have observed for more than a decade: living with his family in a working-class neighbourhood, he had a bad school record and no academic ambition, worked in a deskilled labour-intensive workplace and was flawlessly straight-acting, saying he was sexually 'normal' (read, heterosexual) and attracted to women only. He performed sex acts with men for money but hid it from others in his life, promising himself that he would quit this 'bad habit' one day. Given the weak market structure of queer commercial sex in Istanbul, I was surprised when Hasan really did find a second liaison that night and left, assuring me that we would talk more one day. I do not think I have ever seen him again.[5]

****

Queering Sexualities in Turkey is about people like Hasan: Self-identified rent boys who identify as heterosexual men but develop 'deviant careers' by clandestinely taking part in queer sex work and the intimate economy in Istanbul. It is also about their customers, mostly middle-aged, upper-middle-class gay men from Turkey and abroad. Inevitably, this book is also about the web of relations between these two classes of men and their relationships with other significant actors in their lives, such as families and friends. Nightlife has mesmerising effects on different groups of people, as their ages, ethnic and class identities and bodily differences converge. Travels between the squatter areas and the city centre provide a context through which sexualities and mobilities are connected. The subjectivities of rent boys and gay men evolve in accordance with these 'perverse' mobilities, spatialities and temporalities. The nocturnal culture of transactional queer sex in Istanbul has its pivotal imprint in both rent boys' and gay men's lives, impacting their connections with the rhythm and the aura of the city, public morality and somatic ethics, and the articulations of multiple masculinities, as chapters in this book demonstrate. Male sex work is performed at the intersection of, and therefore provides a unique vantage point from which to understand the workings of significant governing discourses and bodily regimes, including gender identities, classed social contexts, sexual orientations, forms of self-making and intimate relations of power, as well as possible destabilisations and transformations. Briefly, *Queering Sexualities in Turkey* aims to present the reader with the panorama of male sex work in Istanbul and the interpretive universe in which the relations between rent boys and their customers are possible, (un)sustainable, meaningful and worthy.

Critical Urban Encounters

Cities house multifold urban capacities, processes and configurations of segregation. Social, cultural, political and spatial forms of segregation between different clans of urban residents are experienced daily by billions of urbanites worldwide and documented closely by urban researchers in the fields of urban anthropology and urban sociology as well as journalism and news media on television. We live, work, shop, socialise and have fun in deeply and meticulously segregated social and physical spaces in the contemporary metropolis.[6] The city today is mutually accepted and agreed upon as a place of social isolation, exclusion, indifference and 'civil inattention,' in Goffman's classical words. Our urban lives are increasingly built on the principle that we do not see, feel, speak to or touch those people who are not like us in any imaginable way. On the other hand, there are also a bevy of exceptional spaces where different classes, racial and ethnic identities, political persuasions and sexual orientations come across, connect and even interact with each other and realise social potentialities. Joel S. Migdal, for example, calls our attention to such encounters for a better comprehension of current sociabilities: 'the effects of the modernity project can be found not in examination of elites and their institutions exclusively, nor in a focus solely on the poor or marginal groups of society, but on those physical and social spaces where the two intersect.'[7] These encounters and instantaneities are multidimensional. They can be interpersonal, physical and tangible as well as discursive and incorporeal, as Carlos Ulises Decena elucidates, 'the importance of unspoken basis of connectivity for the making and sustenance of socialities [...] forms of connection that cannot be fully articulated but can be shared, intuited and known.'[8]

Highways and mass transportation, state-owned universities, shopping malls and supermarkets, public spaces and shared commons, domestic cleaning and care-giving jobs, as well as sex work, create conditions for such unpredictable contacts and alternative social forms between classes, races, ethnicities, genders and sexual identities. They push the boundaries of social engineering and social imaginary, and generate vibes of uncertainty, instability and incongruity.[9] Journalist Yildirim Turker (2005) accounts for the sense of segregation thus:

> Some of the powerful elites want to transform Istanbul, which they have designated as a chic world city as appropriate to its reputation, from struggles for profit, sharp inequality in income distribution, and its slums (*varos*) to a city similar to a diamond where all pavements are painted and its streets flowered. They are not happy with the voiceless from the slum areas, those who can look at the city only from their shelters, those who procreate fast as an insult to the elite. Having many unreachable hills and unconquerable castles, Istanbul opens itself to the slum people only in religious holidays, it presents its residency as a title that people can get only through money or fame. Nasty kids of slums, the thief youngsters, and their crowded families cannot fit into even their own places. They have started to haunt urbanites though they do not insist on being deemed as one of them. They know that even if they are tamed, they cannot look good in this city.[10]

When I started conducting this research in the early 2000s, middle-class cultures of the modern urbanites and the excluded lifestyles of the *varos*[11] people of squatter areas were differentiated and elaborated via the notion of *delikanlilik*, the codes of youth masculinity with an emphasis on of personality development and honesty. Signifiers of youth were not accentuated haphazardly. Demographically speaking, Turkey has a youth bulge. The population is young and the unemployment rate (especially for the younger urban segments) is quite high. Deindustrialisation, shrinking formal employment opportunities, ongoing migration to the metropolitan areas and the ubiquitous emergence of neoliberal

INTRODUCTION: QUEERING SEXUALITIES IN TURKEY

subjectivity and entrepreneurial selfhood, which make men think that they might have generated profit from their bodily and affective capacities, all contribute to the issues of youth and make them nebulous. While the young men from the *varos* reclaimed *delikanlilik*, it was not quite a success in middle-class urbanites' eyes. The squatter youth were not reviving what the middle classes had defined as *delikanlilik* in the past. They were just trying to escape from *kiroluk*, *magandalik* and *barzoluk* – public insults used to mark (especially) Kurdish, peasant, migrant identities, with their mismatched behaviour and misconduct in the city.[12] Another journalist, Alperen Atik, comments on this differentiation, which was clarified through the embodied modes of masculinity:

> Metrosexuality transformed even the sense of *delikanlilik* in slum areas and a new type [of masculinity] emerged: Neo-*delikanlilik*. This type deviates from the previous generations by their appearance. They put a great amount of gel on their hair, wear Adidas Tygun sneakers, buy new and cheap jean pants from the bargain stores, purchase mobile phones with cameras from the second-hand market, and listen to pirate CDs to have a taste in music. The transformation is complete, with the exception of the earring. Since piercing body parts is a taboo for the slum people, they put fake earrings without piercing their skin. The ambition to be cool (become charismatic) is very strong and it does not matter if this aspiration is second-hand, fake, pirated, faulty, or it may cause balding. What matters is to break the chains of *kiroluk* and to be accepted as an MTV kid. An alternative style of *delikanlilik* emerged with cheap hair gels, jeans from the bargain stores, second-hand mobile phones, amplified loudspeakers, and David Beckham posters.[13]

Rent boys in the early 2000s looked just like what Atik describes. They exuded the air in this portrayal: Trying to avoiding stigma but unable to avoid it completely, stuck between the two marginalising identity positions. I, however, view these attempts to stylise a masculinity based on imitation, not as emulating the hegemonic middle-class-white-Turkish-urban identity (which is structurally unavailable to these men), but as a creative and even inexpungable response to it. What rent boys and other *varoş* kids manufactured was not a cheaper copy of the middle-class taste, not an attempt to straitjacket themselves, but an assemblage of various elements of style and embodiment purloined from various resources and origins, including the middle classes, its obtainable cheap imitations, their own cultural taste, and globally exposed styles and trends, to create a unique impact on their social interlocutors. As Annick Prieur states, the originality and relative autonomy of the aestheticisation of certain predilections may have greater and more effective outcomes than imitation: 'The dominated classes may try to adopt the dominant taste and lifestyle – a strategy favoured by social climbers. Or they may content themselves with imitations or substitutes: Polyester has not the same qualities as silk, but it is much cheaper. On the other hand, a lipstick with the 'wrong' colour is not necessarily cheaper than the one with the 'right' colour, and the length of the miniskirt is not determined by its price. The popular classes have, according to Bourdieu, some autonomy of evaluation in their own aesthetic choices. And among the basic principles of this autonomous taste are a taste of necessity (they learn to like what they can afford), a taste for what is practical and functional, and a taste for what can provide a maximum of effect at minimum cost.'[14] Therefore, the embodied style of rent boys, the components of their exaggerated masculinity, or the expressions of neo-*delikanlilik*, cannot be grasped by the construction of dualities such as good/bad or real/fake. Instead, I contend that what we witness is the production of a hegemonic culture, with its own modes of urban citizenship, gendered identity and self-presentation, and the responses to this hegemonic model by hybridisation, re-articulation and incorporation by rent boys in negotiations with their own sources, references and necessities while they form their own tastes, approaches and judgments.

This process of differentiation and creating a peculiar style taken up by young men who are seen as *varoş* (or the self-identified rent boys) in the context of the social and physical segregation of Istanbul enables them to become subjects who give meaning to their milieus, providing them with a position from which to speak, negotiate the rules of conduct, decide on terms and change the deal when they desire so. In other words, they actively engage in this game of self-transformation and the results, which seem unsuccessful to outsiders, hide the real consequences of the re-stylisation that take places in their lives. In the case of queer transactional sex, the critical urban encounter between differently gendered, aged, and classed identities can happen only because of the emergence of this new subject, whose self-assurance is boosted by his creative reappropriation of style. The *varos'* high opinions about themselves, their bodies and masculinities are reiteratively constituted: They become urban, stylish, attractive, but simultaneously authentic and uncontaminated subjects of masculinity. They learn to invest in their masculinities, bodily and interactional styles, taste in cultural products and sexual and erotic boundaries, which is the subject of this book.

Queer Sexualities in Turkey

Following a social constructionist perspective on same-sex sexualities and homosexual identities throughout modern history,[15] one can discern an ambiguous time in Turkish history when there were no sexual self-identities or medical diagnoses of sexual abnormalities, yet same-sex sexual acts took place and virtually everybody had knowledge of them. This undocumented and thus ambiguous period starts from the late Ottoman Empire and continues for 100 years or more into the temporal realm of the modern Turkish Republic, which was founded in 1923. The new republic radically transfigured almost all spheres of social, cultural and political public life via various developmentalist projects, including Europeanisation, secularisation, Westernisation and modernisation. Not only the empire was abolished and a new nation created, but a new, modern subject-citizen was formed under the influence of Enlightenment ideals by state discourses, policies and practices.

In spite of this grand transformation towards the nation-state, same-sex sexual acts, or the cultural type of 'the homosexual', was not explicitly monitored, regulated, named or criminalised by the new regime. Although the state and governing elite worked meticulously on the structure of the nuclear family, the role of women in public and private spheres and the gendered politics of representation,[16] the modern revolution in Turkey was seemingly too busy to deal with, cure, ban or intervene in homosexuality. Same-sex sexual activities became a significant part of an invisible yet connived urban underground culture. Contemporary scholars trace this hazy time period through local and foreign historians' work, as well as novels and other literary forms.

Among others, the great Turkish author Kemal Tahir's numerous novels and stories and social historian Resat Ekrem Kocu's marvellous, unfinished *Encyclopaedia of Istanbul*[17] and his other books can reveal this unnamed yet fully experienced sexual riptide.

The conceptual framework that provides exact, flawless knowledge of what and how the state watches and regulates must come before the practices of surveillance, navigation and intervention. For the Turkish case, we do not have historical studies showing when (if) the state devised and put together such knowledge about homosexuality and gender-bending behaviours. The Turkish War of Independence, the occupation of Istanbul and Izmir by European soldiers in the 1920s, the intellectual and moral confrontation with the allegedly perverted and degenerated Ottoman past and the pandemic militarisation of World War II (although Turkey did not take part in it) certainly offered the state many opportunities for being alarmed at homosexuality, and prepared for the emergence of the distinct category of the homosexual population (apart from the heterosexual majority). These people might have been dangerous, infringing or cunning from the state's viewpoint. The knowledge that led the state to determine policies of immigration, recruitment principles for the military and the state intelligence unit, and imprisonment due to immoral acts, among others, had not yet been formed before the eyes of the public. Or perhaps the necessary national documents are still inaccessible to enthusiastic historians who wish to unravel the sexual past of the state.

Following Michel Foucault's analysis, it becomes obvious that as the Turkish state did not seem to notice, regulate, exclude or ostracise homosexual people – to our knowledge, at least – it also did not constitute and accentuate homosexual identity and community. Other institutions that might have potentially played a role in the construction of homosexuality as a distinct human type by generating knowledge and discourse, such as legal, religious, military, medical and psychiatric disciplines, participated in the silence and inactivity of the state. Same-sex sexual acts and counter-normative gender behaviours remained an isolated, individual deviance until Zeki Muren made an appearance.

After a relatively nondescript period in terms of homosexual culture in the 1950s, the famous singer Zeki Muren became the first queer public figure in the history of the country in the 1960s. In the beginning of his career, he enacted a kind of alternative masculinity that contradicted the hegemonic displays of manhood of its time. Later, he destabilised gender and sexual norms more obviously, and continued to do so until his death in 1991. People loved him as if he were a national hero and called him 'pasha,' a title used for very masculine military leaders, despite the fact that he was not involved emotionally or sexually with women and performed on stage in women's clothes while wearing heavy make-up. For most of his lifetime, Muren was an open transvestite and clandestine homosexual, a well-respected 'queer king.'[18] Even long after he died, in the 2000s, gay men still recounted memories of how lonely they felt when they believed that they and Zeki Muren were the only homosexuals in the world.[19]

Despite his exceptional queer public display, Muren was not alone in enjoying a homosexual lifestyle in Turkey. The Beyoglu district of Istanbul has long been the focal point of queer lives in Turkey.[20] The country's first popular gay bar, Vat-69 (opening date 1975), and almost all its successors have been located in Beyoglu and its vicinity. By visiting these bars, as well as specific public beaches, parks and Turkish baths at certain times, a new, distinct, modern homosexual person, located within a web of same-sex sexual relations instead of conventional family ties and collegial sociabilities, started to emerge in Istanbul after the 1960s.

Another crucial figure in this history is also a singer, Bulent Ersoy. After becoming immensely popular in the late 1970s as an apparently homosexual man, in 1981 she came out as transsexual and became male through sex reassignment surgery. Though Muren's subversive queer performance was never suppressed by the state, Ersoy was legally banned from performing on stage by the post-coup military government. She was exiled to Germany until 1988, when the new liberal government put an end to the prohibition. In contrast to Muren's highly adaptable, almost officially-sanctioned transvestism, Ersoy's radical transgenderism, with its narratives about surgeries and bodily transformation, along with the political conflict with military power, made Ersoy a trenchant symbol of gender and sexual struggle that is still effective in the 'structure of feeling' about homosexuality or same-sex intimacies in Turkey.[21] For homosexuals, the 1980s was also the decade of brutal police patrols, torture in police stations, harassment in public spaces and bars, and the new stigma that came with the first HIV/AIDS cases.

By the late 1980s, the incipient neoliberalisation of the economy, the further integration of Turkey into the Western world and the strong tides of globalisation paralleled public Turkish culture becoming gradually demilitarised. Along with these changes, modern gay men emerged in major Turkish cities. They tended to imitate a Euro-American style of gayness, embodying body-oriented gay masculinity and declaring a symbolic war against the feminine public image of homosexuality, which more or less stemmed from popular transgender singers.[22] A more surreptitious but better-organised urban gay culture flourished in this period. Men who had sex with men started to identify themselves as 'gay' as in English, while having emotional and long-term relationships, desiring and emulating a straight-looking bodily demeanour and coming together not only for purposes of sex and joy but also for political commitment and activism against homophobia.

The first commercial movies regarding the issues of same-sex sexuality were produced in the Turkish film industry in the 1980s[23] and homosexual stories also began to reappear in Turkish novels, after a long period of silence. Representations of homosexuality in film and fiction increased steadily in the 1990s, and notable examples of queer art became well known: examples include gay authors such as Murathan Mungan and Selim Ileri and Ferzan Ozpetek's critically acclaimed first film, *Steam: The Turkish Bath* (1997).

In contrast to contexts such as North America and Europe, in neoliberalising Turkey it is not a commonly held queer belief that all sexual minorities ought to come out and fight for the right to live as decent citizens, happy with their sexual identities.[24] The normal queer subject in Turkey is not necessarily out and proud about his sexuality and partner(s) or his mortgage, job, and plans to have a baby. Queerness in Turkey has a much more convoluted way of being achieved, performed and approved, however only partially and contingently. Therefore, what Decena offers for the Caribbean context as the *sujeto tacito* (tacit subject)[25] is quite applicable to the construction and exposition of sexual identities in Turkey. As Decena puts it, 'what is tacit is neither secret nor silent,'[26] and we need a more refined analysis in order to think beyond false binaries between out/proud versus secret/shameful.

Gay life in the recent history of modern Turkey reached its peak in the early 2000s, followed by its eventual decline in terms of visibility and diversity in social and physical spaces in the metropolitan areas.

Numerous gay (and to a certain extent lesbian) cafes, bars and clubs opened during those years in Istanbul. Gay-focused businesses were full of hundreds of avid homosexual customers, the popular press and the news media ran positive coverage about the glittering gay bars and their clientele, academic publications and research accounts on homosexuality were beginning to be published, sexual activists became more discernible and respected, and public confusion about the meaning of the concepts gayness and transgenderism abated slightly.[27] In addition to the self-assured gay man lesbians became for the first time visible and came together as a separate social group to discuss their own issues, as they differed from those faced by gay men.[28]

In this formation of modern gay and lesbian social identity in Turkey, three different developments played important roles. The first was the gradual decrease and eventual end of police raids and violence towards homosexuals and transgender individuals.[29] In this sense, it was deemed slightly more acceptable and feasible to open and manage gay commercial venues, especially in metropolitan areas. Visitors to these queer businesses did not have to fear being exposed to the police when they were socialising. The second development was a change in the attitude of the newspapers and the news media. Broadly speaking, the marginalising, otherising and even dehumanising language was dropped and gays and lesbians started to appear in the pages through their own agendas and words, within a framework of tolerance and esteem.[30] A third cornerstone of this process was the diffusion of access to the internet. It enabled gay men and lesbians to become connected to each other, social organisations and groups, and the world, without being revealed in front of heterosexual society or having to come out of the closet unwillingly.[31] In the beginning, European dating websites brought large numbers of people together online, and later Turkish websites were founded and replaced the European ones, becoming even more popular in urban zones and in the provincial towns. Perhaps for the first time in modern history, being gay and engaging in same-sex sexual activities had no social costs or consequences in Turkey.

Current Situation

Today, Turkey is one of the few countries in which homosexuality or counter-normative sexualities are legal, yet they are subjugated by state institutions, including police forces and public prosecutors.[32] Thus, a double life is experienced in terms of same-sex sexualities. On the one hand, the Turkish state and society are becoming more conservative, religious and oppressive, in the sense that they forbid not only certain types of sexualities but sexuality itself, and all its public manifestations are being labelled taboo. On the other hand, same-sex sexualities are performed as they are tolerated within the zones of exception, especially in certain neighbourhoods of the major metropolitan areas. These urban areas, under strict surveillance, provide social and physical spaces in which queer citizens engage in same-sex activities and experience gay sociabilities while the state authorities are able to watch and govern the flow of homosexuals outside those areas. In this double configuration of same-sex sexual cultures, tolerance and intolerance, respect and intervention, freedom and restriction, grassroots diversity and super-imposed uniformity are amalgamate by the participation of the state, the heterosexual public and gay men and lesbians as condoned exceptions.[33]

Subjects who have same-sex inclinations promulgate their own characteristics of flexibility, multifariousness, discretion, self-centredness and even a precarious insincerity, in order to navigate within this compelling binary social structure, oscillating between a globalising tendency for multiculturalism and an imagined insular isle of normality and undemocratic homogeneity.[34] The first step in this process is the formation of modern, Western, Euro-American gay and lesbian identities. These people construct a self-image that does not strive to hide their sexual identities and actions; on the contrary, as Western role models suggest, coming out strategies and narratives play a crucial role in constituting who they really are and to what extent they internalise gay identities.[35] In this Westernised view of sexuality there is a neat border between heterosexual and homosexual affect, culture, eroticism and identity. A person is either gay or straight and the definitions of both groups are exact and stabilised.

There are factors complicating this supposedly neat, yet never neutral, division between homosexuality and heterosexuality. One of the most significant of them is particular to Islam. Islamic doctrines clearly prohibit same-sex sexual acts. Some of the most popular religious discourses and interpretations, as well as the religious public, openly deny and ostracise gay men and lesbians as sinful people. This otherising, robust anti-gay position is visible at least for the Sunni majority, while for the Alevi minority of Islam the attitude towards homosexuality is vague but supposedly more democratic and flexible. As Islam is not singular and unified on almost any subject, it has also multiple perspectives and principles about homosexuality. Despite a lack of the kind of elaborate discussions about religion and homosexuality that exist in Christianity, homosexual citizens in Turkey have to deal with religion in their everyday lives and, to a certain extent, they have to find a satisfying answer to the inescapable question of whether they have faith.[36] Mostly, gay men and lesbians reconstruct themselves as entirely outside of the religious domain, believing in God but disconnecting from religious practices and developing a tacit silence, while some unmistakably reject religious and belief systems altogether.[37]

Another critical factor that shapes the current homosexual *mise-en-scène* in Turkey is class, which is not entirely independent from the social organisation of religion in Turkish society. As it signifies a modern, global, refined, European, elite person whose cultural capital is relatively high, the term gay has a certain middle and upper class connotation in the Turkish vernacular. In other words, being gay in the Turkish context is never only about erotic subjectivity and sexual acts, but always also a matter of social class.[38] According to this class-based understanding of sexuality, a person's erotic and intimate escapades cannot mark or stabilise her sexual identity: defining oneself as gay (or lesbian), sharing intimacy with self-identified homosexuals, or being a part of queer social environments are not enough by themselves to make one gay. One needs to meet a certain set of class criteria to achieve the proper inherently modern gay identity. The most recurrent of these class signifiers are having or sharing an apartment in one of the decent middle class areas of the city, being a college graduate or student, speaking foreign languages, adopting a secular lifestyle, following global cultural flows and fashions, travelling abroad, embodying and performing a specific style that is imbued with consumerism, self-care and masculinity (at least for men). Being gay in this setting is translated into becoming gay through utilising cultural capital and mastering symbolic codes and then buoyantly sustaining them.

What happens when one has same-sex sexual affinities but for class reasons cannot follow the codes of the middle-upper class gay ideal? If such a person is more masculine and has a straight-acting aura, then he is tagged as *varos*. *Varos* in popular Turkish means both the destitute neighbourhoods of informal housing and the poor, working-class people who live in these areas. The word *varos* has obviously negative overtones and it is generally used in a derogatory sense. However, in Turkish gay slang, *varos* is transformed into a word that signifies poverty and the lack of middle-class values but also highlights robust virility and an authentic, uncontaminated masculinity.[39] In this sense, the Turkish case bears a resemblance to contexts in other countries in which the power of working-class masculinity defines or rejects sexual identities, labels and communities.[40] In Turkey, if the person who lacks higher-class qualities is more feminine, then this person is more easily deemed a *lubunya*. This is a term that was borrowed from transgender culture and it simply means sissy or unmanly.[41] *Lubunya* people are easier to match with the famous transgender singers' behaviour by the public, and in some contexts they can be seen as candidates for future transvestism and transsexuality. Class for homosexuals in Turkey is deeply intertwined with desires that govern one's bodily presentations, gendered acts and the modes of interpretation that affect how homosexual subject relate to other people.

Another significant aspect of contemporary homosexuality in Turkey is the state institutions' intervention into the domain of morality through policy implementation at different levels. The most important aspect of this state intervention takes place through the compulsory military service.[42] According to the law, all male Turkish citizens have to spend a certain amount of time in the army, serving for military purposes in the barracks. Only citizens with a predefined, extraordinary medical condition can avoid the service. Homosexuality, framed as an 'advanced psychosexual disorder' in outdated psychological terminology, is among the disqualifying medical conditions. Thus, people who are able to prove that they are gay can be exempted from military service. After experiencing the awkward and torturous examinations held by the military officials, self-claimed homosexuals are entitled to receive a medical document called 'the rotten report,' which marks them as officially recognised homosexuals and tacitly excludes them from public life.[43] Both gay and heterosexual Turkish citizens believe that a person with the rotten report cannot work in state institutions, including public schools, and when such people apply to jobs elsewhere, their homosexuality will be known to potential employers. In other words, gay men in Turkey must find their way between two difficult strategies: performing the long compulsory military service while struggling to pass as straight, or getting the rotten report, which has the potential to destroy their coming-out strategies and exert control over their personal and professional lives.

Despite the fact that the state, especially through the army, acknowledges the existence of homosexual citizens and labels them whenever it can, Turkish law does not recognise them otherwise and does not guarantee them any of the social rights that heterosexual citizens enjoy, including, but not limited to marriage, civil union contracts and partnership benefits such as retirement, heritage, insurance, social security and access to the corpse of their partners in case of death. No Turkish law specifically forbids discrimination on the basis of sexual orientation or sexuality in social institutions, government offices or corporations. In fact, Turkey encourages discrimination through the Ministry for Family and Social Policies (previously The State Ministry for Women), which reinforces the priority placed on protecting families instead of those individuals who opt to remain outside of families, precludes alternatives to the conservative, heterosexual definition of family; and proselytises reproductive policies. The previous head of the Ministry, Selma Aliye Kavaf, even stated in 2010 that homosexuality was a disease that needed to be cured. Although she lost her chair immediately afterwards, this iteration is believed by many to reflect the official state attitude towards citizens with homosexual inclinations. Supporting this assumption of state negativity, HIV/AIDS is still largely seen as a homosexual illness and the non-governmental organisations that aim to prevent infection and to help HIV-positive people maintain their lives are not supported by the state, most likely because the sufferers as well as the charities addressing this illness are labelled as gay.

Issues, Visibilities and Absences

Today sexual minorities in urban Turkey are diverse, consisting of gay men, lesbians, bisexuals, *varos* and *lubunya* individuals, transgender individuals, bears and queers, who are mostly from the younger generations and defend the fluidity of sexual identities in the original sense of the term in English.[44] In addition to the issues that emerge at the intersection of sexuality, Islam, social class, military policy and the state, homosexuals have other issues to deal with in the course of everyday life. Among these issues are the fierce or symbolic violence they face; the continuing (though decreasing) confusion between gay and transgender identities; the murder of both gays and transgender individuals; the homophobic approach that the popular press and even politicians do not hesitate to use out of the blue; the limited availability and despicably low physical standards of queer spaces; the huge secrecy, concealment and insecurity of their lives; the rigid top-bottom sexual duality in terms of physical penetration; the scarce academic and scholarly research about queer lives and sexualities; and the intense marginalisation and exclusion experienced by those intellectuals who think or write about sexualities. Some of these issues are common in multiple international cultures, while some are strictly local and unique to the Turkish context and history.

Despite these limits, the emergence and the rise of same-sex sexual or queer activism also deserves to be mentioned. Lambda and Kaos, in Istanbul and Ankara respectively, have been active since the early 1990s and they have greatly improved in terms of visibility and respectability. Queer college students at different campuses began to come together in the 2000s and they are still the most powerful group regarding the mobilisation of young people against homophobia and heteronormativity. Turkey is a conservative and religious country and its politicians, whether from left or right wings, have traditionally stayed away from any discussion of issues of sexuality, starting with homosexual politics. Nevertheless, in the last few years observers have begun to see a minor shift, especially in the two leftist political parties, the secular-modernist Republican People's Party (CHP), and the Kurdish Peace and Democracy Party (BDP). One BDP parliament member stated in the commission for rewriting the constitution that general provisions, like the one holding everyone equal before the law, should be made more explicit, and that lesbians, gay men, bisexuals and transgender individuals' situations needed to be clearly mentioned in the new constitution. A group of CHP parliamentary members, among them former academicians, held a press conference with families of gay and transgender people and advocated for equal rights for sexual minorities. Another CHP congress member visited the gay and transgender section in a prison and talked to prisoners about their demands. These are small but symbolically remarkable actions, exceptional and meaningful steps in the long process of creating equal sexual citizenship and a democratic sense of identification and representation.

Recently there has been a boom in queer artistic production and representation. Major novelists, among them Perihan Magden, Duygu

Asena and Elif Safak, as well as more independent literary figures, such as Niyazi Zorlu and Mehmet Murat Somer, published popular books,[45] while the queer filmmaker Kutlug Ataman's movie *Two Girls* (2007), which was adapted from Magden's novel, was noted as the first modern mainstream lesbian film in Turkish popular culture. The respected director and university professor Can Candan produced a documentary about parents of queer children, *My Child* (2013), which became a national sensation and was discussed widely by the heterosexual public as well as among queer circles.

In terms of queer visibility, the greatest event that happens in Turkey are the Gay Pride celebrations, which have taken place each June on the Istiklal Street in the Beyoglu district of Istanbul since 2001. Thousands of people, queer and straight, men and women and transgender, young and old, in all their diversity, gather and parade in attire that is quite counter-normative for standard Turkish style. Attendees act out, kiss each other and dance together, activities which in other settings across the city would typically create physically abusive, homophobic reactions. Onlookers can easily detect the carnivalesque, collective spirit that inspires many otherwise closeted gays and lesbians, tired of oppression and concealment, protesting the heterosexist social values with their conspicuous presence in the heart of the city. The police, while normally harsh towards protesters of any sort, do not attack the participants of the Pride, but allow queer citizens to march, and maintain security through surveillance from a distance. Aaron Betsky defines queer space as a 'misuse or deformation of a place, an appropriation of the buildings and codes of the city for perverse purposes.'[46] In this sense, the annual Gay Pride of Istanbul queers urban space and adds another layer to the history and living memory of the cosmopolitan city centre.

At the end of the carnival, the burdensome conditions for queer people in Turkey recommence. There are serious taboos about same-sex sexualities in many spheres of social life. Sports, especially football, is one of them. The first and only out-of-closet gay football referee is not appointed to games anymore by the national federation, regardless of support from many fans' associations. Theological circles, legislators, and the bureaucratic elites are silent about homophobia, if not entirely against having queer members. The world of higher education is also divided and not necessarily inclusionary – if not explicitly discriminating

Photograph 1 A poster that hung in public spaces and some college campuses in the summer of 2015, states, 'If you see someone who is doing the ugly business of the Lot Tribe [the people of Sodom and Gomorrah], kill the actor and the subject.' The Islamic Defence, apparently an online organisation, summons the reader to kill the homosexuals. Source: Cenk Özbay.

against existing or prospective queer scholars. There is no out queer politician at either the local or national level in Turkey. Except for some older actors and writers, there is no single esteemed, accomplished, inspiring queer role model in the country.

The governing logic of the conservative, pious, neoliberal, corporate collective consciousness in Turkey avoids, forbids, condemns, marginalises and blacklists queer people and same-sex sexual acts, as Photograph 1 shows. Though disempowered by much of culture and the state, these people strive to survive, make peace with their identities, congregate, socialise and attempt to change the hostile social order in a bold and electrifying manner. The dynamics of globalisation and the transnational flow of ideas and expressions has brought certain novelties, not only in Turkey but also in the Middle East as a whole, in terms of sexualities and intimacies.[47] It is difficult to say whether same-sex sexualities were freer 50 years ago in Turkey or nowadays because it is almost impossible to fully grasp the clandestine nature of queer acts in the past. However, it is certain that today we talk, think and know more about sexualities, and in this discursive frame same-sex sexualities and queer identities occupy a great place. The Turkish case presents a twisted example simply because globalising, flexible, liberating ideologies are juxtaposed here with a more conservative, authoritarian, subjugating undertow. Thus, it is not entirely possible to foresee which direction Turkish same-sex sexualities will take in the future, but it is obvious from recent developments that the symbolic, social and political struggle of queers against homophobia in Turkey has been ignited.

The Study

Linguistically speaking, there is no equivalent to 'male prostitute' in the Turkish language, and men who are involved in male-to-male commercial sex refer to themselves as 'rent boys' or just 'rent' (as the word is written and pronounced in English). In the course of research in the mid-2010s, I have encountered the usages of *jigolo* (gigolo), *eskort* (escort), and *masör* (masseur), especially on smartphone dating apps. Notwithstanding this recent expansion of terminology, 'rent boy' is the main term that my sex worker informants use for themselves, and clients refer to them this way in return. In everyday usage, these young men either say '*ben bir rent boyum*' (I am a rent boy) or just '*rentim*' (I am rent).

Sometimes they prefer to say, *'parayla veya ucretli cikiyorum'* (I am seeing people for money). I never encountered any other terms, either in English or in Turkish translations (such as *erkek fahise* (male prostitute) or *seks iscisi* (sex worker) used by my informants, their clients, or in mass media.

Analysis in this book draws heavily from eclectic data collected during ethnographic fieldwork. I have been researching queer sexualities, masculinities, and male prostitution in Istanbul since 2003. Based on formal and informal interviews with rent boys, their clients and bar workers, as well as gay men who displayed knowledge about transactional queer sex, participant observation at bars and other public and semi-public spaces, and media analysis, the first period of data collection took place between August 2003 and June 2005 (including 20 formal interviews with rent boys and gay customers). I performed brief follow-up data collection in the summer months of 2006, 2008 and 2009.[48] By interviewing 11 more men and having brief conversations with many others, I have conducted more research in order to discern what had actually changed about commercial sex between men, in the summer months of 2013. I took extensive field notes about the people, settings, conversations and activities that I witnessed. I also tried to read and interpret the meanings of bodily codes and cultural symbols that rent boys employ, in order to better comprehend how material culture is significant in their self-making process.[49] Throughout this period, I was able to observe how queer sex work (like queer sociability, sex and intimacy) was de-territorialised and concentrated on the virtual tools of communication, first using websites via personal computers and then various applications on smart mobile phones. This book is an attempt to present and combine the end results of two different research projects (or one intermittent one) on the changing forms of compensated sex between men in Istanbul over the last decade.

In the early years of my research, there were four bar-clubs that I frequently visited for observation purposes. Bientot[50] was a small dance bar. The upper floor (at street level) had a bar and dance floor. The basement had toilets and a lounge, as well as facilities for staff. Now closed, Bientot was *the* rent boy bar of Istanbul: it did not have a good reputation for its music, atmosphere or cocktails. Most of the time the customers consisted of rent boys and men who looked for transactional sex with rent boys. Prive and 99 were very small bars without dance floors. Although their customers were diverse, these bars were popular among rent boys and gay customers all through the 2000s. SenGel, on the other hand, was established as a low-profile 'bear bar,' with a customer profile of transgender people, bears and 'gay truckers.' Rent boys and their followers also frequented the place. One of the most successful examples of queer investments in Turkey, SenGel moved three times. It not only became bigger and better known in and out of queer circles, its public also changed and expanded. Today it is the biggest gay club in Istanbul, the most spacious queer space in town with the most diverse customers across ages, classes, ethnicities, gender displays and sexual identities. All of these bars are located very close to the busy and cosmopolitan city centre, Taksim Square. During my research, I also went to public places around Taksim Square in which rent boys gather and cruise.

During interactions with my informants, I articulated that I was neither a rent boy nor a client and that I had never sold or purchased sexual services. I have never acted as a customer in order to receive attention from rent boys. In this sense, it was also crucial to elucidate that I was not a journalist who was going to write another sensational story but a researcher affiliated with the university and who was interested for social scientific research purposes. I have never given money to rent boys, but I did purchase food, coffee, tea and other drinks during daytime interviews, and beer at the bars.

I must admit that it was difficult and risky to examine queer sexualities in Istanbul within a context of unswerving conservatism and heteronormativity in the public sphere, as well as the underground character of the socio-spatial organisation of homosexuality. In addition to this difficulty and the abundance of biases about studying queer sexualities, rent boys were not visible figures even when one could reach queer groups and spaces as they revealed and represented themselves. Although I had previous knowledge of queer culture in Istanbul,[51] it required a careful ethnographic plan to regularly frequent the bars and create a sense of familiarity and rapport (which were naturally fragile) in order to talk with rent boys about sensitive issues.

There have been times when I could not even start a conversation about the sexual acts that my respondents performed for money. Especially in the earlier phases of this research, I was too shy to ask my interlocutors direct questions about male sex work, although I was aware of it. As Melissa Gira Grant explains about her research on sex work in another context, 'I did not know if I should be asking. Was it okay to ask? Did she want to tell me? And should she tell me? Would she think I thought I was too good to do what she did? Did my asking, my not knowing, the fact that I had to ask mean I did not have it in me? Was I just one of her customers, asking terrible questions, wasting her time?'[52] To further complicate the social situation, rent boys frequently asked me if I were gay. I never answered this question, in order not to personalise or sexualise the dialogue between us. I either moved on to another question or made a joke like, 'Why are you asking, do you want to marry me?' I believe most of them assumed I was gay (but not sexually interested in them) during our conversations. Beyond this attempted distance between the researcher and the researched, I have always reminded myself that these men were not categorical examples, representatives of a type or abstract units that were similar or dissimilar to others, but fellow humans. Each had his own biography, viewpoints, proclivities, anxieties, and hopes that might or might not resemble others' (or mine). I believe it has been crucial to locate rent boys as unique individuals and not as soulless objects of study in terms of understanding and representing their sexual activities, as well as their multi-layered practices of meaning making.

Following social scientific research principles, obeying certain institutional boundaries, and paying respect even to the common-sense meanings of privacy and anonymity, while studying the intersection of sexual identities and sexual acts – what is intimate versus what is exposed – have always been difficult on ethical grounds. The crisis of representation and the limits of research practice about sexual encounters became most visible after the publication of Laud Humphrey's remarkable book *Tearoom Trade: Impersonal Sex in Public Places*, in 1970. In his book, Humphrey talks about men who used public spaces, 'tearooms' in gay slang (i.e., movie theatres, bushes, restrooms) to have instant, anonymous sex with other men without further interacting with them, 'desiring kicks without commitment.'[53] Humphrey was among the first researchers to reflect on sexual acts between so-called straight and gay men, and to contest the applicability of strict identity categories over erotic practices: 'Tearooms are popular, not because they serve as gathering places for homosexuals, but because they attract a variety of men, a minority of whom are active in the homosexual subculture and a large group of whom have no homosexual self-identity.'[54]

The methodological discussions following *Tearoom Trade* centred on its 'voyeuristic sociology', or how the author collected the licence numbers of unsuspecting informants, chased them to their homes, acquired data on them and even their neighbours, and distorted or disguised truth in order to convince them to be interviewed for another (public health) study while asking questions about the subjects' tearoom involvements – violating standards of what social scientists call 'informed consent.'[55] Doing comparable research in the shadow of Humphrey, although in an immensely different time, place and culture with radically dissimilar people, I have always tried to be vigilant about the respondents' knowledge, agreement and permission. I have also done everything possible to develop a specific sensitivity to the privacy of the family lives of rent boys, who might have acted overprotective and even intimidating about them in order to secure their heteronormative sociabilities.

Rent boys may sometimes act in an aggressive and recalcitrant fashion. I am not talking about an essential quality of theirs, it is not something inherent to them; but, as I will explicate in the following chapters, it is an indispensable part of the cultural repertoire of exaggerated masculinity through which they become legible subjects (in the world and in gay subculture) and engender their social and moral lives. It has been consistently difficult to deal with such overt pugnacity and self-assertiveness as an aspect of 'intimate ethnography,'[56] despite understanding (and reminding myself during conversations with them) rent boys' need for this masculine gender construction as a performative, theatrical aspect of their identities. However, conversational intimacy during this research never turned into an embodied participation to the commercial sexual acts or 'voyeuristic' sociology like Humphrey's.[57]

Organisation of the Book

Certain historical processes and socio-political dynamics, such as globalisation, neoliberalisation, migration from rural areas, cultural engagements with modernity, intergenerational conflict within families, and the current situation of Istanbul as an 'urban failure'[58] definitely impact what is recounted in this book. However, this book is not about the broad picture of male sex work per se in a macro sense, focusing on social change, its actors and effects. Instead, the book concentrates on subjective worlds and interrogates rent boys' individual attempts to navigate experiences, narratives and identity construction, as well as their entanglements with gay men in the rigidly classed sexual economy and the affective landscape of desired and desiring subjects. The chapters present discrepant and sometimes non-linear portrayals, stories and interpretations of what is lived and how it comes to be talked about. In addition to this plurality of plots and perspectives, sex work at each instance involves at least two human beings, often with different backgrounds, emotional and affective compositions, future expectations, aspirations and fears. This unavoidable human factor further marks the non-representational aspect and frailty of a search for a lucid account of male prostitution in Istanbul. Hence, readers should be warned in advance that in dividing *Queering Sexualities in Turkey* into the chapters below, I do not claim complete presentation of each and every aspect that contributes to the definition of male prostitution in particular, or queer sexuality in general, in Turkey. While my attention overall here is on masculinities, sexual identities, neoliberal subjectivity and the city, other important subjects (for example, transgender sex work, the twisted interactions between ethnic-racial identities, the impact of religion, and the profanity of the police) are not necessarily addressed.

Each chapter below has an overarching theme that is singled out from the plethora of issues and encounters it registers. Chapter 2 presents an overview of the interdisciplinary studies on male prostitution and queer sexual economy, with a focus on a number of themes that are particularly relevant to this book. It also gives an outline of four crucial issues that demarcate the rent boys' identities and their bounded sexualities. Chapter 3 provides a detailed account of exaggerated masculinity, the cultural and bodily repertoire that transforms *varos* youth into rent boys and stabilises their surface appearance alongside their interactions with gay clients, transgender prostitutes, other rent boys and their families.

Chapter 4 concentrates on the construction of neoliberal masculinity and entrepreneurial personhood that rent boys enact, which emphasise an adaptable, profit-oriented self-enterprising subjectivity. Chapter 5 discusses how and why rent boys are queer subjects and which social structures they queer by their bodily presence, somatic engagements and discursive acts. Chapter 6 updates the 'straight' rent boy framework with an emphasis on the diversification of sex workers and the de-territorialisation of male prostitution. The concluding chapter reviews and reshuffles the stories and relations in the rest of the book by revisiting some collateral themes and concepts.

CHAPTER 1

SEXUALITY, MASCULINITY AND MALE SEX WORK

They are called 'faggot' if they are poor; 'gay' if they are rich.[1]

[M]any of the boys and young men who sold themselves for subsistence or perhaps just pocket money experienced disgust or at best indifference when satisfying their patrons. These 'prostitutes' differentiated sharply between the sexual services they provided and their personal preferences and love relationships. A large number – as many as a third, in fact – professed to be heterosexual.
Robert Beachy, *Gay Berlin: Birthplace of a Modern Identity* (New York, 2015), p. 189

The emergent interdisciplinary analysis of male prostitution and queer sex work informs the framework of this book. My research particularly builds on a number of recent sociological and anthropological studies that discuss, in one way or another, the identities, practices and social situations that resemble to what I elucidate in this book. Here I will provide an overview of this literature, and then allude to four basic lines of contestation that determine and stabilise that who the rent boy is (not) and what he does (not) do with gay men.

The Burgeoning Literature on Male Sex Work

Feminist sociology of sex work has been concerned mostly with female prostitution and human (female and children) trafficking until recently.[2]

Three arguments are the centrepiece of this well-founded literature: first, sex work must be considered a form of violence against women and should be restricted (if not abolished) by policymakers; second, sex workers provide a service and thus sex work is a form of embodied, aesthetic and affective labour, which should be analysed in labour terms; and third, sex work is a kind of sexual liberalisation which has the capacity to radicalise sexuality and to advance sexual possibilities. There is a rich ethnographic literature, as well as more political and activism-oriented accounts on various forms of (female) sex work, that demonstrates that the lived reality of sex workers around the world is far more complicated than the simplistic analytical positioning of sex work either as liberation, choice, empowerment, autonomy, resistance and legitimate income-generating activity or sex work as exploitation, survival strategy, an outcome of forced migration, human trafficking, slavery and violence.[3]

When we look more closely at men who sell sex to other men, these positions are indeed very hard to apply directly. In spite of the fact that male sex work is still in its incipiency as a field of academic curiosity and activity across established disciplines, research findings show that there are at least six types of male sex workers: The fake ones who steal and blackmail their customers, hustlers who take part in prostitution but are also involved in stealing, part-timers who have regular jobs in addition to their occasional involvement with forms of compensated sex, professionals who perceive this as a form of committed work, poverty-driven sex workers who do male prostitution as a survival strategy ('survival sex' in the literature on female prostitution) and the more affluent and enterprising gigolos who work for agencies in the Global North.[4] Within this most recent and comprehensive framework of male prostitution, rent boys in Istanbul fall into the third group, the part-timers, who do not have to sell sex in order to survive; there is therefore agency, choice, autonomy and flexibility in negotiating the terms and conditions of the sexual interaction.[5] Rent boys are male sex workers as long as they wish. There is not an outsider actor, or factor, that pushes, forces or persuades them into male prostitution.

Male sex work and other forms of queer intimate economy take place in different social settings around the world, across a wide diversity of class, ethnic, racial, cultural and organisational arrangements, representations, fantasies and discourses.[6] Social studies on male (or queer) prostitution, though, are largely limited to the geographical focus of the North[7] and South America.[8] *Queering Sexualities in Turkey* is the first monograph ever published on male prostitution in the region that includes Eastern Europe and the Middle East.[9] Although it is expanding, the existing literature on male sex work is still highly limited and scarce in contrast to research on female sex work, and there is a clear need for more ethnographic, historical and comparative studies to comprehend and theorise the social situation better.[10] Taboos about homosexuality, the relatively late appearance of masculinity studies as an admissible field of scholarly inquiry, the lack of institutional sites for research practice, like brothels, and popular opinions (sometimes myths), such as those that depict male sex work as less exploitative and more egalitarian than conventional sex work arrangements (women sell, men buy, pimps mediate), have probably contributed to this comparative under-representation. However, as Dennis Altman notes, 'across very different societies men grapple with demands of masculinity, sexual desire, economic survival, family responsibilities and status, and the exchange of money for sex plays a role in each of this.'[11] Particularly younger men, in many different geographies and cultural settings, negotiate with societal norms, the rules and boundaries of masculinity, religious dogmas, erotic desire, somatic expressions, kinship ties, codes of honour and public morality as they get involved with transactional queer sex as embodied entrepreneurial selves. Male sex work is but one field of analysis where the materiality of social inequalities, the secrecies of everyday realities and the informalities of power relations are articulated with bodily and discursive gender and sexual practices. By studying male prostitution, we gain crucial insight into the social dynamics behind how dissident sexualities are organised, experienced and interpreted in the heart and the margins of hegemonic masculinities.

This book in general aims to make a contribution to the literature on male sex work with a particular emphasis on non-Western sexual geographies and to add nuance and intricacy to the field of class, sexualities and masculinities in the Global South. In particular, I explicate compensated sex between men of different social classes and sexual cultures that generate, and are fortified by, distinct masculinities. A number of sexual cultures, such as those in Mediterranean, European, and Islamic countries, as well as the rapidly globalising sexual identities, categorisations and proclivities meet and interface in Turkey.[12] Hence,

I am not talking about an essentially non-Western place, culture or form of sexuality here. Instead, I argue that Istanbul presents an amalgamation of the well-studied Western-style gay culture with its own history, typology, boundaries, marginalities and objects. In this sense, Istanbul is indeed a 'sexual' or 'queer' city located in the margin of the West. This sense of the queer city in the margins deviates in obvious but multifaceted ways from the conventional queer centres such as New York City, Los Angeles, San Francisco, Berlin, Paris or London.[13] By Western-style gay culture, I basically mean the emergence of men who call themselves gay (as in English) or sometimes *gey* in Turkish[14] because they engage in sexual, erotic and emotional relations with other men who are supposedly self-identified as gay and are not ashamed of their sexual identity. There are many components of the gay (sub-)culture, including the enclosed spaces of gay bars and clubs, access to foreign or local websites with gay content for various purposes, such as online dating, watching gay TV shows, following gay (or, gay-friendly) singers and groups, and a discrete 'gay slang,' that is shared by the members. Before the emergence of modern gay identity in Turkey there were various sorts of same-sex sexual relations occurring under different identifications and social organisations.[15]

In its secrecy and isolation through carefully planned discretionary practices, male sex work, like homosexual acts, is neither criminalised nor normalised in Turkey. Optimistically speaking, it is the result of a collusion by authorities and society. As I discuss throughout the pages of this book, there is a common silence, an absence of public discourse about the subject and a superficial incomprehension about it. In this sense, male sex work stands somewhere between the concept of 'the will not to know'[16] as a response to homosexual acts in Islamic societies and 'the unspokenness of prostitution'[17] as a way of representing sex work in India. What Carlos Decena conceptualises in his work on the Dominican Republic as 'tacit subjects'[18] fits well with rent boys and the context of male sex work in Istanbul: 'A tacit subject might be an assumed and understood, but not spoken, aspect of someone's subjectivity as well as a particular theme or topic.' While the bewildering aspects of transgender sex workers' lives and female sex workers' long-understood hardships are rarely, if ever, talked about in public, there is an absolute blindness about the actors in male sex work. This tacit knowledge, or state of social blindness, about male sex work hides at least three significant concepts that I contest throughout this book: power, choice, and labour. These are also deeply related to economies of desire, sexual subjectivity, strategies for upward mobility, neoliberal personhood, search for adventure and somatic aspects of fun in accordance with the conquering masculinity, globalisation and economic transformations, migration and the opportunities the internet provides. On an urban scale, spaces of homosocial, homoerotic, masculine and queer sociabilities are available in the city that are known, intuited, felt or imagined by subjects of male sex work.

Bodies, Acts and Identities

When we look at how multifarious same-sex, non-conformist, counter-normative or queer sexual acts are organised in time, place, culture and the diversity of local gender/sexual identifications in each and every corner the world, we may reach a superficial analytical distinction between two basic configurations: The egalitarian model (Western, modern, globalising, normalising) with identical gay bodies and personas, and the difference model (non-Western, non-modern, Middle Eastern, Latin, Mediterranean) with dissimilar men, who embody the conventional gender binary via explicitly masculine and feminine roles, the former hiding his same-sex erotic biography and stigma working upon the latter. In the second configuration, within which Istanbul's queer sexual economy is partially included, the features culturally associated with masculinity become a critical arena of constructing, staging, exhibiting, repeating, emphasising and exaggerating virility. Masculinity begins increasingly to be deemed a skill or a form of capital that some men may invest in and have more, better or deeper versions of. There is, therefore, a hierarchy of embodied masculinity – an erotic market or a 'sexual field'[19] – in which the young men with the most authentic, rough, thuggish and macho performances stand at the peak. As I explicate in the next chapter, this very constellation of masculine acts and demeanour is a carefully defined and meticulously calculated set of performative dispositions, affective intensities, bodily positionings and aesthetic labour of 'looking good and sounding right.'[20]

In his ethnographic analysis of Brazilian male prostitutes, *garotos*, who have transactional sex with foreign gay tourists, Gregory Mitchell argues that performative and affective labours are intertwined in male sex workers' bodily, behavioural and discursive enactments.[21] Mitchell maintains that what *garotos* bring together as elements of their butch and macho attitude is attuned to tourists' fantasies of racialised male bodies:

> *[G]arotos'* performances of racialised masculinity are actually shaped by gay clients' eroticisation of straight men and macho masculinity. This is an example of a *commissioned performance* of masculinity in which economic incentivisation structures and guides the repertoire of masculinity. The end result is that the *garotos'* masculinity consists of a lot of macho straight men trying to perform a version of straight masculinity constructed and desired by gay men. (Mitchell 2016: 38, emphasis original)

In the queer sexual economy of Turkey, racial categories and the racialisation of the male body do not necessarily work in the same way as in Brazil. Nevertheless, a certain number of rent boys implicitly underline their real or imagined association with Kurdishness – the largest ethnic minority in Turkey – with political, social and cultural demands that may or may not include separatism, self-government and spatial segregation.[22] Kurdish rent boys often get racialised on the margins of Turkish social normativity as 'Easterners,' and everything they do or do not do is explained by their Eastern or Kurdish identity. As Mitchell puts it, 'attractions to difference' and 'eroticizing an exotic Other'[23] are organised through the distinction between the refined, Western(ised), 'decent citizens,' Turkish gay men and the disenfranchised children of Kurdish minority – the lusted after outsider within. In many situations being an Easterner also signifies a sense of lack or failure, that is, not being modern enough or having appropriate social taboos, which denote the non-performance of whiteness, middle-classness, or Turkishness. In this sense, some (Turkish) gay men have a specific sexual fantasy of having sex with Kurdish boys, who are supposed to be wilder, more animalistic and unfettered, and unquestionably more masculine. As one of my interlocutors once said, 'When you get used to fucking with the Kurds, you would not enjoy the Turks any more. They [Turks] are smaller [in penis size], more feminine and more [self-] controlled.'

Mazlum is a good example regarding the curiosity about Kurdish men. I heard stories about Mazlum from two of my gay respondents. He was the realised fantasy of the monstrous young Kurdish-Arabic man, who has sex with men for money and satisfied his clients with his extra-large penis, as well as demonstrations of his untamed masculinity. He was from Mardin, a very conservative town in south-eastern Turkey across the Syrian border, and his Turkish was weak, with a thick accent. One of my key informants, Umit, told me,

> I went to this Turkish bath which had rent boys for a short term [later it was closed down as a result of the smothering police oppression] with a queer friend. When we entered the hammam, he shouted, 'Who is the guy with the largest tool here?' Everybody said, 'There is Mazlum.' He came, a heavily Kurdish boy. I could not believe what I saw [his penis]. [My friend] said, 'Well, how much does it cost, it is worthy.' They went into a private cabin [to have sex].

But beyond the exceptional examples, such as Mazlum, and gay men who are specifically (and sometimes exclusively) interested in having commercial sex with Kurdish boys, it should come as no surprise that most clients have distinct (and changing) ethnic-racial 'types' and particular tastes in bodily and sexual predilections, which largely translate into ethnic or hometown identities, such as blond boys of Bosnian or Bulgarian origin (that their families migrated to Turkey in 1980s and 1990s), or young men of Caucasian or Black Sea descent.

Even though the racialisation of male sex workers' bodies in Turkey does not operate in the same way as in Brazil's complex racial and sexual economy, there are sharp similarities between these two otherwise radically different contexts. The biggest resemblance in this framework is the performative characteristic of masculinity from the vantage point of male sex workers. Mitchell says that masculinity of *garotos* in Brazil 'is embodied, commodified and consumed,' and their 'success or failure depends on constructing certain styles of gender,'[24] which is also the case for rent boys in Turkey. This strict dependence on not only the successful performance of a particular gender identity (i.e., straight masculinity) but also the performative, repetitive, superficially coherent yet convincing enough and almost naturalising set of efforts in Brazilian and Turkish male prostitutes brings in the notion of affective labour as a complementary constituent. Affect, for Patricia Ticineto Clough, 'refers generally to bodily capacities to affect and be affected or the augmentation or diminution of a body's capacity to act, to engage, and to connect, such that autoaffection is linked to the self-feeling of being alive – that is, aliveness or vitality.'[25] Mitchell takes it up further by referring Deborah Gould's (2009: 19) usage of the concept:

> [N]onconscious and unnamed, but nevertheless registered, experiences of bodily energy and intensity that arise in response to stimuli impinging on the body [...] For Gould, the language of emotions puts words to affects but doesn't really represent them because affects are unstructured, noncoherent, and non-linguistic, whereas emotions are expressions structured by culture. Most significantly, affects do not come from conscious thought but instead originate in the realm of preconscious. This is similar to what laypersons sometimes speak of vaguely as 'instincts,' 'intuitions,' or 'unconscious' feelings.[26]

Affective labour is about orchestrating affective tendencies, intensities and flows before the subject even recognises, makes sense of or attempts to regulate them. But affective labour may not entirely be anti-social. It, at the same time, may come to mean watching others and learning to use certain bodily capacities and fragilities in accord with cultural and social dispositions, while they also manipulate others' feelings and govern the direction desire follows. Rent boys' relationality with gay men is a simultaneous process of affective (as they command the pre-textual and pre-conscious, such as libidinal drive, erection, ejaculation, touching and other acts during sex, and even gazes), emotional (as they constantly influence others' emotions, play with them and present themselves as unemotional and apathetic, to a certain extent closed to human contact behind a cold mask), aesthetic (as they strive to meet certain standards of manly beauty and the semblance of sybaritic lifestyle), and performative (as they stage a scripted, mediated and exaggerated form of 'proper' masculinity and rule its cohesion without failure) forms of labours. This intersection of forms of labour renders rent boys legible, desirable, meaningful subjects in the eyes of potential clients as it further impresses, satisfies and binds gay men to rent boys. In other words, the possibility of being a successful rent boy is highly contingent on this very skill or investment in the capital of navigating masculine accomplishments and pretences through affective, emotional, aesthetic and performative labours through which they define themselves and locate others.

One critical point in this discussion is about the commercialised erotic experience between men and the designation of sexual identities of gay and straight. As I continually point out throughout this book, rent boys are always too quick, too insistent and even too arrogant to elucidate their heterosexuality. Accordingly, they are indeed straight men, who normally fantasise and desire women, and male prostitution is an insignificant, ephemeral and exceptional encounter that does not harm their heteronormative identity, lifestyle and social networks. Although it may never be clear enough to come to a conclusion, after years of witnessing rent boys' affairs and listening to stories about their escapades with gay men, I can say that some rent boys in the long run opt for heterosexual identities, while another group pick a queer way of life and come out eventually as gay men. For me, however, the way rent boys and gay men talk about their sexuality, negotiate sexual and class boundaries and situate their somatic experiences within potential real-life implications are more interesting than straightforward findings on identity (re)formation and (re)socialisation. Rent boys' construction of their heterosexuality bears serious parallels to what the sociologist Jane Ward's recent theorisation offers:

> [A] New way to think about heterosexual subjectivity – not as the opposite or absence of homosexuality but as its own unique mode of engaging homosexual sex, a mode characterised by pretence, disidentification, and heteronormative investments [...] when straight white men approach homosexual sex in the 'right' way – when they make a show of enduring it, imposing it, and repudiating it – doing so functions to bolster not only their heterosexuality, but also their masculinity and whiteness.[27]

Under the right circumstances, alongside legitimate excuses and explanations and especially while obeying the gendered dichotomy of sex roles (i.e., the penetrator versus the penetrated), queer sex does not harm the presumption of heterosexual masculinity. On the contrary, queer sex turns into a reinforcing asset that may bolster heterosexuality as a solid end product after all sorts of sexual experiments, challenges and tests. Most of my rent boy respondents verbalised this belief many times and put their 'queered' heterosexuality over the 'untested' straight identities of their peers and family members, including those of their fathers, in an invisible hierarchy of masculinity.

Ward underscores the gravity of the whole cultural (infra)structure of heteronormativity in which we live and explains how queer sexual acts without undertaking social identity, the case which she calls 'heteroflexibility,' as an effect of belonging to the heterosexual culture. In this view, the importance and pleasure of straight sex comes secondarily after the comfort zone drawn by the institution of heterosexuality. In this regard, the heteroflexibles 'are generally content with straight culture, or heteronormativity; they enjoy heterosexual sex, but more importantly [...] they enjoy heterosexual culture. Simply put, being sexually 'normal' suits them. It feels good; it feels like home.'[28] Being, identifying or masquerading as straight or as gay is not an easy and linear formulation about with whom one has sex with. Sexual identity does not even determine the gender of sexual partners; instead, it defines the whole socio-cultural universe within which one lives, including, but not limited to, family and intimacy. [S]traightness and queerness are not simply matters of sexual object choice; they also carry a vast array of cultural requirements and implications that, in turn, shape how people orient their bodies and move through space. Because heterosexuality is the default sexual orientation, reorienting oneself in the direction of public queer legibility takes some significant effort. As queer theorist David Halperin puts it, being gay is 'a resistant cultural practice that gays must learn from one another.'[29] Nonetheless, most rent boys are not the willing subjects of resistance. Most of them are attached to the prevailing ideas, norms, and rules in society, without open confrontation that would cast them off. They choose to love the sin, as they hate the sinner and fear becoming him at the end. They gingerly learn to invest in and improve themselves, while protecting who they are. Everything, including the greatest challenges, such as queer sex, turns into nugatory details in this project of reinventing self. These intertwined senses of the 'entrepreneurial self'[30] and the incorporation of a 'neoliberal masculinity'[31] provide a critical conceptual perspective for my analysis in this book.

Gul Ozyegin in her recent book about the changing grounds of gender, love, romance and sexualities among the upwardly mobile members of the 1980s generation in Istanbul, argues that in the midst of multiple dualities 'between West and East, modern and traditional, secular and Islamic,' these young people cultivate classed and gendered neoliberal selves:

> [I]t is not sexual selves alone that are in the process of being made, for the domain of romance and sexuality is also a space in which class aspirations are disciplined and regulated. These are the grounds upon which new gendered class aspirations operate, as a means of measuring, monitoring and signalling one's social position to others and of differentiating and marking masculine and feminine identities. This domain and the relationships within it, often experienced as a realm of uncertainty and a source of anxiety, paradoxically offer a clear lens through which we can understand the forging of neoliberal selfhood and its intimate connections to gender, sexuality and class.[32]

Following Suad Joseph's conceptualisation of 'connectivity,'[33] though which (Middle Eastern) subjects are differently positioned than their Western counterparts, as they put greater emphasis on familial ties and other close interpersonal relations in defining who they are, instead of the prevailing discourses of self-autonomy and independence, Ozyegin asserts that her respondents (heterosexual, gay, lesbian, secular, pious college students) exhibit patterns of connectivity in their neoliberal self-formations, their relationality in midst of social intimacy and their attempts to develop new notions of femininity and masculinity, 'in a deeply patriarchal and paternalistic society.' She further maintains, 'While connectivity does not exclude the possibility that individuals understand themselves through the language of autonomy, it is the connective self that is most desired. In societies such as Turkey, the key component of selfhood is a relational experience with members of one's family.'[34] My analysis at this point deviates slightly from Ozyegin's account. Both the not-upwardly-mobile and disenfranchised young rent boys and the upper-middle-class gay men imagine, reflect and use the meaning and (dys)functions of familial relations in dissimilar ways than the elite college students who are enthusiastic to renegotiate the domain of 'patriarchal masculinity' and 'normative femininity' for their bodies and lives. Rather than focusing on recasting themselves through their involvement with and relations to others, men I talked to emphasised instantaneous pleasure, short-term calculations, satisfaction of erotic desire, material gain, conceitedness and self-indulgence, immediate benefits and 'saving oneself' as soon as they can.[35] However, as Ozyegin insightfully cautions us, the 'individualising forces or ideologies of the autonomous self'[36] are strengthening alongside connectivity; the opposite is also true, in that for my respondents (especially rent boys), the capacities (and ghosts) of family play a certain role despite, and in contrast to all the discursive intensity of self-concentration, self-reinvention, and self-expansion.

Ozyegin's upwardly mobile and academically successful heterosexual male college student informants, who were from relatively less-educated milieus where traditional small-town values reign, regarded their fathers and the type of masculinity their fathers represented in a condemning, if not reprimanding, fashion. '[T]he father as both a symbolic figure and a specific person, who, for these young men, serves as an example of an undesirable outcome, and they envision alternatives for themselves [...] They use the parental model as an example from which to differentiate themselves [...] They perceive themselves as closely linked to a new lifestyle predicated on self-discovery via extracurricular activities, travel and romantic and sexual exploration, allowing them to map desires that are more ended and ambitious than those of their fathers.'[37] At the other end of the spectrum, rent boys also reflect on the sense of masculinity they inherited from their fathers and elder kin, expand the cultural repertoire of being a man through social and sexual experiments and, in contrast to Ozyegin's respondents, play with and destabilise heteronormativity by dealing with gay men in economic, social, cultural and sexual ways. While Ozyegin's college students mention 'risk taking' and 'entrepreneurial viewpoints' in connection with their heterosexual relations with women students, their (future) business lives and (self) employment, rent boys, as I elaborate in Chapters 3 and 6, radicalise and bend risks towards bodily and social dimensions and develop a sense of self-entrepreneurialism not based on academic merits or business capacities, but on their erotic capabilities and physical attractiveness, as well as steadiness and morale.

The Mainstay of Rent Boy Identity

Between the years 2003 and 2015, I spoke to many rent boys, as well as gay and bisexual men who were involved with male sex work as service providers or customers in Istanbul. In these divergent, mostly informal and short, conversations, certain themes have been quite common, in spite of rapid transformations in the social context in which transactional queer sex is embedded, including the actors' self-definitions and changes in the organisation of physical spaces. Among these themes, the capacity and limits of the male sex work market, questions around the sexual identity of the male sex worker, whether rent boys take the passive role in penetration or they are 'top only,' as they incessantly reiterate, and their relationships with gay men are especially indicative of the relations between the actors who are entangled in the scene of sex work.

Is the Market Lucrative Enough?

Starting from the very beginning of this research, and in stark contrast with other settings that scholars of male prostitution examine, I have always believed that the amount of money exchanged around sex between men in Istanbul was quite low, and that for the great majority of the men involved, these amounts of money cannot sustain a lifestyle. Hence, I believe there must be other reasons, inspirations and sources of motivation to explain why heterosexually identified young men are having sex with gay men. When I asked Ata (in his early fifties) if he thought rent boys were having sex with gay men, not for the money they would receive after sex, but in exchange for other things within a complicated relation and symbolic exchange, he agreed:

> Sure, what else did you think? Is it possible to feed all of these rent boys by paying them for sex? Where's the money? We, gay men, are not the Turkish army, right? But you may say the following and then I would agree: there is a tiny group of people who earns and spends too much money, or the squanderers, give cash and make the rent boys fuck them. Yes, exactly. But shall I ask, how many are they? This type of people is countable by fingers; [they are] just a few. The situation is simple: Here are the rent boys. You approach them at bars and, of course, they ask money for sex, let's say 100 US dollars, or 100 euros. You can always negotiate the

price, though. You can take him with you in the morning for free, or worse, let's say for 20 Turkish liras. On the other hand, there is this other boy that you find, have sex and, then he leaves. While he is leaving, he asks money from you. It depends on your generosity, 15 or 20 liras, whatever you can or are willing to give at that moment. I am saying this to show that here, his real intention is not to earn money, but to take something from you after having sex. Or, another situation for you, chatting online with a *varos* boy. Everything is set forth: where are you from, the location of the house, phone numbers, etc. He even says he was top only, that he did not like to kiss, [he is into] the sexual stuff [only]. Then, after everything is agreed upon, he says he wanted money. No! You know what, he wants to come and fuck me, but he has to try his best chance. Of course, I am a seasoned gay man. I never say anything about my financial conditions to them. [The rent boys asks] Do you have a car, no. Do you own this apartment, no. I have a second, older cell phone only to talk with *varos* boys. The thing is, the rule of the game, a rent boy should always ask. He can take something with him or no he can't, it does not really matter. Better, of course, if he can get something. You should be smart and not give him the chance though.

Veli (in his late forties) offered another perspective on how he was able to manipulate rent boys and convince them to come to his place and have sex without paying them cash but by offering food instead. In this way, the gap in class identities of the sexual encounter around male sex work becomes crystallised. Veli spoke of a particular and recurring experience that defines and fixes his and rent boys' class positions. I have heard similar lines of stories from many gay men I have talked to.

You know I am 43 years old now, though I do not show, do I? I have accepted myself, I am into very young men, sexually speaking. Imagine even your age group would not desire me. What about the teenagers, forget it. Cenk, do you think I have another way? I have nothing to do but going for rent boys. Gay culture in this country pushes me to do so. You know, I have had sex with many rent boys. Before this latest boom of rent boys, there were fewer [of them] and I knew all of them personally, even their [real] names. Of course, it is not possible any more. My point is that I have never paid a cent to one of these rent boys. Write this. Veli has never paid them. Is it because of my beautiful face? Surely not. One should use his mind. We are smart, experienced educated people. We are the gay people who could survive in this country despite every hardship. We have seen and coped with every possible problem so far. Who are the rent boys? Some loser *varos* boys who could not even complete their education, shaking their dicks in front of us, thinking naively that they were great [at sex]. They should not conquer us; we should not let them. You ought to know the rules, otherwise, the hunter may be hunted. What would an experienced (*kasarlanmis*) rent boy say if you go to and ask him how much [he charged for sex] at the beginning of the night? Of course, he would say 100 US dollars. Don't rush, wait, hang out, drink something, look at other rent boys and trigger the competition. At the dawn, they will eventually come near you. They would again ask me for money, a lower amount, I never even answer them. The most I can do is buy the kid a beer, and commence conversation. You know I cook well. I start to tell them the dishes I make. They love it because these people are hungry, they are [poor] peasants. Has he ever seen a dish like the ones I cook in his life? For example, I tell them there was beef and cornbread I cooked at home. Now imagine, at 4:00 am in the morning, he is hungry, can he resist this? Most of the time he comes, what else he can do? At home, I hide perfumes, toothpaste and shampoo, whatever they can take with them when they leave. In the taxi on the way to home I always say I had a brother who was a cop. The rest is the well-known story. You know I do not earn money to spend on these cheap boys.

From the rent boy's perspective, though, receiving cash sounds more significant and it has a central role in male prostitution that gay men seem to fail to understand. Burak (aged 24) exemplified, for example, how rent boys also develop strategies and form typifications for the customers in a similar way to gay men.

Cenk: How many people have you have had since September?
Burak: (Pause) One minute (Pause) five, are you asking for the ones that gave money?

C:	Are there any that gave no money?
B:	Of course.
C:	Okay, all of them.
B:	Then let's count it, I have received money from five people, and four without money.
C:	Then what are the non-paying for?
B:	They can buy drinks or give me the taxi fare. Or some of them say I do not give money, but I can give you gifts.
C:	What sort of gifts?
B:	I don't know. (Pause). Cologne, t-shirts, sneakers, CDs, exported drinks, etc. For example, I took a silver candlestick from this guy's home and gave it to my mother. She liked it very much. She put it in our living room and she shows it to everyone and says, 'My son bought it.'

Although Burak accepted that he might get involved in same-sex sexual relations sometimes without receiving cash, he also said he made fun of a gay man who offered him a bed for that night and breakfast for the next morning: 'The younger guys want to have sex for free. Once, a boy came to me and told me that he wanted to have sex in exchange for bed and breakfast. I said, 'What you were talking about, were you a hotel or something?' Then I asked him how much he would charge if I were a customer. He said, 'Generally, a young guy does not offer money to have sex. He probably waits around until the morning to get someone for free. But if he asks I would directly say 80 liras, 100 liras.' When I asked about the extent of negotiation, Burak approved, 'The final price is determined for the specific person. And, you know the saying, the penis gets erected for the face [of the partner]. I would normally ask 100 or 120 liras for old guys, for hairy guys. If they negotiate well and there are not many options for me around, I would go for 80 liras. No less than that.'

Who is a Rent Boy?

Murathan Mungan (born in 1955) is a famous author/poet and public intellectual in Turkey. He is gay and, unlike other queer celebrities in the country, he has always been out. During the late 1990s and the first half of the 2000s, he was also quite clear about his affective and erotic attraction to *varoş* boys. Indeed, he was the first one who brought the term *varoş* into the higher cultural nomenclature of same-sex relations in Turkey and inspired me to look more closely at rent boys and male sex work, although he never mentions that these sexual relations are cash-mediated. Still, it is challenging to see such a public/intellectual figure talking about his cross-class, intergenerational queer escapades reputedly full of love and passion. For my purposes here, his remarks on rent boys' divergence from middle-class values and gay men's expectations is significant because in these romanticising comments, the class and sexual aspects of the imagined difference are erased. A *naturally* and *essentially* different masculinity is formulated in order to highlight the dispositions of somatic affiliation. In an interview for a widely read national daily newspaper, when asked about his preference for *varoş* boys over the well-educated [gay] guys, he said,

> The family education of the *petit bourgeoisie* steals the heart, love and emotions to a certain extent. For example, most of the men from this class cannot make love. Even when they are naked, their clothes are still on. Even their eyes and their gazes are covered. They come to the bed with their mothers, fathers, aunts, uncles, friends and everybody else. They think about the explanation they would have to give them. They cannot undress [...] People not belonging to this class, those not-well-educated, not contaminated with this education, feel free to experience their raw nature. Really, the lower-middle-class boy, or the *varoş* boy, makes love better than the others. Because they leave themselves to the language of their nature. They do not insult their bodies and skins with the wrong learning [of middle-class values].[38]

The phrase 'raw nature' (*ham doga*) here brings the notion that *varoş* boys are innately more animalistic, natural, authentic, uncontaminated, and hence closer to nature, in the sense of their masculine bodies and identities. I will elaborate on this gendered notion and its implications throughout this book. Being a peasant and migrant in the city are equalised with being purer, more naïve, impervious and with holding essentialist values that somehow get lost in urbanised, modernised Turkey. Mungan used this naturalistic gendered imaginary in order to exalt rent boys, the sons of migrant families. *Varoş*, in this sense, turns into a space that does not belong to the city, a space where middle-class morality and societal values have not yet penetrated and contaminated. The difference between *varos* boys and the middle-class urbanites (and gay men) moves from being about unequal opportunities and backgrounds and turns into something about unchangeable essences and natures. *Varos* boys bear the essence of masculinity, while the others have lost it. Gay customers of male sex workers agree with this idea:

> I think what Murathan Mungan says is true. Rents are clearly more masculine than the gays. Yes, they are; why do you look surprised? [They are] living in *varos*, they have a distinctive male culture there: the coffeehouse, playing soccer, having fights, swearing. Never mind the gays, we know that they are retarded. Even the straight rich kids cannot be as masculine as *varos* boys. At the end of the day, they are educated, they are refined and clean with all good manners. A rich person cannot escape from this. You can have a [decent] conversation with rich kids, go out and have fun. However, you have to go to the rent boys if you want to be fucked well. The son of a good family cannot fuck me as well as a *varos* kid does. For me, it is not important whether he was gay or not. I don't care; it is totally irrelevant. What matters is if I found him attractive and if he could satisfy me. [The question of] gay or straight: I don't care (Ata, in his early fifties).

Veli (aged 43), on the other hand, used a kind of liberationist gay discourse that describes *varos* boys as actually gay or desiring to be gay, but unable to come out because of who they are (culture) and where they live (location):

> For me rent boys are also gays, but of course they cannot call themselves gay in their uneducated, narrow-minded environments. In those places, if you were a homosexual, especially if you were a little bit effeminate, you would turn into a transvestite. Otherwise, you cannot survive. If we cannot get rid of this trouble [being a transvestite] rent boys and other *varos* boys cannot become gay. Is it important? Actually, no. I know who he is. He sleeps with me. Then, who cares whether he says he was gay or not? [...] I am not sure if we fall in love with their masculinity or the class and

educational differences we have. Because only *varoş* boys can be this mind-blowingly masculine. The white Istanbul {the middle classes} does not provide us what we love. Since we are all Turks, it is not race. Then, it is about being a *varoş*. The lower-class masculinity is different from the educated classes. But it is still ambiguous for me why I find this difference attractive.

Another issue that was brought up by my interlocutors was about the agency of rent boys: Whether these young men are seduced or induced victims or whether they are knowing subjects who are responsible for their decisions, choices and actions. Virtually everybody I talked to stated that they believed in the agency of rent boys and their capacity to read the situation and respond accordingly to protect themselves and maximise their advantage.

> If the there is someone above who manages the circulation of rent boys, they may catch some of the novice rent boys for their own use. However, I don't think this is the situation. Rent boys are not like female prostitutes, their stories are not about touching bottom and there was not any other way. A rent boy fucks a faggot. Well, what's wrong with it? He does not lose anything even when he does this for free. In the story, he tells that he did this for money. Okay, fine, no shame. Also, he can always deny. I think rent boys are aware of their situation, the consequences of their actions, the meaning behind it, and what they want. They act according to this knowledge. Take, for example, this new fashion. They wear stretchy, tight t-shirts on their skinny bodies, pants with really low bellies, the t-shirts in their pants on the waist, without a belt. They can exhibit the lines and size of their bodies from the neck to the groins. This fashion emerged in one or two weeks. Before, they never put their t-shirts into their pants. You know this was an *amele* (labourer, redneck) thing to do. Go and look at them now. All of them look like this. Obviously, this is not a coincidence. They learn and they think what they are supposed to do. They know what they are doing. (Kutay, in his mid-forties).

Kemal (in his early sixties) stated that he not only thought that rent boys were active agents with capacities for decision-making and taking responsibility, but that gay men in this relationality were the used and exploited ones.

> It is shameful for a gay man to have sex with a rent boy in exchange for money. We cannot say this in public. I am telling you now, because you will change my name. Someone around us knows, of course, but it is not good to be publicly known in this way after this age. I said it is not good because we frame it in this way. What is wrong with it? [It is] like buying massage, you are paying for and buying a service. Nobody talks about it, but there is also something dangerous about it. You can be robbed, physically injured or even killed. And we still continue to be with rent boys despite the risks. It shows us that we have a desire, whatever the stakes. And the desire is for real men. For rent boys, this is a not a crime. I mean it might not be good but it is okay. In the worst scenario, he can say he regrets and he is not going to do it again. He walks away. It is the dirt in his hand, he can just wash it. Gays are the used part here. But of course, we also want them. We seek beauty and masculinity, not education and status.

It is not entirely possible to learn how to do (male) sex work as if it were a static structure, pedagogical behavioural model or a repertoire that fixes cultural, social, economic and sexual acts. Each client has his own rules, priorities, tastes and displeasures. Satisfying each single customer, although rent boys seem not to care about that, is another challenge in the normative regime of the sexual economy. Rent boys have a tendency to state that they are unaware of the governing and regulating patterns of sex work, and that they move according to their instincts and beliefs about the right thing to do. I contend that they gradually learn what to do (i.e., how to negotiate, how to relate, how to have sex) by practising and repeating. Then they solidify and naturalise their skills – the unwritten straitjacket of male sex work. However, as Judith Butler famously argues, every repetition has the potential to destabilise the supposed original and differentiate from it. Each act of compensated sex offers another venue for the participants to reformulate and adjust the script. This is also true for gay clients because while they complain about the sameness and tediousness of the sexual acts they perform, they still say they are excited again each time they meet another rent boy, as Abidin (aged 37) said,

'Every person is another test.' (*her insan bir imtihan.*) That may be one reason why gay men in Istanbul hunt for a new person to have sex with each time, and, in most cases, only have sex with each person once. The very few 'regulars' are either in love with a particular rent boy, so that they want to see him again (and again), or have enjoyed a rent boy's sexual performance and prefer not to take the chance of trying another one.

Sexual Repertoire and the Top-Only Rhapsody

I agree with Kevin Walby, who prefers to refer to the relations between male escorts and their customers as a 'touching encounter' because 'it suggests two meanings, both physical and affective [...] A focus on touch can help reorient the literature referred to as queer theory away from abstract starting points toward a greater understanding of how discourses of sexuality are made sense of through processes involving concrete interactions and gestures.'[39] In the case of Istanbulite rent boys, however, touch is not such a simple subject. Rent boys claim that they are 'top only,' meaning that they can insert their penises into clients' bodies through anal and oral sex, but do not allow their clients to penetrate them. Rent boys also claim that they never touch their client's penises or allow their clients to caress their bodies. There is almost a pre-arranged masculine choreography that regulates what sorts of touch are allowed and which bodily acts are rejected in the intimacy between the rent boy and the gay customer. In addition to the top-only rule, for example, some of the rent boys I talked to stated that they never kiss their clients on their mouths, and some told me that they do not 'make out' with clients, rather limiting their sexual activities to oral and anal penetration.[40] Aykut (aged 27) recounts how his negotiations with the customers are structured around sexuality, nationality and age:

Cenk: How much do you charge?
Aykut: 100 liras if I will fuck, if not [just oral sex] 70 liras. If he were not Turkish, I would also ask for the taxi fare.
C: Turks do not pay for it?
A: No, they do not. Actually they do not pay this much either. This is my tariff in order to protect my reputation.
C: So there is negotiation?
A: Of course. This is Turkey. You bargain for the price when you buy a cucumber from the farmer's market, our

	cucumber is also subject to negotiation. It does not come for free.
C:	What is important in the negotiation? How do you determine the price?
A:	(Pause) Age comes first. As the age increases, so does the money, excuse me (older) faggots are richer and they become more desperate to find someone to screw them. So, if {he is} a *balamoz* (an old homosexual) I would directly ask for 100 euros. Excuse me, but I need to get whatever I can.
C:	I see. What else affects negotiation?
A:	Real men always pay less because they can always be with gay men for free. If there is demand, gays can even fuck them. So, they are double-sided (versatile), like a full treatment. If the guy were effeminate, woman-like, then I would ask for more because gays would not want to be with them. Two sisters cannot be together, right? Real men do not really fit us because we are too masculine for them, or worse, they would want to fuck us, which is impossible. I don't do that stuff. However, most boys do [being penetrated] and charge accordingly. It is a different rate. The overall manner of the client, the cuteness of the rent [boy] all affects the negotiated price. Yet again, if he is ugly, older, or more effeminate he should pay more. There is nothing he can do. If he is a cute boy, like the tourists, all smooth, then we can go for cheaper amounts. You know, sometimes you should give your penis a reward. Overall, we make more money with the tourists, sometimes $50–100. But it is different to fuck a guy who is the age of my grandfather, like he's 50 years old. That's torture.
C:	So there is an element of pleasure with some customers?
A:	Of course, it is a natural thing.

It was interesting and intriguing for me to hear that a rent boy who defines himself as unquestionably heterosexual admits that he gets pleasure when he is sexually involved with other men. I asked Aykut how he could manage to have sex with men that he was not supposed to enjoy. He said, 'I try not to think of it. I imagine women in the pornography. I think of him as a woman. I always prefer oral sex at least in the beginning when I can close my eyes and concentrate. I think they already know about this. There is a natural balance.'

Another respondent, Furkan (aged 25), points to an additional difficulty when rent boys are with younger and physically more attractive customers:

> Furkan: That is confusing. I honestly do not prefer to fuck the younger ones. Because they do not want to give money. I guess it is something about their psychology. They cannot accept that we screw them for money. They think they are still beautiful. Also, I am afraid that you may get used to fucking the younger ones. I think it will be difficult in the future to quit if it turns out to be a habit.
>
> Cenk: That means you take pleasure with the younger guys?
>
> F: Why would I not, am I not a man? Who does not take pleasure?
>
> C: Have you ever had sexual relations with girls?
>
> F: We sometimes fuck with transvestites for free. It is really funny, we are free for them only and they are free for us only, for the rest of the people we are all for money. And some of them are really beautiful. I have also gone to the women prostitutes two or three times. So, yes, I know how to fuck a woman. But for me, to fuck a nice young boy or to fuck a woman is the same thing in terms of pleasure.
>
> C: But only to fuck, nothing else, right?
>
> F: As I said before, nothing else could happen, I can only fuck, even if Erman Toroglu [a national soccer commentator, used to be known as a tough guy] comes.

Emre (aged 25) also speaks in the same way, with an emphasis on sexual experiences with men:

> I love women. I do this thing [male sex work] only for money. It is like a second job for me. And that is it, there is nothing else, and there cannot be. My inside [love] is for females only. You would

like to fuck a guy because you need money, or worse, you are horny. So it is temporary. When you are young, you need experience, you need money. I have been around [in the male prostitution] for four years and I have seen everything in this time period. I have seen Istanbul. What have my parents seen? There is a song called 'Istanbul has ruined you.'[41] It is like my story.

Deniz (aged 24) admits that he slept with men either for money or for his bodily satisfaction. When we were talking, he told me he would have sex with me for free. I responded by saying that I was not looking for a paid sexual relation and he said, 'Who wants your money? There are the guys I want [to be with] and those where I do it for money. Don't confuse the practices for work and for piety.'[42]

The Relations Between Rent Boys and Gay Men

Rent boys approach and interact with gay men in four moods: in an unforthcoming and impersonal way (most frequently), in a kind and civilised manner (with the hint of professionalism), in a friendly and sociable fashion (implying that the rent boy might hang out with the client), and in a desiring and embracing attitude (not necessarily sexual, more likely social, i.e., indicating that he might become a fellow gay in the future). When I talked to rent boys about their relations with gay men, my interviewees were generally dismissive, saying that it is not probable or plausible to have human contact with gay men because there are too many differences involved.[43] Ulas (aged 22) says, for example, 'Some gays want to talk. They say, "Tell me, I am listening." I ask them what they want me to talk about. He says "About your life." I do not have a life to tell you about. I am not that kind of [a person] (*oyle bir sekil degilim*)'.

Mert (aged 26) answered in detail, when I asked what he shared with his customers:

Mert: We are total opposites. Most of them are rich, having good jobs, speaking in foreign languages, educated, drinking imported alcoholic beverages, wearing colognes, clothes, etc. They are friends with famous people. They have different lives than what I saw in my family. What they wear, how they talk, they are all intellectuals, clean,

Cenk: Then it is difficult for you to be friends with a gay person?
M: Very different, what is a friendship? You should share something; you should be able to talk to each other. What problems do those gay men have? How can they understand my life? I have many problems, like how I could not pass the university placing exam, how I am unemployed, the [compulsory] military service, etc [...] These are my problems, right? They are preoccupied only with getting fucked, going out, drinking French champagne. Motherfuckers (*orospu cocuklari*).
C: I guess it is very difficult to share intimacy with these people that you do not like?
M: [Laughs] It is different. I do not think about that aspect of it, I concentrate on my pleasure when I am with them. Can I solve the problems of this country? Actually, I understand that being from different worlds does not create an obstacle for fucking. I do fuck anyway, brother (*ben her turlu sikerim abi*).

The encounter between a rent boy and a gay man is first and foremost a bodily and intimate one through prescribed identities. These people prepare different parts of their bodies through a number of techniques and to the extent that they believe in self-disciplining. However, their concern with fighting the signs of ageing and mis-performance also manifest in diverse ways. Transactional sex is possibly one of the most intimate types of economic exchange: These people have sex, make love, take a shower, sleep, talk, cuddle, drink, eat and have some time alone with one another, while all the concepts of social power we use in the outside world may become illegitimate, insufficient, or irrelevant. Vulnerabilities, sensitivities and embodied memories come to the surface and become visible. Rent boys in general refuse to talk about their affective or social experiences with gay men. Emir, a 20-year-old rent boy, is an example of the standoffish attitude:

Cenk: Do you talk with gay clients?
Emir: When?
C: Before sex, or after, or other times?

E: Do we talk about what? I would not be involved in gay chat with them. Gossiping like women?

C: Should it be gay chat? What about their lives, your life?

E: (Pause) Well, it depends. Of course, sometimes there is conversation. We are all human; you might be worried about something at that moment, or in need of talking. They are generally willing to listen to me. But I feel there is always an abyss. They always tell me, finish your school or let me find you a job as an answer to what I say. Thanks God, I do not have any complaints [about my life] [...] Of course, I would want to have a place in a better neighbourhood, a better job, or a beautiful girlfriend. But I am not ashamed because of what I have now. Generally, gays are good people, especially tourists, they like me and they adore everything I do. It is strange. I really cannot understand how a man distances himself from masculinity this much and then falls in love with someone only because he is masculine.

C: They fall in love with you, too...

E: Oh yes, you cannot even guess how miserable they become. I cannot comprehend it at all. I think in this way: okay, you are a man, almost 40 years old, having a house near the Bosphorus, having a good job, a comfortable social milieu. Books, chats, culture. Everything seems to be fine. But you are a faggot. You give money to young men to fuck you, and then you cry until the morning and tell them, 'Please do not leave me'. He tells me he could give me whatever I want. This drama happens only because I am a handsome boy, because I am a *delikanli* (rugged, young and masculine). This guy does not even think that this boy has a mother and a father, has a family of his own, lives far away and works for a few pennies. So he does not realise that it is not possible for me to adapt his lifestyle. He cannot understand my way of living, either. He cannot see that he is not my equal and thus we have no future together. He does not tell himself that I may want a girl in the future, or to marry in the end and have children. Older, mature men call me, send me text messages and follow

> me in the bars. That is so sad. How blind they are. Now, I have learnt that I should not give my phone number to these guys ever.

Mendacity is an inseparable part of the erotic economy in queer Istanbul. Both rent boys and their clients lie to each other for different purposes and through diverse plots. Manufacturing fake identities or imaginary social positions was the most frequent kind of deceitfulness I observed. Gay men usually present themselves as more powerful, significant and wealthy than they actually are, while some strive to conceal their real identities and social status due to the risk of blackmail, harassment and stalking. Rent boys, however, never give their real name and surnames, and generally produce scenarios that they think gay men would find more enjoyable, for example, by making up jobs that they do not actually have (i.e., being a mechanic, working at bicycle shop, or being a security officer) or painful stories of poverty, disability in the family or orphanage experiences. Both sides generally approach each other with a certain level of unreliability and disbelief, as they all want to impress their interlocutors and manipulate their feelings.

****

In this chapter, I have laid out the scholarly discussions and research findings about male prostitution, queer sexuality and masculinities. Then I presented four central issues in determining the characteristics of the rent boy identity and rent boys' manifold relations with gay men, with a focus on rent boys' and gay men's own accounts. In the next chapter, I will explicate the material, symbolic and relational components of the style of 'exaggerated masculinity' that boys engender and embody in their attempted transformations from ordinary *varoş* boys to successful and desired male sex workers.

CHAPTER 2

RENT BOYS AND THE CONTOURS OF EXAGGERATED MASCULINITY

> I always lied, and for me this mendacity was the most exhausting aspect of the job.
> Rick Whitaker, *Assuming the Position: A Memoir of Hustling* (New York and London, 1999), p. 39

I am wandering through Taksim Square. This place has long been accepted as the heart of greater Istanbul, which is one of the megacities of the Global South, with 16 million inhabitants occupying more than 350 square miles of urban land. The word *taksim* means 'to divide,' and the name comes from the Byzantium, Genoese and Ottoman water channels that used to be centralised here. Remnants of the antique water distribution system are still visible although nobody seems to care in the hustle and bustle of this extremely crowded city centre that is awake 24/7. Similar to the old water distribution system, the mobilities of contemporary Istanbulites intersect at Taksim. The most visible public space in the country, Taksim Square functions like a magnet that pulls millions of bodies to itself for numerous unutterable reasons. This is, among many others, the geographical hub of queer life in Istanbul, as well as the male sex work that takes place in the city.

I wandered through Taksim Square during evening hours, especially after 10 pm on Friday and Saturday nights and early on Sunday mornings. This was long before the Gezi Uprising that took place in the square in the summer of 2013. Taksim was not yet as politicised[1] as it became after the insurgent occupation to protect the small Gezi Park against the government's intention to destroy it in order to build a shopping mall with luxury residences. The park itself, particularly from the late 1990s to the late 2000s, was a dim and clandestine meeting point for homosexuals, rent boys, transgender people and other queers who seek illicit, semi-public, uncontrolled, mostly transactional sexual encounters.[2] Thus, it was not deemed as an especially decent, family-friendly place on evenings and nights by middle-class Istanbulites. In general, the Taksim area has been perceived as a space of decadence and vice, housing female sex workers, homosexuals, transvestites and transsexuals, bachelors, gypsies and the Roma people, Kurdish migrants, criminals, drug dealers and delinquents of all sorts, street kids and other 'undesired' populations of the city. Whoever cannot find a place for herself elsewhere, whoever cannot fit into the existing spatial and moral norms, whoever is excluded from the mainstream urban networks and seeks a sense of freedom to be herself, comes to the Taksim area. This scene of multiple otherness and social marginality is consolidated by the presence of a small number of Christian (Armenian and Greek) and Jewish minorities in the immediate surrounding area. Sexual, political, ethnic, religious, intellectual and subcultural undercurrents meet here to further bolster the public image of the alternative and precarious urban centre in the eyes of the 'normal' majority. This sense of risky urban space was the case until the mid-2000s, when the spirit as well as the economic organisation started to change.

I am heading towards the always-crowded Istiklal Street, which is a major promenade connecting Taksim Square and the Tunnel area. It is full of intermeshing people from all classes, ages, genders, ethnicities, religions, sexualities and cultures representing Istanbul's social diversity. During the course of this research, the 1.5-mile street has been transformed from a significant local cultural centre, with numerous bookstores, art galleries, cafes, theatres and independent cinemas, to a hyper-consumerist touristic scene with giant stores of global brands, chain restaurants and several Starbucks coffee shops. The transformation was not only about the cultural topography of the zone; rather, the publics of the promenade have radically changed. Today, Istiklal Street looks like any other shopping district in any other urban area of the world, with an ambiguous historical décor (authentic and artificial parts are intertwined), strict police surveillance and a welcoming attitude towards families with purchasing power and no obvious political symbolism or ambition. Since the bookstores and cinemas have shut down, the intellectuals, bohemians, graduate students and hipsters have migrated to the neighbouring Galata-Karakoy zone, or to Kadikoy across the Bosphorus, rapidly gentrifying the historical Genoese-Ottoman buildings and streets with new and expensive cafe houses and art shops.

I walked on Istiklal Street at night. Among the carnivalesque crowd, an attentive eye notices some young men strolling meaninglessly or leaning against walls or closed shop windows, checking the passers-by out. It is obvious to these attentive eyes that these young men, who carefully prepared themselves for the peak hours of transactional sociability, reciprocate with curious gazes that speak the same language of the looker. Around midnight these young men suddenly disappear from the street. Then the bar time starts.

After paying the entry fee (around $10) I enter Bientot, the most famous and best-frequented club of rent boys in Istanbul. Bientot is very close to the vivid Istiklal Street, as well as a tavern that was well known among transgender people, and the only gay sauna of the city. Bientot, like two other similar bars, is a 'limitative and disciplining'[3] space, in the sense that types of people there (i.e., rent boys, transvestites, clients) are set, their roles are prescribed (i.e., who dances, who looks, who buys drinks) and interactions between visitors are relatively stabilised (i.e., negotiations, flirting, cruising, kissing), except during sudden fights and police raids, when the music is switched off and the lights are turned on[4]. Especially gay men (whether clients of rent boys or not) told me repeatedly that they do not 'have fun' in Bientot the way they regularly do in other gay bars. They come here just to see or talk to the *varos* boys in the prescribed ways that are available to them.

In the approximately 1,300 square feet main dance area, Bientot is full of its usual crowd: Several single gay men of all ages, some mixed friend groups, several transvestites and more than 70 rent boys hanging out in the usual 'social choreography'[5] of the place. In general, everyone seems to know each other. Everyone, generally except the rent boys, drinks alcoholic beverages and rests against the walls surrounding the dance floor enjoying music (popular euphoric Turkish pop songs of the day), while rent boys dance in a unique style without drinking, unless a client is generous enough to buy them a drink. The other two bars with a similar reputation among rent boys, Boogie and SenGel, do not have very different spatial and social organisations, except that SenGel is larger in terms of space and is also very popular among Turkish bears, who normally do not mingle with gay men and lesbians.[6]

Here is a candid quotation from field notes I took immediately after arriving home from Bientot:

> A small but shocking place [...] Very high volume of music, really bad ventilation, the smell of alcohol, the smell of sweat, the smell of cologne, the smoke from cigarettes [...] You can't escape from the piercing looks into your eyes. These looks are so masculine, you can tell, but they are also very inviting and flirtatious, which contradicts with the assertive masculinity. The dancing bodies are very close to each other. They are very straight looking, like the ordinary boys on the street; but, on the other hand, the male-to-male intimacy of the dance destroys the desired heterosexual ambience. It seems like they are straight boys in a gay club, dancing together passionately.
>
> A topless waiter with very thin eyebrows asks if I want beer. At every second, another person touches me; it is impossible to trace who he is. It is very crowded inside. Finding a wall to lean on is the only getaway, but it is not possible to escape from the insisting looks, they eventually find and check you out. After a while, I realised that the rent boys around me keep rotating, as long as I don't talk to them. It is very difficult to follow the movement of rent boys. They have lure in their eyes as well as toughness and even threat. Like smells, the feelings I receive from them are hybrid, ambiguous and atomised (17 April 2004).

Introducing Metin

Metin was one of my key informants. I met nineteen-year-old Metin in the summer of 2004 and I somehow kept in touch with him until 2011. He was living with his parents, grandmother and three sisters in Sariyer, one of the less-urbanised northern districts of Istanbul. The family was from a small city on the Black Sea coast. When they migrated to Istanbul in the mid-1980s they built a squatter house without permits, and since then they have lived in the same house, although there have been expansions and remodelling, which are typical in squatter slum houses in Istanbul.

Metin had an older brother who was married with a baby and lived close by. They saw each other very frequently and this older brother was the one Metin felt most intensely attached to. He had a large family including his uncles, aunts and cousins. Metin was not a good student, but he was able to get his high school diploma. A six-foot-tall, handsome young man with an easy smile and green eyes, Metin was a popular rent boy on the weekend nights when he was not working with his father at their family business of selling canned natural water door-to-door. Carrying the heavy containers from an early age had helped to develop his body. Sometimes he complained that he could have been taller if he had not had to carry the containers almost every day when he was still growing up.

The economic crisis of 2001–02 hit Metin's family hard. His father was fired from the landscaping company he had been working for, and he could not find another job for a long time. His mother was a retired domestic cleaner. Following her husband's unemployment, she had also looked for jobs but wasn't able to find any because of her relatively advanced age. Then the family started the water business, using a large amount of informal credit. That is why everybody in the household had to work in the shop, in order to serve more people and make as much money as possible. Like many other people in Istanbul at the time, Metin was tired of financial difficulties and felt deeply insecure and pessimistic about his future through the aftershocks of the economic crisis. In the ensuing years, his family started to improve their business and paid their debts back. Meanwhile, Metin's father's political views shifted from the Turkish nationalist centre-right to the Islamist AKP, and he became supportive of Prime Minister Tayyip Erdogan. The rest of the family, including Metin, kept their conservative-but-not-radical opinions of political and social life in Turkey.

In most cases, someone of the 'old' type of rent boys (prevalent roughly between the early 1990s to the late 2000s) would start doing male sex work either by the initiation of a friend or a distant relative, generally a cousin. Metin was initiated by a friend. For a long time, he would not tell me the story of how his rent boy career started. He used to say that he did not remember how he was initiated, but I soon realised that he rarely forgot anything. After a while, he recounted a vague story about how a slightly older friend, a junior fisherman also from Sariyer, took him to a gay club for the first time. This friend of Metin was not gay; neither was Metin. They went to a gay club because it was the only place that did not require that men have a female companion in order to gain admittance.[7] Metin said he did not particularly like or dislike it there; he was rather nonchalant about the place. This indifference demonstrates Metin's more flexible moral boundaries. His straight peers would have been disturbed by gay men's presence and possibly would have reacted in a hostile manner. This was not the case for Metin.

While at the club, as Metin later comprehended, his friend found a client and left. He hung out alone for another hour with different people approaching him as he observed. He adapted himself to the environment, refused all the men, and left the club. Eventually, he learnt about the money involved and began to think that he could also become a top-only rent boy, have sex with gay men, preserve his masculinity and earn some extra income.

> So, yes, it is interesting that I was never surprised. Of course, I knew the stuff about the perverse guys using smooth boys. I mean pederasty [*oglancilar*] and other things. Like all other members of Turkish youth, I grew up protecting my ass. [Laughing] But [I did] not [know about] the other way, I mean effeminate homosexuals and the young men. When I figured it out, I thought it was not big deal to fuck some men. I could do that for money. That's what my thing is: money. If there were no money, I would never be involved. I believe that's my difference from other rents. I know they are doing everything for money or for stuff. Some do that for drugs or clothes. Some even have sex for mutual satisfaction. That is gay.

Metin, when I knew him, was a clever and exceptionally complex person. He was well aware of the performative aspects of 'being' a rent boy and 'doing the rent boy stuff,' at the right place, at the right time in front of the right audience. We first met at SenGel one night. He had worked at the water shop that day and as a result was very tired. He was sitting in the lounge, not actively seeking a client, and was in a talkative mood, as he generally was. He interpreted my initial attempts to approach him as a potential client's manoeuvres and hinted that he was not interested.

When I explained to him that I was not a customer but a researcher, he found this quite entertaining (unlike the typical rent boy reaction) and started talking to me about his life – partially and selectively, but in a coherent fashion. He was always one of the most open rent boys I talked to. He was clear about what about him caused gay men to try to be with him in an unceasing demand, the weaknesses and strengths that gay men had, and the 'fake' or 'theatrical' nature of the male sex work that he and other rent boys perform. He was also one of the most articulate rent boys on the nature of self-marketable masculinity.

> Well, I am not doing anything [special]; just being myself. And that is what they [gay men] like. So, if I have this [asset] why should not I use it, right? I am a man, I don't know how not to be a man, and that's what they actually crave. I know I have good looks and my eyes are nice and the other features. But you know what? They actually look for masculinity. If you are not cute but masculine enough you can still sell yourself because you know if you are ugly they may find you 'charismatic.' But if you're not tough, manly enough, then it does not matter how tall or well-built you are [...]
>
> Of course I know how to play this game. There are certain things that you must do, again and again. For example, disguise yourself. Don't tell, don't give information about yourself, not even the phone number, where you live, don't be interested in their [customers'] lives and don't ask questions about them. You are not supposed to care, right? When they insist on talking, which they always do, look as if you're disgusted and got bored, pretend you're not listening. When they talk, look at the other direction. Everything starts with this attitude. Most gays would fall in love with you just because you act this way. Do not do the gay stuff [...] gossip, clothes, etc.

In the early hours of one morning, a group of people, including Metin and I, were sitting and talking at the Burger King at Taksim Square. That restaurant was popular because it has a large rooftop and is open until 4:00 am. I had finished my fieldwork in the gay and rent boy bars and Metin was done with a tourist customer at one of the nearby hotels. The topic of conversation, as was frequently the case when gays and rent boys managed to have a conversation, was whether rent boys were straight guys or if they were just repressed and concealed homosexuals. During a heated discussion, Metin said, 'There must be other ways to understand [sexuality]. Okay, I am different from my father [a heterosexual] but I am also different from you [gay men]. So it is not the gay versus normal [*sic*] thing, there must be other types.'

In the seven years that I knew him, Metin experienced many different situations regarding his identity, relations, future expectations and dreams. I will come back to Metin's life later in the book.

Introducing Rent Boys

From the late 1990s to the early 2010s, rent boys became increasingly visible in the queer social spaces of Istanbul. Rent boys engage in different forms of compensated sex (Agustin, 2005) with other men. They construct their masculine identities through their clandestine homoerotic involvements. They invent and practice an embodied style that I call 'exaggerated masculinity,'[8] in order to mark their manly stance and handle the risks that same-sex sexual activities pose for the reproduction of their masculine selves. In the rest of this chapter, I examine how these heterosexually identified rent boys assemble and perform exaggerated masculinity in order to negotiate the tensions between their local, socially marginalised environments and a burgeoning Western-style gay culture while they conduct their risky sexual interactions with other men.

Jeffrey Weeks' historical study shows that there was no distinct (sub) culture of male or homosexual prostitution during the formation of the modern homosexual identity in the late nineteenth century in England.[9] On the other hand, Albert J. Reiss details norms, rules and codes that governed the interaction between young male prostitutes (peers) and homosexual men (queers) in the late 1950s in Nashville in the USA.[10] Reiss' cultural framework of male prostitution corresponds with Maurice Godelier's definition of culture: 'the set of representations and principles which consciously organise the different aspects of social life, together with the set of positive and negative norms and the values that are connected with these ways of acting and thinking.'[11] Timothy M. Hall's analysis of local forms of compensated sex among men in Prague[12] also employs a cultural framework similar to Godelier's. This culture forms three loosely defined and flexible types of men: 'the barfly', 'sex for pocket money', and 'the kept man,' using different strategies and entailing multiple subjectivities.

Here, I follow a similar cultural approach in order to understand how the contested identities of rent boys in Istanbul are shaped and stabilised, and through what strategies they navigate their masculine selves. Rent boys come from lower-class neighbourhoods in the outskirts of the Istanbul metropolitan region. These zones started to be called *varos* (a term somewhat similar to the Brazilian *favela*[13] and the French *banlieue*)[14] in the 1990s by the middle-class Istanbulites and the mass media. Rent boys (aged between 16 and 25) are mostly sons of recently migrated large families that have coped with dislocation, poverty and cultural exclusion. They speak Turkish with different regional accents which show their symbolic marginalisation and lack of cultural capital. Through performances of a muted authenticity, rent boys self-fashion their masculinity to produce a niche for themselves within a highly stratified, increasingly homonormative gay culture in Istanbul. This self-fashioning via the embodied, stylised, continuously refined, exaggerated masculinity operates through an 'outsider within'[15] position amongst self-identified gay men in Istanbul. Most of the rent boys I have talked to emphasised that because of this very position of 'within the gay culture, intimately close to gay men; but not being one of them, radically different from them' they were able to see 'what is wrong with' gay men or gay culture. In a reflexive manner, some of them said they were also able to perceive what was missing or malfunctioning about their lives as an outcome of their interactions with gay men.

Varos boys narrate a story of the authenticity of their real selves while they strive to become rent boys, which they claim is a temporary and transitory position. Exaggerated masculinity is a critical part of this construction in the context of male prostitution. *Varos* boys transform themselves to achieve the rent boy identity through a discursive process, in which they reiterate the rules and characteristics of being a rent boy, and simultaneously through a bodily process in which they learn to do, improvise and enhance exaggerated masculinity. On the other hand, this reconfiguration of authenticity through the creation of a rent boy identity alleviates the socially excluded *varos* background via the bodily rules and practices that I will detail below. It enables rent boys to connect both materially and symbolically with the upper-class milieu through their encounters with local and foreign gay men.[16]

The globalisation of modern gayness has produced the desire and mechanisms of adaptation associated with Western gay identity, space, culture and community in the non-Western world through a compound process of imitation, hybridisation and reconstruction, while it has made different, if not counter to, subject positions and subjective mediations available through the fragmented experiences of differently modernising societies.[17] In the Istanbul case, the identity of the *varos* is a highly marginalised social identity vis-a-vis the mainstream culture of the middle classes. When they attempt to enter the spaces of Western-style gay venues in Istanbul, *varos* boys are discriminated against and rejected because of their alterity to the apparently modern, urban and liberal lifestyles that the middle classes have long adopted.

As a form of representation, the rent boy emerges in the liminal space between the *varos* identity and the local reflection of the global, homonormative and seemingly uncontested gay culture: a rent boy neither becomes gay nor stays a *varos*. This is not necessarily the actual story. Instead, the construction works on the assumptions of a binary: the imagining of an idealised, top-only hetero-masculinity and the idealised, refined, feminised homosexuality. Both sides mediate male sex work through this story, which is based on representation of distinct social imaginaries. Rent boys animate a dynamic process of cultural hybridisation and theatrical displays of exaggerated masculinity as a response to double marginalisation. While they strategically use their *varos* backgrounds to underline their masculinity and consolidate their authenticity in order to attract gay men who are supposed to have fantasies of having sex with 'real' heterosexual men, they concomitantly take advantage of their encounters with middle-class gay men and empower themselves in their *varos* environments. In this sense, the agility of the identity of rent boys permits its subjects to be enriched and strengthened in the symbolic hierarchies that they face in both *varos* and gay cultures. Masculine embodiment and its deliberate and nuanced uses become crucial in rent boys' symbolic and material culture.

Varos Identity

After the 1980 military coup, neoliberal reforms in Turkey transformed Istanbul's position within the country as well as the city's own socio-spatial organisation.[18] The population in Istanbul has expanded by almost 400 per cent and has recently approached 12 million people. Urban segregation and social fragmentation have escalated and reshaped Istanbul as a space of contestation in which previously silenced social groups including Islamists, Kurds and queers claimed legitimacy and public visibility (Kandiyoti, 2002; Keyder, 1999, 2005).

Varos was one of the names given by the middle-class, tax-paying, law-abiding resident citizens of Istanbul, or as Norbert Elias puts it 'the established,'[19] to the illegal squatter settlement neighbourhoods around the city and the migrant people who built houses and worked at temporary jobs in the informal sector.[20] The term was used in a sense of borderwork in order to draw boundaries between the Istanbulites, who are imagined as modern, urbanised, secular and Westernised versus the peasant, insular, religious, uneducated classes that lack the forms of cultural capital necessary to amalgamate within the urban culture. In this sense, *varos* became synonymous with a regressive, 'pre-modern' subjectivity that is abject and disenfranchised.

In the 1990s, the term *varos* started to designate urban poverty instead of backwardness and rurality, while people living in *varos* areas were increasingly identified as the 'threatening Other.'[21] *Varos* was constructed as a space where radical Islamist fundamentalism, Kurdish separatism, illegality, criminality and forms of violence met. Through media representations, *varos* was otherised in terms of culture, economy, ethnicity and politics. Accordingly, the 'dangerous' *varos* quarters of the city were believed to house beggars, terrorists, gangsters, smugglers and other components of the informal economy.[22] At the same time, inhabitants of *varos* reclaimed and appropriated the word as a way to identify their own cultural position as distinct from the Istanbulite. For the first time, *varos* culture appeared not as a humiliating discourse directed towards the *varos* people, but as a resurgent medium to voice their own subjectivity, however fragmented and disputed it was.[23]

Rent boys are the children of *varos*.[24] They tactically constitute their identities as *varos* to underline their differences from their gay clients, not only in terms of sexuality, but also in terms of class position. In this sense, being *varos* refers to an embodied cultural difference as well as a certain gendered meaning regarding masculinity. Rent boys repeatedly state that they are 'real' men because they are coming from *varos*. In this way, the *varos* is naturalised and linked to an inherent masculinity that gay men do not (and cannot) have. In other words, being *varos* becomes a sign of an uncontaminated, natural, physical and authentic masculinity, while beingn gay stands for feminine values and norms such as culture, refinement and cleanliness. In a symbolic order of masculinity, *varos* boys become 'naturally' and unchangeably masculine, while gay men's bodies represent a modern, inauthentic and imperfect masculinity.

Tactics of Masculinity

In addition to the symbolic significance of *varos* in creating a 'naturally' virile character, rent boys also employ tactics to maintain their masculine identities vis-a-vis gay men. The most important strategy is being 'top only'. Thus, rent boys claim that they engage sexually with other men only by playing the top (active) role. Protecting their bodies from penetration and becoming sexually available only as tops allow rent boys to reclaim their incontestably masculine identities. The gender of their sexual partner does not make a real difference either for their sexual repertoire or for their erotic subjectivities.[25]

Another way that rent boys secure their masculinity is through their heterosexualising discourse. When they talk, rent boys position themselves in relation to imagined girlfriends, fiancées, or long-term lovers-to-be-married with whom they have on-going emotional and sexual affairs. When challenged, this discursive heterosexuality and the spectre of women enable rent boys to prove their 'real' heterosexual identities. In order to distinguish themselves from gay men and to buttress their masculinity, rent boys also humiliate and denigrate gay men. It is important to note that rent boys' homophobia is, in most cases, a performative 'utterance,'[26] used to help maintain their masculine identities. It does not really prevent them from mingling, negotiating with and having sex with gay men in other situations.

Masculinity has always been a contested subject in the construction of queer sexualities in Turkey.[27] However, rent boys' 'top only' positions and homophobic utterances are only one aspect of the exaggerated performance of masculinity. In contrast to the archetypical macho sexual pose of Latin America,[28] rent boys do not brag about their sexual escapades with gay men. Instead, they have an evasive manner about their queer sexual practices. In addition to homophobia, the silence of rent boys about their homosexual involvements coincides with the tradition of the strict separation of intimate affairs from the public sphere in some Muslim societies, what Murray calls 'the will not to know.'[29] Accordingly, rent boys have a will not to divulge.

Within the framework of interpenetrating Western gay culture and local constellations of gender and sexuality, masculinity matters for rent boys and gay men on another level: the appeal of passing and acting straight.[30] Gay men in Istanbul have an increasing obsession with the straight-acting and straight-looking self-presentation, which demands a certain degree of heterosexual masculinity for erotic engagement. This fetishism of 'more masculine' attributes and bodily gestures contributes to a hierarchy in which feminine qualities, as in effeminate men, are deemed inferior and unwanted, while masculine traits are presented as rare, desired and superior. The negative attitude towards effeminacy and the desire for more masculine attributes contribute to an exaggerated masculinity and a desire to prevail as the 'most masculine' in the gay culture of Istanbul. Rent boys take advantage of this erotic climate and reposition themselves in the eyes of their potential clients. In other words, rent boys convert their erotic and sexual positionality into social and economic capital through their use of the encounter and desire between different masculinities.

The Interplay of Masculinities

Since gender is conceptualised as a continual 'doing' rather than as a natural 'being,'[31] gendered subjectivities are constituted through 'the repeated stylisation of the body, a set of repeated acts within a highly rigid regulatory frame that congeal over time to produce the appearance of substance, of a natural sort of being.'[32] Gendered subjectivity comes into being via the constellation of bodily performances within the 'regulatory frame' of the heterosexual matrix. Rent boys subvert their regular and 'normal' heterosexual script with male prostitution, while they simultaneously try to re-stabilise it by enacting an exaggerated masculinity — a style that requires a well-defined gendered performances before different audiences, as in Decena's words, 'in their past socialisations and present negotiations of daily life, the body and the regulation of its significations functioned to communicate, demand legitimacy and create boundaries with others.'[33] The omnipresent sense of risk inaugurates the possibility that the exaggeratedly masculine identity will be questioned and imperilled. In this sense, the rent boy's masculinity is a delusional and insecure subject position that needs to be repeatedly asserted and proven, while it continuously introduces new risks to be contemplated by rent boys in order to achieve their heterosexual and masculine status.

In her seminal work, Raewyn Connell demonstrated that multiple masculinities coexist and interact in a society at any given time.[34] The encounter and dialogue between a *varos* boy and a middle-aged upper-class gay man might be seen as a manifestation of what Connell called the relations between divergent masculinities. These relations ought to be seen through the prism of power. The culturally exalted hegemonic masculinity brings complicity, subordination, intimidation and exploitation into the relations between different masculinities. The exclusion of same-sex desire is critical for the constitution of hegemonic masculinity.[35] As a model, an ideal or a reference point, hegemonic masculinity – in relation to the heterosexual matrix – affects all other ways of being a man, including its imitations (as in rent boys) as well as the resistant or alternative versions (as in queer masculinity).

In the eastern Mediterranean region, configurations of masculinities take shape between the Westernising influences of modernity and the history of Islamic culture and tradition.[36] The case of rent boys in Istanbul is not an exception. This study shows that critical elements of the social context, including belated Turkish modernity, incomplete urbanisation and persistent poverty, the increasing effects of globalisation and cosmopolitanism, Occidentalism and the desire to be Western, and the contested meanings of locality and tradition, must be taken into account when one attempts to understand the ramifications of the globalisation of modern sexual identities in Istanbul in the 2000s.

Playing with Fire: Elements of Rent Boys' Style

A weekly TV show filmed the gay sauna near Bientot with hidden cameras in early 2005. After recording each possible proof of male prostitution (including negotiations for prices and actions), the programmers tried to talk with the manager of the sauna about the internal organisation of the place, while he kept refuting that he hired the rent boys. During the interview the camera focused on a young rent boy, half naked in his towel, arguing angrily with another one about the recruitment of new rent boys that they already knew. He said,

I told you not to bring everyone here from your neighbourhood. Look at me. I only bring my brother. You may have a fight with one of them in the future and he can go and tell people, including your father, what you do here. You are playing with fire. I told you this before. Don't play with fire.

As rent boys have a will not to divulge, they certainly want to keep things hidden. Thus, this warning against 'playing with fire' is neither unique to this rent boy nor restricted within the walls of the bathhouse. It offers a useful framework to better comprehend a rent boy's unceasing physical and social negotiations with other rent boys, gay men and transvestites. Being a rent boy is a conditional and fragile identity. It surfaces between contradictory discursive and sexual practices, which subvert the line between homo and heterosexuality. It is a contingent performance that links the *varos* culture of Istanbul and the ostensibly global gay lifestyle. It is an interplay of competing working- and upper-middle-class meanings and signifiers. Through the incessant practice of risk taking, a rent boy invests his heterosexuality as well his social position and kinship networks, which are likely to be harmed by an undesired disclosure, as the rent boy quoted earlier fears.

Here I follow Agustin's proposal to define and study prostitution, sex work and compensated sex as a culture in order to expose previously under-researched links with systems of inequality and the production of social meaning.[37] Wright also highlights the 'percolation of queer theoretical concerns' and 'an array of cultural studies interventions' into the sociology of masculinities in order to pose new questions about masculine performances, cultural practices and 'engenderment' processes that men undertake through the routes of non-hegemonic masculinities in diverse settings.[38] Hence, I frame exaggerated masculinity as a product of the culture of rent boys in Istanbul. Rent boys learn, practise and transform exaggerated masculinity through the mechanisms of social control and self-governance. The process of the construction and reconstruction of exaggerated masculinity is constantly under threat of disappointment and failure.

As 'discretion was indeed the hallmark of homosexual prostitution,'[39] risk appears three-fold in animating exaggerated masculinity by rent boys. First and foremost, rent boys' involvement with male prostitution must not be revealed to their friends, family or extended relatives.

Otherwise, they cannot sustain their ordinary lives as young, decent and respected members of their community. Secondly, while the rent boy reproduces *varos* culture as corroboration of his 'natural' masculinity, he must also play with and transmute it symbolically in order to have a subject position within gay culture instead of being abject. It is a nuanced middle space between the two unwanted identities that a rent boy must navigate carefully: staying an unmodified *varos* or becoming (too) gay. While connecting closely with gay men, rent boys' third risk is about protecting their heterosexuality. Said differently, although rent boys have sex with gay men, they are not supposed to have a gay identity. In sum, a rent boy has to meticulously control and manage risk regarding his bodily acts, behaviours and relations with other people in order not to be exposed while balancing between the discrepant meanings of *varos* and gay positions.

In this framework, I will now outline the elements of how rent boys sustain exaggerated masculinity through their risk-taking activities and their entanglements with different segments of the culture of male sex work in Istanbul.

The Body

The first point of risk that rent boys take into consideration focuses on their bodies. Almost all rent boys have skinny/fit or athletic/toned bodies. They say they are physically in good shape because they regularly play football (soccer) and/or run. Although the number of gyms in some *varos* neighbourhoods has risen recently, and these places provide an important opportunity for masculine socialising, most rent boys do not go to the gyms. Their unwillingness to do so is related to three factors. One of them is financial; they simply are not able to pay the fees. More importantly, they think that their gay clients like their bodies slim, lean and definitely not overly-muscular, or hunk. They also believe that they look younger this way. The third reason is about rent boys' belief that the pills and other artificial protein supplements they would take to sustain a muscled appearance will eventually decrease the power of their penises and consequently terminate their virilities. They always make jokes about the impotency of their overly-muscled, bodybuilder friends.

Hakan (aged 22 at the time of our interview) said, 'the body is everything we have in this [job], of course we need to take care of it'. Rent boys have a certain tension concerning their bodies in order to keep them in good condition, to seem young(er) and not to lose their virility through developing an overly-muscular look. As another rent boy (Baris, aged 24) told me, 'There are always a few muscled types, the bodybuilders, or the athletes. But, yes, their downsides do not always work well. It is not a good thing at all.' Can (aged 25) explained his attention about his body: 'I think my body is okay. But I always have an eye on it, especially for my tummy. If I keep eating heavily on dinner for a while, it can go crazy, really fast, on the middle of my body. [To stop] I just don't eat anything but salad for dinner until my belly is gone again. I also try to exercise and I know about the many benefits of regular exercise, but I cannot do that for most of the time. So, yes, trying to control my eating habit is the only thing I can do right now.'

Body hair is also an issue in the male sex work scene. Some rent boys are naturally smooth. The others try to deal with their body hair as the presence, absence and excess of body hair may send different messages to customers and can create different problems. Metin explained, 'I guess I am lucky. I have a few hairs on my chest and the rest is pretty bare and blondish. I don't think I will ever get it shaved either with razor or wax. I know some guys have fur and somehow they have to get rid of them. Football players also cut their hair. But waxing still looks a bit feminine to me.' Mert (aged 26) said, 'Independent of what the customers like, I have a tendency to shave my chest, intimate parts, and legs especially during summer. I have dark skin and dark hair. Being hairy is a disadvantage. It looks old and immaculate on you. I simply don't like myself; after I am done with hair, it [makes me] feel better, my self-confidence revives. Nobody has ever complained that I shave. But I know some gays look for really hairy men.' Murat (aged 23) added, 'I trim my body hair [with a shaving machine]. Being fully smooth is not something I like. Also, a smooth rent boy probably implies a passive sexual role. I don't like it natural either. Trimming is the best option for me and for the customers. I use a razor for my genital area like everybody else.'

Attire

Another significant issue in the material culture of rent boys is what they wear and how they look overall. A typical rent boy wears a t-shirt, denim jeans and sneakers. Most rent boys wear dark-coloured, long denim jeans in both cold and hot seasons. They almost never wear shorts, even when it is unbearably hot and humid in Istanbul. Akif (aged 18) sarcastically stated that 'real men never wear shorts; jeans are the best.' For their upper parts, they commonly opt for white. 'White is better because it looks more attractive when you are tanned. Also, it shines in the dark bar and makes you more visible among others,' according to Metin. Black tops are also very popular because black is deemed to be more masculine and mature. Rent boys also wear some bright and lively colours, such as red and yellow, in order to be seen in the bar, but dreary colours, such as grey or brown, are not worn.

Rent boys do not wear earrings, as Okan (aged 18) told me, 'Earrings would spoil masculinity.' They are more tolerant of wristbands, chains and rings, but earrings are identified with gays and/or foreigners. Some of them use fake earrings that do not pierce their ears, in order not to look as *varos*, and take them off when they go home. Rent boys in Istanbul insist on wearing sports (tennis) shoes and sneakers even on snowy days. This is another tactic they use for negotiating with the *varos* label. Their shoes are mostly cheaper imitations of the famous sports and designer brands, unless they get them original from clients as gifts. Metin said,

> Nobody likes or wants to be with a guy with muddy boots on his feet. Of course, sometimes it might be cool to wear a nice pair of boots but it is always better to have sneakers. It is like of a uniform. I am not talking only about gay men here; I mean our kids enjoy wearing them for themselves. Everybody wants to be cool in the neighbourhood, among his friends. But of course, you should also be careful about your underwear and socks. You should not look like a child or a fool.' Can said, 'I have two sets of underwear. It was really difficult to explain it to my mom [who washes and arranges them]. One group is the cheap boxers that I normally wear. The other group is more expensive, always black, and tighter, you know, outline your package. She [my mother] always has a funny face and looks disgusted when she brings me my clean underwear.

Cologne

Perfumes and colognes are significant manifestations of rent boys' risky relations with their gay clientele. It is always good for a rent boy to have the fragrance of a charming perfume, because it increases his attractiveness when his client has to whisper into his ear in the noisy bar. Perfumes are very expensive for rent boys' budgets, but sometimes they receive them as gifts after satisfying a client with their sexual performance. Whether it was stolen from a client or given to the rent boy, it proves the rent boy's popularity and sexual activity. As Burak (aged 24) told me, 'If you smell [of] perfume, it shows that you recently got some work done'. The risky point is about the gendered quality of the fragrance. Accordingly, the fragrance must smell masculine because otherwise it cannot contribute to the exaggerated masculinity that the rent boy displays. However, rent boys generally do not find the perfumes that gay men use attractive. In this smellscape, they are not masculine enough − mostly too androgynous − for rent boys. On the other hand, a client who uses a very masculine perfume for himself endangers a rent boy's masculinity, because it implies that the gay client was not a feminine man and that he could turn active through sexual penetration. So rent boys construct a narrative in which their client was effeminate enough to use a less masculine perfume for himself and thus did not threaten the rent boy's masculinity. However, he gave the perfume specifically to the rent boy to show his gratitude. Of course, this narrative's veracity can always be questioned. Hence, using a masculine perfume is a risky action. Its absence or the presence of a more androgynous fragrance points to a failure. Its presence indicates the dilemma of being a 'bottom' or finding a really generous gay − which is rather difficult.

Most of the rent boys that I talked to said that they were totally against stealing or any other kind of criminal activity. On the other hand, they also revealed that they were not against asking for or even stealing colognes from gays' houses after they have sex. Perfumes clearly are the exception for rent boys' moral stance against the act of stealing. Metin said, 'When I see a nice perfume I ask for it. Honestly, if he does not want to give it to me I will try to take it anyway. I don't think this is stealing.' Hakan also noted that 'I am not interested in anything else, but if he has a nice perfume I will take it [...] He can buy another bottle easily and I will smell nice. Good deal.' Murat (aged 23), more poetically, stated, 'A perfume is a seduction on the air. It is a connection between the rich's life and mine. I can take it, I can use it and when I smell it I remember what I did and I enjoy it. It makes my life more beautiful.' Can added, 'I hate the cheap, imitation stuff that is sold in small shops on the Istiklal

Street. I can wear imitation shoes or t-shirts, but when it comes to the fragrance, I respect myself. I don't want that cheap stuff. They are so different than the real colognes. I think it is a part of this rent boy thing.'

Dance

Dance is another risky subject in the context of male prostitution in Istanbul. Rent boys have to dance in the bar in order to be seen by clients. The particular motions and gyrations of the boys' dancing give the impression that they are carrying out a predefined script and performing a task, but not reflecting pleasure or moving in a relaxed manner with the music and the rhythm. In other words, when rent boys dance, they perform another requirement of their work. Their dance is never visibly homoerotic, although their bodies are fairly close and sometimes touch each other.

This has its own sense of bodily humour: If a rent boy puts himself at the back of another, the one in the front bounces in sudden panic, in an anxiety to save his back (his bottom), as in Metin's joke above about protecting one's ass. This move manifests a rigid top–bottom code concerning the control and defence of your own back and a constant search to attack others' backs. If a rent boy oversteps the boundary of touching another's back or exhibits signs of pleasure, other rent boys explicitly disapprove the act and call him a pervert; ergo, humorous pleasure that comes from sodomising others should be limited to activity with gays and not with other rent boys. In the bar, this is the main reason behind small quarrels or physical fights amongst rent boys. Thus, bodily movement is dangerous to play with, although avoiding it altogether brings social exclusion, because a rent boy ought to dance. He needs to show himself in order to charm his audience. A motionless rent boy renders himself invisible, which seriously reduces his chances of finding a client. As Anil (aged 20) said, 'Dancing is the moment where we get the gays. We attract them when we dance. They love watching us.'

Most importantly, a rent boy has to dance without looking feminine. Okan said 'It is better not to do it [dance] if you do it like a girl.' Riza (aged 21) told me, 'You should not shake your ass like a belly dancer. Arms and legs must be straight. The gaze is also important. Don't look into eyes.' There are strict performative codes that most rent boys obey in order to protect the masculine image during the dance: the body should not be curved or shaken too much, and it must repeat the same rough movements without flexibility as in a collective military training. It must show strength. Shoulders and arms should be kept wide open, and the waist should move only back and forth, imitating the sexual act of penetration.

Dance is controlled and regulated by the surveillance of other rent boys. As long as they can perform it according to the unwritten rules of exaggerated masculinity, dance guarantees and consolidates rent boys' masculine identities, and makes them the centre of attraction before potential clients. However, I also saw some great dancers who seemed to really enjoy doing the moves for the sake of the action. Metin was one of these rent boys. When I asked about dancing, he said, 'For me the whole thing is being able to dance. I really lose myself and every night when I am here, I give myself at least an hour to dance. I mean dancing only; not looking for customers. If someone comes to me I just say "please wait" or "drink something, it is too early." I really love to feel the music in my bones. Even for the songs that I don't particularly like. Actually, my music taste is not the one that plays in the club. But, still, it is fine. Being able to dance without thinking about anyone and without delimiting myself is worth it.' Okan (aged 18) on the other hand, said he never danced and always stayed in the rear, looking at others and making eye contact with the customers.

Friendship and Intimacy

As we saw earlier in this chapter in the words of the indignant rent boy in the bathhouse, taking part in male prostitution or being seen while cruising is very risky. This necessary concealment paralyses friendship mechanisms amongst rent boys. Most of the time, they come to the bars or other cruising places alone or, at most, in the company of one other rent boy, who is supposed to be trustworthy (mostly one's kin, for example a cousin). They usually know other rent boys personally, and they have an intimate network of gossip and information exchange. They also spend time together chatting and dancing in the bars, but they always wind up alone while working or cruising. The solitude of rent boys might be seen as a tactic to increase their chance of negotiation for higher prices or as a part of the tradition of mendacity about what they do for how much. It actually protects them from unwanted rumours and from the dangers of unexpected disclosure. Baris (aged 24) elaborated, saying that 'I know some people in the bar, some other "rents" but I never see them out of the bar. Nobody knows that I am coming here in my neighbourhood. I must be very careful. When my regular friends ask where am I going, I tell them I will hang out with my cousins at Taksim.' Mert (aged 26) added, 'If you go out together he [a friend] can say that Mert let the guy fuck him, Mert was bottoming, etc. If he won't say it today, he will say it tomorrow. This is how it works. So it is better to be alone instead of dealing with gossip and lies.'

Another point that poses a risk to exaggerated masculinity is about emotions and sexual attraction between rent boys. In order to sustain fraternal heterosexuality, homoeroticism must be tamed and eliminated.[40] In male prostitution, who is feminine (gay) and who is masculine (rent boy) is rigidly defined. For rent boys, intimate relations are allowed only between these distinct gendered groups and not within them. Therefore, the possibility or manifestation of any kind of affect, eroticism or sexuality between rent boys subverts their masculine positions as well as their 'naturalised' heterosexuality. Just like the uneasiness when they dance together, the risk of emotional and bodily intimacy, as well as the ways it might be talked about, create a certain tension and prevent rent boys from becoming further attached to each other.

After watching and talking to many rent boys for years, I have come to the conclusion that they frequently do enjoy intimacy with other rent boys, even when they refrain from talking about it or confessing themselves. There are two lines on this subject. Deniz (aged 24) delineated one:

> I know many "rents" that kiss each other, or touch others' parts on purpose while they act like those things never happen. Also, they sometimes fuck. If it comes out they say "I was very drunk and I do not remember what happened", or "I was high." Well, it is not true. Some [gay] men like the "tableau" [...] A number of rent boys make out together and the guy watches you without participating, or maybe participates later. So if a rent boy participates in a tableau for money, he intentionally has sex with other rent boys for money.

In addition to this more evident line of relationality, there is also a subtler context of romance between rent boys. Metin said,

Sometimes these men [rent boys] are actually gays. They just hide it. And, you know, gays can fall in love with other men, including other rent boys. I know it sounds confusing but what I say is I know rent boys who became gay and then boyfriends. If you understand that not all rent boys are as "normal" as they say, then you can see that there is love, sex and gossip between rent boys.

Metin never admitted it to me, but I always sensed that he had an unspeakable and unreciprocated feeling for his apprentice, Berk (aged 17, eight years younger than Metin). Berk was a reserved and reticent high school student. After several months of being a rent boy with Metin on and off, he gave it up and was conscripted into the army. This was in 2010, during which I did not see Metin as often as I used to. Despite the infrequency of our contact, I observed that he was affected by the disappearance of Berk. I have never been able to convince Berk to talk to me.[41] Therefore, I cannot ask him about Metin. When I asked Metin later, he said that Berk had never answered his calls when he was in the army.

Alcoholic Beverages and Drugs

For rent boys, their young age is but one factor that needs to be grappled with in the face of the need to appear more mature and masculine than they really are. Drinking alcoholic beverages in the bar is a vital chance to look like an adult and demonstrate toughness. Soft drinks and soda are not preferred, because they look juvenile and gentle. Beer is the drink that rent boys prefer, mostly because it is the cheapest and the most masculine beverage (except the traditional *rakı*, which is not the best option for a bar because it requires two glasses). Beer is easy to drink while dancing, and, more importantly, it does not make one drunk easily.

Alcohol, like drugs, is a risky issue for rent boys. Mixing different beverages, drinking tequila shots quickly or taking drugs can make a rent boy dizzy – sometimes almost unconscious. As Emre (aged 25) noted, 'Gays try to make you drunk by buying you many drinks. They want to use you when you are drunk. If you are new here, they can easily entrap you. You can have sex for no money, or worse things can happen.' These 'worse things' that Emre mentioned may lead to losing the masculine pose and toughness which has been carefully constructed. When they are very drunk or 'high,' rent boys might take the passive role in sexual intercourse, which may result in rape, as Emre implied. Hence, although drinking (and drugs) is an integral element of the bar culture and a good way to expose masculinity for rent boys, it might be quite risky for sustaining this lifestyle.

Transgender Sex Workers

My framing of risk for rent boys' exaggerated masculinity includes their multifaceted relations with *travestis* – transvestite and transgender sex workers. Almost all the rent boys that I talked with had had sexual experiences with transvestites. A rent boy and a transvestite can become friends, sexual partners and even lovers. The stories told about rent boys and transvestites range from scandals, such as a drunken rent boy who was raped by a transvestite, to some poignant love stories. Despite the fact that they are on two different sides of sex work, neither rent boys nor transvestites pay to have sex with each other. As Aykut (aged 27) said, 'We are free for them, they are free for us. For all the rest, only money talks.'

While transvestites enjoy the young virility and 'real' masculinity of rent boys, the latter are happy to show how masculine and sexually active they are by having sex with the 'girls.' In most cases, a transvestite mentors an inexperienced rent boy and teaches him how to have good sex. Although it seems a mutually satisfying relationship, these escapades with transvestites are indeed very risky for rent boys. Transvestites can easily ridicule a rent boy for not having a sufficiently large penis or for not achieving a fulfilling sexual performance. Emir (aged 20) said, 'I saw many guys like this. Everybody knows that they ejaculate really fast or it [the penis] is really small because one of the girls talked about it. They can still convince some clients, especially tourists, but it is more difficult to find a client for them.' Such a public display of physical or sexual inadequacy would permanently destroy a rent boy's masculine respectability and reputation.

In the real world of interpersonal relations, there are gay men and *travestis* with distinct modes of embodiment and social identities. However, after the mainstreaming of the internet, many cross-dressing (CD) people began to present themselves according to their different gender identifications. Therefore, the more visible border between gay men and transvestites has tended to evaporate in recent years, as more gay men act in masculine ways in daytime and become CDs at nocturnal erotic economies.

Practices of (Un)Safe Sex

The last component of what I conceptualise as risk for rent boys' construction of the exaggerated masculinity is about 'sexual risk'[42] and bodily health. All the rent boys that I conducted interviews with had knowledge about STDs, HIV, condoms and how to use them. Nevertheless, my conversations with both rent boys and their clients testify that rent boys have a certain disinclination and resistance to concede their vulnerability by using a condom during sexual intercourse. They prefer to have *dogal* (natural) or *ciplak* (naked, without a condom) sex, especially when the client asks for or pays more for it. Ilker (aged 19) told me, 'I use it [a condom] sometimes. It does not really bother me. I prefer cleaner gays, so it is not a big threat for me. I know many rents do it without condoms with tourists because they pay more. It is crazy because there is a higher chance for a foreigner to be sick.'

Rent boys' negative attitude toward condoms might originate from their practical difficulties with using them, or, more likely, the construction of their masculine self-identities rejects expressions of fear and self-protection while it promotes courage and adventure. Rent boys interpret the sexual encounter as an opportunity to challenge and prove their manhood, as Hakan (aged 22) said, 'Little boys might get scared of it, but for me, it is not the case. I know how to fuck a guy without a condom in a safe way. It is not necessary for me to put one on. I can protect myself.' Also, some clients opt for unprotected sex with younger rent boys who they believe do not have a long sexual history and are thus 'cleaner.' On the other hand, Akif (aged 18) noted, 'probably because I am younger, they ask my age and how many times I did it [having sex]. Then they say "It is okay with you, you are clean," and I don't put a condom on. That's what they want.' Thus, rent boys' desire to demonstrate their courage and fearlessness operates along with some clients' demands for unprotected sex and produces a risky encounter for both sides.

Unprotected, risky sex has become a much more acute issue in the years I have been conducting this research. In the queer networks of Istanbul, there is knowledge that many more people have HIV/AIDS now, but despite this particular knowledge, unprotected sex has become hegemonic, especially outside of middle-class, urban Turkish gays. As Abdullah (aged 30) described his trip to the gay sauna in

Taksim: 'There were 20 or 25 Kurdish boys, very young, 16 to 20 years old, all naked. They have bigger penises than average. They were engaging in unprotected sex with the customers.' As I was really surprised to hear this, Suleyman (aged 30) further explained, 'With these [*varos*] boys it is impossible to orient them to have a condom. It is so unbelievably absent from their minds. They do not even think such a thing. Asking about it actually harms the conversation or the attraction between him and you. He would probably think that you were sick and he would run away.'[43]

****

In this chapter, I have explained how rent boys in Istanbul have developed cultural, bodily, symbolic and material strategies both to challenge tacitly and to negotiate inventively with the social norms of hegemonic male sexuality[44] and hegemonic masculinity.[45] The top-only sexual positions whereby they make themselves sexually available, the protection of their bodies from penetration and the distance they place between themselves and feminine attributes by the way they dance, smell or dress, can be seen as attempts to save the penis-and-penetration-centred hegemonic virile sexuality. On the other hand, the enactment of exaggerated masculinity and the production of a story of authentic manhood via *varos* culture are manifestations of their complicity with the hegemonic forms of masculinity in Istanbul, despite their dissident sexual practices.

Is it acceptable for the embodiments of hegemonic masculinity or its imitations to operate alongside queer sex? Is it possible for one to reclaim his privileged heterosexual status while he engages in compensated sex with other men? Gary W. Dowsett and his colleagues note that the definitions and conceptualisations in which masculinities have been theorised are in need of reconsideration and recalibration since 'the prevailing formulation of masculinity represents a failure to engage with the creative meanings and embodied experiences evident in non-hegemonic sexual cultures, and with the effects these meanings and experiences may generate beyond their boundaries.'[46] In this sense, rent boys and their ambivalent sexual acts and identifications provide an excellent case for such inquiries regarding their involvement with the active meaning-making process of sexuality and masculinity. In response to possible challenges towards their heterosexual and masculine self-identities, they use exaggerated masculinity in order to be able to continue their everyday lives as heterosexual members of their families and kinship networks. A rent boy's transactional sexual experiences 'were known not be known' in the heteronormative framework of 'active not knowing.'[47] In other words, exaggerated masculinity repairs and masks the subverting effects of compensated sex for rent boys' heterosexuality and makes them closer to the hegemonic ideal of masculinity. They perform an assiduous self-governance via symbols and implicit meanings through different and contradictory class positions, gender identities and sexual acts.

Rent boys constitute exaggerated masculinity relationally and strategically at the nexus of the contradictory contexts of local *varos* culture and the impact of the global gay culture. Risk, in this sense, is central in understanding the mechanisms of exaggerated masculinity, since it is a fragile, insecure, playful combination of various bodily acts, gestures and symbols. At another level of risk, rent boys and their relations with their gay clientele in Istanbul might be seen as an example of how globalisation has the potential to destabilise and imperil local constructions and operations of heteronormativity in the non-West. In order to cope with the discourses of linear outcomes and the homogenising effects of neoliberal globalisation or carnal economies, there is a need for more research in divergent geographies about new openings, possibilities and hybridisations in gendered subjectivities and sexual identities as a result of globalisation's reshuffling within local entanglements of power, gender and sexual relations. The following chapters will pursue this goal.

CHAPTER 3

RENT BOYS' INTIMACIES IN NEOLIBERAL TIMES

> Until one after the other they each finally disappeared. No one knew where. They all wanted, at least in gloomy hours, to get out of this life.
> John Henry Mackay, *The Hustler: The Story of a Nameless Love from Friedrichstrasse* (San Bernardino, 2002), p. 252

For my informant Vural (aged 24) it was not as gloomy engaging in transactional sex with gay men as it might have been for the male prostitutes in Berlin that Mackay describes almost a hundred years ago. Instead Vural, as a self-defined 'rational and smart' person, formulated the actual interaction of sex work (when and if it happens, depending on his own decision) as a 'win-win' equation. He insistently believed that he did not 'lose' anything in this equation.

> When I ask myself why I am so addicted to this place that I come here every week, I think I see this as a form of accumulation. Let me tell you. It is like a game that children play: Every day I spend here {in the rent boy bar} I have fun, right? I dance and sometimes I drink free beers, gays buy them for me. How much do I spend to come here and turn back to home? Nothing. The bus is free for me because I have the unlimited monthly pass. So it is literally free for me to come here and have fun, right? Then if I have someone {a client} {it is} again the same game.

Do I somehow ejaculate every day, do I masturbate? Yes, of course I do. Will I come with this guy? Yes, either he will treat me [oral sex] or I am going to fuck him, and then I come at the end. So I do not lose anything again because I was going to ejaculate [even if I were alone] anyway. It is more pleasurable if somebody gives you a treatment, right? Plus, they even give me money: 50 or 100 liras, sometimes US dollars or euros. I make money out of my pleasure. Do I lose anything? No. I make profit without doing anything. Is this being a faggot? I will break the mouth of the person who would say this to me. I would make his mother cry hard. I am just having fun here and making money [without losing anything].

In this chapter, I examine rent boys with a special focus on their lives, their customers and their sexual relations. The rare phenomenon of seduction and the abuse of young, modest, innocent and virile boys by the 'pervert, immoral, old, and rich' gay men took a different shape in the social imagination of Turkey in recent decades. Before the late 1990s, the male prostitute (if imaginable outside of some marginalised literary work of fiction writers) was a sexual fantasy that the public figure of the old rich gay men, who was somehow exceptional, sophisticated, artistic, and even famous, could only occasionally achieve: having sex with a real straight man, initiating him into the underworld of homoerotic encounters by the help of money, fame or power relations, even living with such a man as a kept boyfriend. With the opening of the first publicly known and advertised gay bars, this exceptional and exclusive erotic experience turned into a regular sexual service that ordinary, and increasingly 'out,' gay men could purchase. The service providers, the objects of gay men's fantasies, started to call themselves 'rent boys' or just 'rents,' without translating the term into Turkish language. Gay bars' institutional yet highly flexible and insecure support (if not their active involvement) increased the perceived 'normality' of the sexual encounter between the middle-class, urban, Western-looking gay men and rent boys from the slums (*varos*) outside of modern urban life in the 2000s. On the other hand, more gay men were assaulted, beaten or killed by men who they took home to have sex with. This toxic knowledge circulated amongst gay men, while the mass media widely covered these tragedies as 'gay murders.' This discursive frame triggered a powerful sense of precariousness and fear, and hence made the sexual fantasy seem even more dangerous, unpredictable and risky than it might have actually been. It also became more attractive and meaningful from the viewpoint of some gay men.

When I conducted this research about the relation between the urban middle class, self-identified gay men and rent boys, who call themselves 'normal' and rarely 'hetero,' but never gay, was more balanced and stabilised. The discourse of danger, fear and risk was a little bit volatilised. My gay participants expressed clearly that they had learnt how to deal with rent boys without being robbed, beaten or killed. Rent boys also mentioned how deeply they were disturbed by the social stigma of criminality and vileness associated with male sex work. They highlighted to me that they were quite careful not to force or harm anybody and not to take any money or valuable objects without the client's permission. They also noted that they believed in God and in the code of the honour of manhood, and that such unwritten rules of morality directed their conduct. Both gay men and rent boys yearned to believe that the gay murders were a myth and both groups were unwillingly involved in this representation, which seemed to belong to a long gone past.

In fact, gay murders were not a myth, and many people suffered from multiple forms of violence, mediated through transactional same-sex sexuality, eroticism and intimacy. This is a significant point regarding the everyday realities of male sex work that not only the police and criminologists, but also social scientists should examine. However, my true concern throughout this research was not the criminal and risky aspects of the queer sexual encounter, but instead a set of questions, including: how the typology of rent boy becomes possible, known and representable; how rent boys resist (or consolidate) gendered, sexualised and class hierarchies in order to construct subjectivities; and how this relational process is reshaped in accordance with structural changes (for example, the neoliberalisation of Turkey and the strengthening of neoliberal subjectivity) and the interventions of people who occupy important places in gay men's and rent boys' lives, such as family, friends, relatives and colleagues.

The Encounter Between Multiple Masculinities: Experiments with Neoliberal Subjectivity

Raewyn Connell[1] has shown that masculinity differs not only as we travel from one culture to another (as in 'Turkish masculinity' versus 'Italian masculinity') or from one historical epoch to another (as in masculinity in Ancient Greeks versus contemporary masculinity), but that, more importantly, multiple masculinities coexist at any time, in any given culture. The most critical component of Connell's multiple masculinities framework is the emphasis she places on power: multiple masculinities are not juxtaposed without contact, dialogue, interaction and reciprocal transformation. Instead, different masculinities are relational, this relationality can transmogrify masculinities, and the gender structure can only be comprehended through a lens of social power. In this sense, there is a dynamic, transformational and hierarchal power relation between forms of masculinity that are defined by different criteria. In each cultural context, according to Connell, there is a major form of enacting masculinity (or being masculine) that is underlined, exalted and promoted.[2] This particular form becomes hegemonic, and people start to try to become and act that way, imitating as much as they can and reshaping themselves as they are enjoined by the normative gender ideology to do so. I also think that the hegemonic form of masculinity, with the values, qualities, norms and capacities it requires and represents, is an almost impossible ideal, an unreachable goal or an imagined unity for most of the male population in most societies. Men who strive to find their places in the social order while they simultaneously project their gender identities sometimes unwillingly and even unconsciously yearn for and follow the model of hegemonic masculinity. Those male subjects who are somehow able to realise the hegemonic ideal, or to get close to it, embody this gender identity by being labelled the 'real man' or the 'most masculine man.' If other male subjects fail to achieve this gendered ideal for any reason, they either have a tendency to glorify and emulate it, or they clearly refuse to take this cultural ideal as a model, criticise and challenge it and look for alternatives.

Connell calls the first group 'complicit' and 'subordinated' as they do not raise any oppositions to incorporating hegemonic masculinity even when they fail, while she defines the others as 'marginal' and 'resistant' masculinities – those who look outside of the hegemonic frame to produce new gender forms. In this sense, hegemonic masculinity is a dynamic formulation that affects all male subjects (and bodies). A man repositions himself in terms of gender identity according to the rules and demonstrations that hegemonic masculinity presents and forbids, or the questions it poses about the nature of manhood in public and private domains. It is noteworthy that the framework is based on an ideal (even a delusion for the majority), and there is no relation of force to make people enact hegemonic masculinity. On the contrary, a particular type of doing masculinity becomes hegemonic in time and place as more people are seemingly convinced that it is to their own benefit to imitate its codes as far as they can. In other words, men who attempt to animate hegemonic masculinity are willing subjects to be governed by the gendered codes of conduct and meaning making.

Each culture produces its own features and limitations regarding the workings of hegemonic masculinity. Roughly speaking, a white, Judeo-Christian, athletic and able-bodied, heterosexual and married (preferably with children) man who has a decent job and can earn enough money to take care of his family (the dependents) and maintain a middle-class lifestyle is closer to being deemed a 'good man' or 'real guy;' examples of hegemonic masculinity in the Global North. Non-whites, Muslims, members of the working classes, queers, men who choose not to marry or have a child, the disabled, the overweight, college drop-outs or the unemployed, the actual majority of the male population, are excluded from the symbolic power zone defined by the characteristics of hegemonic masculinity. Those non-hegemonic masculinities do not present the best routes to sustaining the gender imbalance and dominating women, which Connell posits as the main function of the gender order. In other words, in any given social setting, hegemonic masculinity is the form of manhood that enables men to subjugate women in the most sophisticated or efficient way. The men who are not within the symbolic influence of hegemonic masculinity have two paths to choose from: they can either strive for integration into the domain of hegemonic masculinity or play by its rules, in spite of their own deficiencies and incorrectness, or they can accept their already marginalised position and further challenge the hegemonic models of manliness. The significant point in this analysis is the aspect of social change. Hegemonic masculinity can and does evolve and adapt. For example, the election of the first African-American president in the United States can be interpreted as a crucial reform in the perceptions of men who are willing to take the president and his way of life as a gendered model. A non-white president or political leader would probably not have the same effect in the Global South. Values and taboos associated with hegemonic masculinity are mostly contextual and intensively culture-specific.

Despite this contingency, Connell emphasises that hegemonic masculinity has only one cross-cultural and trans-historical component: Heterosexuality. A mode of masculinity which is not exclusively entangled with emotional and sexual relations with women cannot become hegemonic anywhere, says Connell. This is the only unchangeable aspect of her hegemonic masculinity framework. Thus, heterosexuality and hegemonic masculinity are co-constituted and recurrently consolidate each other. This principle is articulated by the core of Connell's structuralist gender theory: the purpose and meaning of hegemonic masculinity is to guarantee the continuity of the gender regime, in which men are (and will remain) more powerful than women. In this sense, 'crisis tendencies' are manoeuvres for men's control over women (and some other men). Whenever there is a crisis of masculinity, or implications of change regarding men's emotional, bodily and relational beings, the social process ends with the adaptation and strengthening of masculine privilege or the recuperation of hegemonic masculinity.

What is the capacity for manoeuvring of hegemonic masculinity in an encounter in which women are almost absent or insignificant except in their transient, spectral effects, such as the case of rent boys in Istanbul? As I explicated in Chapter 2, rent boys simultaneously differentiate themselves from both the cultural universe that they claim they belong to (i.e., slum social networks, poverty, social exclusion, Turkish or Kurdish nationalism or a reactive religiosity that is based on strict gender segregation) and the gay lifestyle and they unsuccessfully try to avoid any possible intermingling (i.e., refined consumer tastes, Western references, the sense of individual freedom, liberated sexuality global connections) by enacting 'exaggerated masculinity.' This is a deeply insecure and sensitive identity construction. It stems from bodily, discursive and relational performances and convoluted tactics and calculations. As most respondents told me, this carefully managed process, with all its performative rituals and norms, helped a slum (*varos*) guy to get rid of his lower class characteristics and remake himself as a skilled rent boy who is open to the world. It also enables them to stay heterosexual ('normal') and definitely 'not gay' despite the fact that they disobey the most basic principle of hegemonic masculinity, exclusive heterosexuality, by developing homoerotic intimacies and experiencing same-sex sexuality. Exaggerated masculinity, with the cultural mechanisms it compels and the risk management it demands, allows rent boys to yearn for, appropriate and imitate hegemonic forms of masculinity even while they challenge its number one rule by their actions.

When gay men and rent boys meet at one of the popular locations[3] it is an encounter between two classes and social positions, sexualities, bodies and manners and two gravely different symbolic worlds which normally would not bump into each other. It is also an encounter between two masculinities. This encounter between rent boys and their clients constitutes an embodied and contextual example of the interaction between multiple masculinities. What Connell describes as the various gender cultures of masculinities and their dialogue in a broad, sometimes abstract sense materialises here through bodies and erotic-somatic economies, in addition to symbolic categories of social identification. We all make and creatively reshape our identities by playing with axes of social inequality and difference, such as class, sex, gender, sexuality, the body, 'race' and ethnicity, location, religion and belief systems, language, ability, citizenship and nationality. Those axes that reproduce social inequality do not generate isolated and independent social identities. On the contrary, social identities and our multiple locations in the matrix of domination coexist, intersect and are manifested through difference.[4] Hence, it is clear at least at the complexity level of twenty-first-century societies, there is no separate class analysis from gender, and there is no politics of the body without an analysis of sexualities. These categories are all inherent in each other, and they act on the same bodies with different emphases according to the needs of the context or the requirements of the public as they are articulated within broader mechanisms of social exclusion.[5] Multiple and complicated others who are produced by the convergence of identity elements, as well as normalities, which are consolidated and which subjects are encouraged to obey, only become possible and legible through these intersectionalities. Looking through the lens of social diversity and intersectionality, it becomes impossible to define masculinity as an all-encompassing, ahistorical, over-generalisable 'super' concept for each theoretical gap we are able to find. Masculinity can only be thought about, theorised and searched for with other social determinants like race, class, the body and sexuality, and how it operates alongside the construction of subjectivities.

As I have elaborated previously in this book, the rent boy is a discontinuous identity position that becomes possible in contemporary Istanbul through the interchange of at least two kinds of masculinities ('slum masculinity' and 'gay masculinity') that impact certain male bodies while simultaneously detaching from both of them and being marginalised by them. *Varos* boys *become* or *perform* the rent boy identity between two different and indeed contradictory masculinities when they accept or negotiate for compensated sex with other men. Rent boys can be present only between these two masculinities, slum and gay, as they simultaneously destabilise and subvert them. They constitute flexible, vigilant, unstable and playful subjectivities and by doing so, they implement the personal and interpersonal principles established by neoliberalism in the last quarter of a century. This is the most exceptional and significant aspect of male sex work in Istanbul, although transactional sex between men can and does happen everywhere in the world.[6] Rent boys incorporate the basic qualities of the neoliberal masculine subject (i.e., pragmatist, opportunist, cost-conscious, cunning, flexible, tolerant and 'open') and transform themselves accordingly. As they perform a line of neoliberal masculinity, they demonstrate that these qualities are not meant only for the global managerial class of the elite and the privileged as it is imagined by social scientists, but rather these 'symptoms' are available as subjective capacities to men from the disenfranchised, lower social classes as well. Neoliberal masculinity, as rent boys exemplify, becomes an attainable gender practice for all willing subjects, and not an epidemic for the superordinate classes only. Masculinity, once again, ends up at the centre of this embodied, relational and discursive process.

The Reshaping of Neoliberal Masculinity

Neoliberalism has prevailed as the new economic-ideological order of the planet, especially after the fall of the Berlin Wall in 1989. Not only has it reconfigured the components of the economic sphere (i.e., economic capacities and organisation of the state, deregulation and exchange rates, global trade balances, quotas and tariffs and the uninterrupted financial flow around the world), but it has also transformed what are known as parts of the cultural field, including the ways how individuals tend to interpret these economic and cultural structures, channels of expression, mediating society and subjectivity. The body, eroticism, sexuality, pleasure, satisfaction, affect, illness, health, integrity, void, disability, scars and other facades and different interiorities of intimacy, which are crucial to the constitution of subjectivity, have become an inseparable part of the economy through neoliberalisation. Without being able to keep its dark and invisible secrets, intimacy has been articulated with the complex of economy and public culture. If neoliberalism also means 'the commodification of everything,'[7] we must be able to predict that who we are, how we identify ourselves and relate with others, what parts of us we deem as the most indispensable, what qualities we have that we tend to think as more disposable, what should be kept more clandestine and more publicly known about our lives, how we draw our boundaries and how flexible these tend to be, is going to be transmogrified and commodified just like urban goods, social security systems and public services – the most recognisable symbols of neoliberalism worldwide.

What is masculinity? If the answer is about getting a gender identity and thus relating with other sexes and genders, or, in Connell's words, enacting the politics of the reproductive arena through bodies' capacities of learning and repeating of certain performances, using the biological make-up in specific ways, referring to a cultural repertoire, struggling, proving, challenging, facing with challenges, doing what needs to be done and internalising the boundaries and the forbidden zones; then we can think that this is an entirely social process that is deeply interconnected with meaning-making, that is produced and reproduced every moment and imagined differently by diverse publics. In this sense, being and becoming a man and staying masculine cannot be independent from the neoliberalisation that diffuses across each possible domain of life.[8]

Turkey started to experience waves of neoliberalisation in the 1980s.[9] This socio-economic transition brought a fragmentation of hegemonic masculinity. New and alternative forms of social power produced new and multiplied models of hegemonic masculinity, in deep contrast with the unique 'successful' and publicly exalted style of manhood that was exemplified by the governing republicanist-étatist elite in the pre-1980s period. In this period, the hegemonic representations of masculinity were multiplied, and different social groups produced their own ideals of 'successful and decent' manliness in a sometimes conflicting juxtaposition. This also helped the change towards a more negotiable, denaturalised, changeable conception of masculinity. This discursive change was strengthened by the public debates on 'the new man' and an alleged masculinity crisis in the 1990s. New masculine subjectivities became available for men to take up, including the emotional man, the 'White Turk' man, the Kurdish man, the Islamist man, the intellectual man, the globalised man or the urban hipster, among others. In the 2000s, these divergences became less significant and less telling, and articulation with neoliberal citizenship became more common.[10]

My aim here is not to provide a full account, or even a summary of the relation between neoliberalism and masculinity, such as Connell accomplished in depicting global (business) masculinity despite the risk of overgeneralisation and normativity.[11] Although neoliberalism, like globalisation, produces a master narrative that is self-realising and applicable to virtually every place in an ahistorical, decontextualised and depoliticised sense, various experiments with neoliberalisation are entangled with the changing social structure, the power of political opposition and resistance and the legitimacy of radical thinking in each society. Thus, it would be meaningless to strive to insert a timeless, ubiquitous definition of masculinity into the centre of the neoliberal transition while neoliberalism generates divergences and differentiation at large.

In the remaining part of this chapter, I will talk about what I have heard and observed from rent boys and their clients about the impact of neoliberalisation on masculine subjectivities (or the constitution of neoliberal masculinity) through male sex work in Istanbul. The rent boy identity is maintained vis-à-vis two distinct forms of social exclusion: being homosexual and being from *varos*. As Turkey shifted from a pre-1980s semi-socialist, statist economy and relatively closed, insular society, first to a full capitalist, nearly open society, free market and reformed state regime in the 1990s and finally to an entirely neoliberalised, Islamised, oppressive and intolerant social mode in the 2000s, ideas and discourses about the neoliberal individual and the ways it has been talked about have imprinted the rent boy identity. In other words, rent boys now have some of the idiosyncratic features and performative qualities of neoliberal subjectivity, which is by definition larger than any specific class or social group. It is possible to notice that some characteristics of neoliberal masculinity which are visibly different from previous modes of subjectivity have crystallised through the self-creation of rent boys and their instrumental relationality with gay men.

The most important point during this process of the neoliberalisation of masculinity is the transformation within the conceptualisation of gender that men experience. The male subject stops seeing himself as a natural, authentic, uncontested, unmarked, essentialised and centralised human being, and starts to think of himself as culturally constructed in language among other bodies, socially encoded and performed in encounters and interactions with others. He is now one person among many others. Men, in other words, started to perceive their gender identities and performances as open to criticism and challenge in a reflexive sense, something presentable in different ways in front of various audiences, something that they and others can manipulate, speculate about and encourage to change. Men's bodies and masculine identities become more tangible, more human and eventually instrumental, with an array of new functions and socio-economic benefits as everything else becomes commodified. Rent boys and the formation of the idea of male sex work in Turkey is one of the clearest examples of this transformation. To observe rent boys' meticulously calculated and enacted exaggerated masculinity used to alleviate their insecurities and strengthen their legitimacy enables one to better comprehend the reordering of masculinity as a gender identity as commercialised as femininity in neoliberalisation.

Also crucial in the manifestations of neoliberal masculinity is the increasing consciousness of male subjects of their bodies and body politics: clothes, accessories, underwear, hairstyle, body measures and being fit/muscled, pale or tanned skin colour, body hair and facial hair, bodily movements and displays of energy and dancing practices have become critical issues in a previously unforeseen way. The male body is intertwined with advertisements and global consumer culture mediated through social dispositions of class. The body gives an idea of who the man is and what his position is in the culture of neoliberal masculinity. As one of the respondents (Baris, aged 24) told me, 'This [job] is about your body. Of course we are always busy with how we look and how we actually are.'

The binary, biological and mutually exclusive social system of sex and gender, in addition to the social and political capacities of heteronormativity with its power to render the gendered and sexualised alternatives unimaginable and unintelligible, is also destabilised through the expansion of neoliberal logic. At least for some segments of society, heteronormativity becomes more obvious and less binding. Rent boys, for example, negotiate illicitly with the heteronormative idea that they ought to have sex only with women in order to have and sustain normal, decent and respected heterosexual identities. They strenuously claim that as long as they can control it and do not let it pervade them, having sex with other men (for example gays, transvestites or tourists) would not harm their heterosexuality. Aykut (aged 27) exemplified rent boys' relationship with counter-heteronormative assumptions: 'We need to be realistic. Personally speaking, if I know myself, nothing [bad] can happen. I am a healthy man and that [having sex with other men] cannot change this. I am committed to my relations with women and I dream of getting married one day. But this [gay sex] is different, one should not mix them up.'

Nationalist ideologies and watchful nation-state protectionism are irrefutably heteronormative, if not clearly hostile towards same-sex sexualities, because signs of homoeroticism may eventually destabilise the innocent brotherhood and homosociality that connect (male) citizens. Homosocial fraternity stems from a neat divide between heterosexuality and homosexuality that each citizen is personally responsible for observing and defending. Neoliberal logic, on the other hand, fortifies the possibilities of commodification of the male body and presents it as more of a desirable, demandable, negotiable, buyable and sellable object. Neoliberal masculinity prescribes the flexibility and mutability of the imagined walls between homo- and heterosexuality. Such a departure from the constitutive binary and the exclusive nature of sexual identities might be seen as one of the most radical differences between neoliberal masculinity and other forms of hegemonic masculinity. Rent boys, as paradigms of an embodied neoliberal masculinity, with their presence, relations and representations, subvert the established mutual dichotomy between homo- and heterosexuality and make the allegedly safe domain of sexualities ambiguous.

In a similar vein, neoliberalisation forces masculinity to leave the insular, introverted, conservative, gender sociability and mutates it into a more dialogical, communicative, diverse, respective, multicultural and cosmopolitan gender position. Neoliberal masculinity rejects a gendered capital that is blind to differences, unaccommodating, obtrusive and recalcitrant. It promotes a form of subjectivity that welcomes novelty and divergence, is open to acting in accordance with new social combinations, creative adaptation and pleasure seeking. The neoliberal man is one who does not live the pre-fixed life within boundaries but transmogrifies with each new social contingency and re-identifies himself according to the situation. Rent boys perform and showcase neoliberal masculinity in this sense: they are not unchanging, 'essential' men; they are instead mutative men who are able to use essentialism even when it is not real. When I talked to rent boys, they stated that their activities, such as using urban space, being mobile within the city, being present in gay bars or rent boy bars, communicating with people of different ages, cultures, religions or classes and even the sex work itself empower their masculinity. It does not castrate them. The things they witness, which could easily be interpreted as 'degeneration' or 'immorality' from a more conservative viewpoint such as their parents', turn into new experiences that enrich them and make them stronger and more active. Metin once elucidated this point:

> What has my father ever seen in his life? When I compare [his and his father's experiences] people I talked to, places I visited, private relations among other things, are incomparable. I have tested my manhood in every possible situation and I have always won. Nothing could ever harm me. If something does not kill you, it strengthens you. [Being a rent boy is something] like that.

A Self-Destroying Representation: Is it Possible to Talk About Rent Boys?

Under what circumstances and through which cultural mediations do rent boys become visible in the eyes of the public? More importantly, how can a public know about the idea of male prostitutes, their deviant careers, their back-alley presence in the city, their perverse mobilities and the discourses about queer sexual economy if the members of this public are not interested in having compensated sex with rent boys? If they are curious about or interested in the subject matter, how has this inquisitiveness been formed and guided?

As I have recounted in Chapter 2, on one of the weekly episodes of a reality documentary show on a national TV channel in Turkey, audiences saw the police walking into a gay sauna with a hidden camera and heard negotiations between rent boys and police officers. Readers of a national weekly news magazine might have encountered cover stories that examined the 'increasing decadence around male sex work in Taksim Square.' Millions of people in Turkey, whose only imagined common denominator is 'normalcy,' had access to a representation of the rent boy identity and its contested, constructed reality. Examining these representations and the discourses that circulated during these historical moments could critically challenge notions about the conditions of men's involvement as sellers in sex work and compensated sex, the (dis-)identification of rent boys and gay men and all the tacit associations with masculinity, sexuality, pleasure, social morality, public order and health, the informal economy and the diversity of urban life.

Sex work has traditionally been framed as an absolute departure from one's dignity and emotional-spiritual integrity, a rupture between the body and self, and the last and lowest survival strategy that the poor victim has; a high risk situation that is open to danger and violence, exclusion and separation from social networks, including family, friends and kin. It represents a radically different and more substandard life than one might have had. Common-sense ideas about sex work also produce a deeply sexist discourse. Those performing the oldest job in the world, who are subject to the painful experiences I mention here, are believed to be women. In the Turkish context, while men can and are supposed to do everything in order to earn money and take care of their families, becoming 'dirty' and agreeing to be used for money are reserved only for women.[12] That possibility does not exist for men; men's capacity to sell sex to other men is unthinkable. Even if it is thought, there is no possibility to express it in the language.[13]

The discursive construction of rent boys impairs the gendered and sexist approaches to sex work in a significant extent. Rent boys in Istanbul are not victims, and they are not in miserable conditions; they do not have to sell sex, it is not a survival strategy for them.[14] Rather, all my observations and their narratives have verified that they can otherwise live with their families, relatives and friends without involvement in queer prostitution, which only generates small, irregular amounts of money. Rent boys are willing to have compensated sex with men, but they carefully articulate their precautions and negotiate and develop strategies. Some of them try transactional queer sex only once and never do it again, some of them quit after a couple of years, but in the end most of them leave the scene and turn back to their normal lives, while a remarkable minority eventually adopt gay identity. The image of the young and healthy man who is attracted to women consciously doing male sex work and calling himself a rent boy when he does not have to, subverts everything we know about prostitution as it is represented in common sense and popular culture. When rent boys describe their same-sex compensated sex experiences as not harming, decreasing or terminating their masculinity but rather enriching them, their recounting creates an alternative sense of combination of masculinity and sexuality, whether the audience is convinced or not. The absolutely heterosexist structure of the public's image of sex work is revealed at the moment rent boys are acknowledgeable and the audience starts to think that 'it were possible indeed.' In this sense, what Decena contextualises in the Dominican Republic is also relevant for rent boys in Turkey: 'narrating sexual practices allowed these men to elaborate on their values, revisions of traditional Dominican identity and erotic investments in masculinity and power.'[15] Furthermore, rent boys exhibiting their bodies and verbalising their experiences make the public revise and redraft its views on gendered morality and the rules of masculinity.

In the existing (but very few) literary and poetic discourses about rent boys, narrators tend to hide their partners' sex worker identity and instead emphasise their 'real' manhood or lower-class identities through codes of passion and love. Alternatively, journalistic language can be employed from time to time to underline the social problems around the male sex work issue. For example, poverty and inequality might have reached a critical point such that some of the poor men started to sell sexual labour. Rent boys may also be depicted as innocent victims who have no knowledge of the city and the dangers they might encounter, so that immoral homosexuals can easily persuade and take advantage of them. In general, this public attitude or media language proceeds with the implications of complaint and calls for official intervention (i.e., will the police and authorities do anything about this?). In this framing, rent boys never appear as active, conscious, wilful subjects, who highlight their masculine performances and learn how to market these gendered qualities. Contrary to what the journalistic accounts insist on saying, rent boys in Istanbul are hardly victims or naïve novices in the queer erotic economy.

Instead of exploring how fictitious and wrong those representations are, I think it is more important to examine the imagined audiences and ways of knowing that influence them. What would an ordinary person who occasionally comes across such a literary product or journalistic account think about the poor, young, migrant rent boys who let other men use their bodies in exchange for money? What are the relative positions and meanings of slums, Taksim Square, poverty, homosexuality and urban life in this discursive construction? What are the comparative mechanisms for meaning-making regarding the subjectivities of rich gay men and the disenfranchised *varos* boys? In what ways could an ordinary person know about the revealed aspects of illicit sexual encounters that are no longer intimate but public, and how does she use this knowledge? Would she ever rethink herself, her knowledge, her tendencies, questions, answers and limits as a moral being?

Those fragments of representation distract social reality and contribute to perceptions of difference in society. Beyond everything, the fragile identity of the rent boy destabilises and obscures the strict, mutually exclusive character of homosexuality and heterosexuality. As long as the concept of rent boy is not verbalised and rent boys' aspirations, strategies, ambitions and subjectivities are neglected, the discourse about naïve, poor migrants who are seduced is deepened and expanded. Alternatively, an artist or a celebrity can present his sexual relations with these young men as imagined and embodied ties between the socially excluded slums and the modern, urban world of global culture. Verbalising the discrepant existence of rent boys, however, means there are alternative encounters, unpredictable and clandestine contacts and queer exchanges in socially segregated Istanbul, where previously unseen social actors engender new desires, tactics and opportunities to be included in middle-class norms and escape from poverty. Hence, representing rent boys in public and talking about them inescapably weakens, problematises and unsettles multiple presumptions about gender and sexualities, as well as social class, urban life and the socio-spatial organisation of the city.

When we think male prostitution in Turkey through Michael Warner's conceptualisation of public and counter-publics,[16] it is quite obvious that different portions of the public in Turkey are not interested in discussing or understanding homosexuality (or any other form of dissident sexualities and their public manifestations). Most of the time, non-heterosexual sexual identities and relations can only be talked about as targets of national censorship policies in Turkey. The public is silent, and Turkey is void in terms of discussion of sexualities with a few rapidly vanishing exceptions. Sexuality, sexual subcultures and the social organisation of erotic pleasure are constantly pushed out of the public sphere and into the zone of privacy and intimacy, although uncompromising social, religious and state control intervenes there, too. Nothing about the body, intimacy or eroticism is left untouched.[17] In this oppressive environment, the rent boy is far less known than the more publicly recognisable figure of the homosexual man. In spite of distressing marginalisation and superimposed de-politicisation, gay men and representations of homosexuality have been tamed and moderated to a certain extent. They have become, within sanctioned boundaries, harmless in the eyes of power. In this context, the figure of the rent boy is much more dangerous, confusing and insecure. Knowing who they are, where they come from, what their backgrounds are, how they negotiate with clients, what forms of human capital they have and invest, what types of risks they calculate and what they do in intimate spaces, in addition to the actual experience of encountering a rent boy and having sex with him constitutes a 'counter-public.' Warner expounds on the existence of multiple publics instead of a single one. Thus, the public which does not let homosexuality into the field of intelligibility is not the only one. It may be the strongest, the most central or hegemonic public against many alternative, counter, dissident or abject publics that have lesser impacts on representative channels, ways of thinking, and the formation of common sense. In this equation, homosexuality is avoided iteratively and rent boys are positioned as unthinkable by the hegemonic heterosexual public, whereas an alternative, or queer, public, in which homosexual experiences are verbalised and rent boys become legible subjects, becomes possible.

What might it mean for rent boys to become visible and knowable and represented in the public sphere? If the public is hegemonic in itself and not open to other voices, thoughts, stories and languages, one is rendered visible only through his resistance, destabilising acts and challenges against discursive boundaries and principles. Then one can only exist within the structure of this central-hegemonic public, with its pre-determined rules and representational routes. For example, rent boys can appear either as the seduced and abused poor youth, or as the dangerous, murderous slum people who commit crime and kill homosexuals. When a celebrity author talks about his escapades with rent boys and the transformative effect of this on his political and artistic subjectivity, rent boys immediately turn into migrant, Anatolian, unspoiled, natural, animalistic slum guys, who cannot even speak Turkish and express what they feel in a proper way. In this discourse, they can only appear as slum youth and make sense only from the slum identity position. They cannot become smart, calculating, strategic or resistant subjects who feel themselves at home in the centre of Istanbul, who are able to initiate relations, set the rules and form boundaries and taboos and who do not play the subaltern role. At the moment they are able to appear as rent boys, as wilful subjects, as young adults who know what they are doing, they turn into impossible representations.

Revisiting Masculinity Studies through Rent Boys

Masculinity studies has a history spanning a quarter of a century. Stemming either from the internal dynamics of this burgeoning transdisciplinary field or from broader developments in social sciences, new forms of understanding and interpretation have evolved. Looking more closely at rent boys, who are involved with an informal and counter-normative subculture through compensated queer sex and perform a kind of border-work[18] to sustain their clandestine identities, enables us to better comprehend two of these interpretations that have recently been pertinent to masculinity studies.

First of all, critical social studies on men and masculinities cannot avoid the neoliberal turn that is taking place in other social disciplines, including but not limited to sociology and anthropology. Understanding how masculinities evolve under the uncontested power and effect of neoliberalism regarding the changing forms of sociability and gender identity constitutes the basis of this approach. Scholars have highlighted the connections between masculinity, social and economic development, opportunities of employment and labour relations regarding the larger framework of the economy and intimacy.[19] The relationship between (un)employment and masculinity positions social class as a critical issue in the formation of analysis of gender and sexualities. The impact of neoliberal regimes on masculinities, for example, in producing the end of the traditional breadwinner role through chronic unemployment, becomes more meaningful and telling when we ponder the effects of neoliberalism on men who are classed and gendered and sexualised at the same time. In this sense, transactional homosexual sex in Istanbul is, in fact, classed. The encounter between the rent boy and the client (local or tourist) is a classed one, in addition to the fact that it is a sex-mediated, embodied and dialogical encounter. When rent boys talk about their customers, or vice-versa, they highlight the differences between themselves and the other men. Otherness and difference are narrated through religion, ethnicity or sexual identity; However, class is almost always the single most significant determinant in any story I have heard. A rent boy says, for example, 'I did not quite understand how gay he actually was. He was as manly as we are. I don't understand how this happens.' A gay customer says, for example, 'gay men cannot be as masculine [as rent boys] even when they want to. Rent boys have to be [masculine] because they are [from] slums. They struggle and fight physically there. They grow up masculine.' Both of them verify that neoliberalism expands the economic field in place of other spheres (i.e., social, cultural, moral or political). This tendency underlines class identity and consolidates the ties between masculinity and money, occupation, poverty and other material and financial components of life. At the same time, masculinity becomes a form of human capital that subjects can invest, calculate, develop, market and convert to other types of capital, including the economic. Codes and signs of masculinity, ways of social embodiment, discourses and practices of performing masculinities become increasingly commodified. A rent boy, as a neoliberal subject, imagines reflexively where, in which ways and against whom he can use his particular (exaggerated) masculinity, and he recalibrates it if and when necessary. Masculinity is included in a symbolic hierarchy with a number of qualifications, such as 'more,' 'real,' 'full,' 'wrong,' 'half' or 'spoiled.' Its exchange value and price are assumed and then paid for in market relations.

Another point that occupies a central position within critical masculinity studies is the increasing role of intimacy in the formation and reshaping of masculinities. Until recently, scholars had not considered intimate spheres to be as necessarily integral to the making of masculinity as, for example, relations of power, hegemony and domination.[20] Men are products of subjective and intersubjective relations with women and other men as much as they are the embodied outcomes of sexuality, fantasy, pleasure, fear, shame, violence, trauma, pain, honour, memory, nature and biology. According to this perspective, affective tendencies, emotional ties and the complexity of desire play a crucial role in the construction and performative display of masculinities.[21] Masculinity is not only demonstrated and proven in public, it is also reproduced and legitimated when the subject is alone, thinking about himself, looking at the mirror, fantasising about his life or reforming himself and his relations.

Examining rent boys in Istanbul brings similar themes to the fore. Homosexuality is generally placed within a framework of bodily desires and their implications (for instance 'homoeroticism' and 'desiring your own sex'). However, rent boys say they do not desire other men. They pretend either to hide their suspected queer desires or to boost their heterosexual façades. Sex between a rent boy and a gay man is supposed to be free from emotions, somatic desires, eroticism and passionate involvement; it must be completely 'cold and metallic.' During our conversations, most rent boys repeatedly made this point in almost an automatic fashion. Nevertheless, pleasure and desire do not always work in the direction that heteronormativity dictates. In the first phase of our chats, rent boys told me that they did not want to have sex with men, that they desired female bodies and that when they have sex with men they do not get pleasure at all, rather thinking of it as work. As we kept seeing each other, they might mention what type of man they enjoyed, under what conditions and exactly what they liked doing in the company of other men.

While the position of rent boy subverts the absolute duality between homo- and heterosexuality, it also makes the structure of desire, which normally stops one from oscillating between these two, more flexible and ambiguous. During the course of my research, I have witnessed some rent boys incorporating same-sex desire and developing gay identities, moving out of their family homes in *varos* neighbourhoods and becoming urban queers, while others stopped performing transactional queer sex, got married and had children. These experiences tell me that pleasure, bodily indulgence, affect, shame, pride, love and sympathy are articulated with power, intimidation, benefit, advantage, sovereignty and subjugation in the modality of masculinities. Rent boys in Istanbul also demonstrate that hegemonic masculinity is mediated through intimacy and forms of carnal knowledge while the production and sustenance of masculinity can be an ongoing, reflexive and contingent process.

CHAPTER 4

QUEER IN THE SPATIAL, TEMPORAL AND SOCIAL MARGINS

Something I never like is this 'gay vs. man' discussion. I believe there are only women and men. A man fucks, and a woman gets fucked. That's it. And then, [there are] some men who act like women, behaving as if they had a woman's soul. You call them gay [and] homosexual. There is no need for that. They are still men, who act like women. We are the real men; actually they [gay men] are not even men. They are something else. It is so simple [...] but also confusing. Fuck that.

(Riza, aged 21)

I remember the first few times I came to the Taksim area. I was not that young, I must have been about 13 or 14 years old. It was something so exciting for me. I felt myself really liberated. I could have screamed in the street, run or laughed crazily. I got this feeling that nobody would care there. Suddenly, I felt released. Somebody or something freed me when I got there. I remember I told myself I could sit somewhere and watch people passing by without doing anything else for hours. I saw a woman with green hair. I never forgot that. It was fun. It wasn't like my own place. There, everybody is the same. Our women are covered; everybody works hard. They are tired and pale because of too much work. If you do something different than them, if you become a little bit unusual in terms of your hair or clothes or the music you listen to, people start to chase you and disturb you. They would say, 'Hey, are you a faggot or what?' In Taksim {you can} do whatever you like and nobody would stop you and ask stupid questions or follow you to catch you alone and beat you. Now, I am a grown up, but sometimes I still feel that freshness, that sense of freedom when I come here.

(Deniz, aged 24)

I am absolutely sure that not all gay men are bad people. That is so stupid to say such a thing. {If you think so} It means you are not experienced enough about life. You haven't met {a sufficient number of} people. 'All normal people are good and all gays are evil,' well, I am sorry but that is not true. You can be hurt by your own. Their {gay men's} lives made them, some of them, tougher, smarter. I mean these people have sex with other men and live with this. Come on, it is not easy. I mean in this society. This is not Sweden or the United States here. And doing this for 40 years, 50 years. That's not easy. That lifestyle gives them some abilities that clearly we don't have. Some kind of sense. So you need not find it strange. You need to respect. I do not say that you have to like it. But then, nobody's forcing you to do this {male sex work} right? [. . .] I am not saying that I love gay people. I think every man needs to marry a woman one day and found a family of his own. So, theirs {gay's} is not the right way. But it is his decision. You have to respect. And you know what, some of them are actually decent guys even though they are faggots.

(Furkan, aged 25)

When I was a kid, I watched the movie *Eskiya* {*The Bandit*, 1996}. There, for the first time, I saw the Taksim area and the Beyoglu area at night. Everywhere was dark but there were things that were going on. Dirty stuff, mysterious stuff, bars and women and men, narrow dim streets [. . .] I was deeply impressed. It was curious to wonder what was going on in Taksim at night. I was thinking to check it myself.

(Can, aged 25)

As the quotes above demonstrate, rent boys in Istanbul are troubling the boundaries of the social, moral, spatial and temporal order in which they are supposed to live in. They also transgress the linguistic order by identifying (or simultaneously concealing) who they are by using a purloined word from English. It is notable that gay men in Turkey also use the English term (gay) instead of the Turkish equivalent, *eşcinsel*, which is generally deemed rather outdated and funny, or boring and too technical and medicalised to refer to a personal self-identity. Sometimes, new, inexperienced boys who are not familiar with the customs of the queer subculture of Istanbul may call themselves gigolos or escorts, but they are warned and corrected by the older boys. If their interlocutor is stubborn enough or pretends not to understand the meaning of the term (like me) and continues to ask what they mean by rent boy, they say 'having sex for money,' 'a fucker for money,' 'a kind of gigolo' or 'male escort' in the vaguest possible way.

In this chapter, I discuss the rent boys of Istanbul as queer subjects in at least two ways. The first domain of the constitution of (queer) subjectivity for rent boys is about sexuality and sexual identity. In spite of the fact that they insistently identify themselves as 'normal,' men or, infrequently, hetero, they have sex with other men on a regular basis, do not adopt the gay identity and claim that they do not experience a transformation based on – or triggered by – their sexual experiences. Thus, they destabilise heteronormativity and make it more flexible than it is supposed to be. The second significant point about rent boys' queer subjectivity is their acts of deviation from the spatial and temporal meanings of heterosexuality and heteronormativity and their capacity to produce queer spatialities and temporalities in the city. Here, I use the concepts of queer spatiality and temporality in the way that Judith Halberstam summarises them:

> Queer refers to nonnormative logics and organisation of community, sexual identity, embodiment and activity in space and time. 'Queer time' is a term for those specific models of temporality that emerge within postmodernism once one leaves the temporal frames of bourgeois reproduction and family, longevity, risk/safety and inheritance. 'Queer space' refers to the place-making practices within postmodernism in which queer

people engage, and it also describes the new understandings of space enabled by the production of queer counterpublics.[1]

In other words, rent boys in Istanbul subvert the imagined balance between erotic practices, sexual identities and regulations about the usages of time and space, while they embody an inconsistent, in-between and oscillating position, through which they produce their sexual subjectivities. Rent boys are queer subjects not only because they have clandestine sexual relations with men as they claim to be straight, but also because they are at locations where they are not supposed to be, they are together with people they should not interact with, doing things that they are absolutely forbidden to do. Rent boys become queer through relations of sexuality, time, space and identity construction, just like other social groups that 'liv[e] outside the logic of capital accumulation:'

> [R]avers, club kids, HIV-positive barebackers, rent boys, sex workers, homeless people, drug dealers and the unemployed. Perhaps such people could productively be called 'queer subjects' in terms of the ways they live (deliberately, accidentally or of necessity) during the hours when others sleep and in the spaces (physical, metaphysical and economic) that others have abandoned and in terms of the ways they might work in the domains that other people assign to privacy and family [...] For some queer subjects, time and space are limned by risks they are willing to take: The transgender person who risks his life by passing in a small town, the subcultural musicians who risk their livelihoods by immersing themselves in nonlucrative practices, the queer performers who destabilise the normative values that make everyone else feel safe and secure; but also those people who live without financial safety nets, without homes, without steady jobs, outside the organisations of time and space that have been established for the purposes of protecting the rich few from everyone else.[2]

At this point it is crucial to remember what Lee Edelman underlines about the impossibility of *being* a queer: 'The queer must insist on disturbing, on queering social organisation as such – on disturbing, therefore, and on queering *ourselves* and our investments in such organisations. For queerness can never define an identity, it can only ever disturb one.'[3] In the same vein, David Halperin famously writes that queerness acquires 'its meaning from its oppositional relation to the norm [...] Queer by definition [is] whatever is at odds with the normal, the legitimate, the dominant [...] There is nothing in particular to which it necessarily refers. It is an identity without an essence.'[4] Here I contend that rent boys are queer subjects because they simultaneously expose how homosexuals *become* homosexual and heterosexuals *become* heterosexual through the normalisation processes associated with each identity, in addition to their distanced and unscrupulous attitude towards these two sexually regulating categories, discourses and erotic regimes.

In this sense, the queer subject can be related with a mode of disinterestedness or passive resistance. Passivity turns meaningful within the quality of resistance against heteronormativity, which is effective in every aspect of individual and social life. Resisting in an active way, imagining confrontation, verbalising it, telling others, struggling and conflicting all denote a process of identity-construction, such as 'being a gay' or 'being a feminist.' Yet rent boys do not have such an intention. On the contrary, they have a tendency to pass through these processes in secrecy, without self-realisation, public contestation or approval-seeking. If we remember that the affirmative feature of identity-construction and self-struggles for identification contradict what queer might mean in Judith Butler's sense of the term, we can better comprehend how rent boys' disinterestedness may position them in the centre of queer modes of apathy and inertia. Most of rent boys do not really care about dominant heterosexual ideals, such as founding a family, having a rewarding business, being a good citizen of the country or loyal children of their families, at least in the short run. Heterosexuality here surfaces as the operating backbone of the institutions that are articulated through such ideals and regulatory myths. Institutionalising heterosexuality and these ideals, which rent boys seemingly ignore, produces, locates, consolidates and secures heterosexuality as a requirement. Rent boys become queer citizens because they do not meet heterosexual and *heterosexualising* ideals and expectations due to their indifferent and uncompromising attitudes. They are somewhat on hold, uncommitted and disconnected.

Examining the fragile queer identity of rent boys requires a departure from the current presiding perspective in the literature of sexuality studies in Turkey or the sociology of sexualities as it is practiced in Turkey, which grasp sexual subjects only within the disciplining binary of homo- and heterosexuality without any evident attempt to problematise it.[5] Looking at rent boys and their bodily, erotic and social experiences around male sex work in Istanbul may demonstrate that a number of sexual subjects position themselves outside of the sexual polarity between being exclusively gay or straight. While the subjects are present in certain urban spaces at certain times, the sexual duality may not work for everyone, every time in an encapsulating sense. Therefore, talking about rent boys is not a meditation about who is gay and who is straight in the sexual economy of contemporary Istanbul, nor it is an attempt to produce knowledge about 'the homosexuals,' which is a socially constructed group. The very figure of rent boy impairs the coherence of the long-assumed border between homo- and heterosexuality and evaporates the assumed ties between the sexual subject and sexual community on the brink of marginality. Although it is possible to make interpretive comments about the current make-up of heterosexuality or homosexuality by studying rent boys, it would be wrong to draw conclusions about them or construct analogies between rent boys and the members of these broader groups. In other words, rent boys are not smaller, representative parts of a larger social (or sexual or subcultural) group. A young man who is acting as a rent boy for a given moment, who identifies neither as gay nor as straight, pushes the researcher of sexualities to expand the sexual binary, explore other territories and develop new questions. If homosexuality can be performed in such an arbitrary and exceptional way, if heterosexuality is done in such a flexible and open-ended fashion, it becomes impossible to claim that the all-encompassing sexual binary constitutes a coherent structure surrounding all subjects.

Researchers have noted that queer theory and queer studies underline the problem of the subject in the sociological research tradition. For example, according to Adam Green,[6] the subject whose existence sociology recognises and researches is counter to what queer theory presumes as the unfixed, denaturalised subject, as it appears in the normalising regimes, cannot be reduced to each other. We can only think about these two models of subjectivity in constant tension. In such a mapping, sociological thinking would accept rent boys in Istanbul as either gay or heterosexual (or within any other identity category) and then select research questions and look for the answers; a queer perspective would disregard this binary and examine how rent boys become gay or straight temporarily, how these sexual identities are undone by the persistent contradiction between actions and words and how rent boys fail to conform to one category and end up somewhere in between. There are definable, recognisable and knowable sexual minorities (for instance, gays or the transgender community) in the classical sense of the sociology of sexuality. For sociological research that is inspired by queer studies, however, the real question is about the unknowable aspects of the assumed subject, her different modes of knowing and expressing herself in certain social situations and the cultural mechanisms that render this subject measurable and understandable. Thus, a queer sociology would be interested in shedding light on what the subject, following the pronunciation 'I am a rent boy,' discontinuously does and fails to do, how he accomplishes gendered and sexualised ideal(s), what constitutes the gap between the ideal(s) and ever-shifting performance of the subject, how the subject simultaneously enacts and unravels homo- and heterosexuality with his bodily and discursive acts and thus how he renders the sexual binary exceptional, imagined, unnatural and contingent in a significantly performative manner.

The Rent Boy

When they talk about their other lives and forms of sociability at home, rent boys mention that these domestic spaces are insufficient in size for their large families, which sometimes consist of about a dozen people, and how these informally built homes on the outskirts of the city are badly ventilated, misshapen, too crowded and packed with stuff and produced with cheap materials and incorrect techniques. Physical perception and cultural understandings generally intertwine in these accounts to generate the sense of distance from what they witness in the middle-class homes (or luxury hotel rooms) they visit to have sex. In this sense, distance also signifies geographical and symbolic differences: 'my place is too far from Istanbul [...] It is outside the city [...] My home is where there is no life [...] You could not even know where it is.' In rent boys' narratives their normal family lives and homes are radically different from what they experience in queer temporalities in the city centre. When they tell me that '[w]hat happens here, stays here,' or that '[i]t is a different universe there, here is entirely different,' rent boys tacitly highlight the symbolic distinction that produces meaning, constitutes subjectivity and controls and reshapes relations. There, at home, outside Istanbul, they have a life consisting of crowded families, unchanging (though actually mild) poverty, suffocating social limits, small comfort zones, jobs that they find meaningless, horrid schools and relatives and friends that they are never fully content with. Here, on the other hand, in Istanbul, at Taksim Square, at gay bars, in gay men's homes, at expensive hotels where tourists stay, they have another, more somatic, more pleasure-oriented hedonistic cornucopia, a life in which they can escape who they are and forget where they come from. Instead, they have stories of fictitious identities and non-existent conditions, where the future becomes ambivalent, unsettled and definitely more exciting.

Rent boys thus have two parallel lives. At home, as young men, they are almost at the bottom of social hierarchies that are based on age, kinship and status. They are the ones who are ordered around, controlled, disciplined, watched and punished. They are seen as inexperienced by the elder men at their households, and nobody listens to them. However, among the queer circles in the city centre, they turn into sovereign masculine subjects who rule, decide and have secrets and boundaries that people must approach with undeniable respect and intimidation. Here they are the ones who have the last word. This is a contradictory narrative, because what makes them more, *even exaggeratedly*, masculine here is their background in *varos* areas, their capacities to perform real, intimidating slum manhood, while back there their masculinities are rendered insignificant, weakened, spoilt and oppressed. What makes them praised male, genuinely masculine subjects are the circumstances in queer spaces and temporalities. Being a real man at home in the slum does not add any value and just makes them ordinary, while it engenders a form of symbolic capital, an erotic investment which they use and convert into other values, including money, in the queer spaces and erotic economies of the Taksim area.

The critical factor that links the two parallel and unconnected lives as rent boys navigate between them is sexuality, which makes these two subjectivities unaligned and differentiated. The formula that governs their double lives is actually simple: Embody heterosexual normality and stylise your actions in a way that not only to stops public inquiries, but prevents even the silent questions in the neighbourhood and among your peers; conversely, have compensated sex with men while protecting an out-of-context, somehow constellated masculinity and not identifying as gay. Discursive and practical acts concerning sexuality, such as displaying, preserving, fortifying and securing heterosexuality in different settings, create and give meaning to the two cultural milieus that rent boys oscillate between. Heterosexual masculinity in its exaggerated style both separates and reconnects these two milieus and makes them more permeable. The rent boy safeguards his masculinity and keeps it away from possible challenges at home, and he re-masculinises himself by using his 'authentic' masculinity (which is neutralised and normalised at home) via his relations with other men. This performance of masculinity, which he aestheticises, stylises and embodies enables him to come to Taksim Square, find customers, have sex and then resume his heteronormative life. In this sense, although it looks extremely contradictory and self-repudiating, this over-sexualised masculinity gives rent boys coherence in their lives: an unfixed queer subject that sustains a coherent narrative across various spaces, sociabilities and temporalities.

As I have discussed in previous chapters, the oscillation between here and there and between queer subculture and slum neighbourhood morality cannot necessarily be circular and mobile. If their queer escapades with men became public at home, this could be risky for rent boys in terms of sustaining their masculine normalcy, their unspeakable condition of legibility. Yet, of course, this is not a simple, linear or predictable process. It depends on contingencies and interpersonal power relations at stake. I came across many instances in which rent boys' engagement with queer sex work became public, though they were ultimately able to subdue the issue in the name of preserving their respectability. For instance, my respondent Nihat (aged 28) lived in one of the lower-class areas with his family and worked at a flower shop in one of the chic middle-class neighbourhoods. He said he occasionally went to gay bars and had sex with other men and that sometimes he got paid. He told me that almost everybody around him, including his brothers and his boss, but definitely not his fiancée and her family, knew about these queer sexual encounters, and among those who knew, none of them particularly liked the idea. Still, he maintained that people around Nihat deeply believe that he would not destroy himself and would stop when he needed to. In Nihat's case, as well as in many other accounts, it appears that there is a presumption that queer sex might be empowering and masculinising as long as you are the top (penetrating) partner. As I have outlined before, such an emphasis on top-only roles in penetration and protection from gay stigma is prevalent in diverse sexual geographies, including the Middle Eastern, the Mediterranean and the Latin American.[7] It is not possible to generalise this idea as though it were an accepted part of heterosexual masculinity to penetrate another male in Turkey. I rather argue that most rent boys that I talked to use this strategy as an alternative explanation if or when their same-sex sexual relations become known to others. It is a heteronormative legitimation of the queer sexual practice of male sex work. This is therefore a one-way sexual and gendered transfer: While the real masculinity from slums is imported into Istanbul and polished in order to be marketed and exchanged in the informal sex work economy, all signs of queer encounters must stay in Istanbul and not move to the slum areas. While queer culture in Istanbul is interested in and keen to further experience slum masculinity, the genuine neighbourhood heteronormativity is positioned against the possibility of importing queer sex and *queered* gender performances.

Sexuality for rent boys is not a meaningful and continuous life sphere through which to define themselves. On the contrary, it signifies an exceptional, disposable, 'for once and one time only' and inconsistent experience. If the concept of sexual orientation presumes that sexual acts that take place in one's history on a regular basis form and reshape one's (sexual) identity, rent boys' sexual practices point to a situation of 'sexual disorientation,' or a failure to orient sexually.[8] Thus my question is whether these disoriented sexual practices, their constant repetition and the iterative way in which they are discussed can make them a precondition of identity-formation. In other words, can repeated exceptions, recurring acts and reiterated explanations make a sexual identity? I argue that it is possible to trace the cracks of the gap between what the subject does and how he talks about it through the sexual acts that rent boys perform in a queered temporality and spatiality.⁹ The queer subjectivity of rent boys stems from the queer potentiality of this gap and their disoriented contingency.

It is striking to note that these young men call themselves 'rent boys,' which implies a state of temporariness. Such temporariness delineates not being owned, permanent, transferable, sustainable, foreseeable or inflexible. The lifestyle and emotions of the rent boy, which has no sense of the near future, institutionalisation, durability or rootedness, resemble what Halberstam describes as the 'queer way of life.' It is not just the body, skin or sexual performance of the young men that is described about as 'rented' for a short term, but the term also, maybe more tacitly, refers to the subversion of the social norm in both spatial and temporal frameworks in a queer direction. The tacit emphasis on disconnection and disorientation are inherent in the sexual, bodily, erotic, temporal, spatial, relational and class conditions.

Looking for Hegemonic Masculinity Among Rent Boys

As I have explained above, Raewyn Connell emphasises that heterosexuality is a cornerstone of the constitution of hegemonic masculinity, and thus non-heterosexual masculinities are destined to become marginalised, since they do not contribute to male power over women, the single structural fact of the patriarchal dividend. This knowledge also reveals the central dilemma of rent boys in Istanbul: what is the subversive potential of not incorporating into, or indeed weakening, heterosexuality for the hetero-masculine subject? Can a rent boy claim that he animates or yearns for hegemonic masculinity while he performs queer sex and male prostitution? How can we explain the contours of hegemonic masculinity when it departs from compulsory heterosexuality?

The most remarkable characteristic of rent boys in a broader effort to interpret masculinities is their capacity to transform heterosexual masculinity from a normal, natural, unmarked, unchangeable and invisible essence to a skill or form of capital that they can manipulate, use, recalibrate, convert into money in a safe or non-threatening way as long as they know themselves and are able to control the bodily and emotive dynamics of their encounters. Masculinity as we know it is deconstructed in queer compensated sex: Rent boys think about their masculinities, change the way they relate with masculinity, unthink and unlearn their preconceptions about being a man or being *more* manly or doing masculinity. Queer subjectivity becomes crystallised when rent boys distance themselves from the modes of masculinity that they are socialised into and performatively imitate, and when they reinterpret and participate in new processes of normalisation at the intersection of gender, sexuality and class. Sometimes, specific enactments of symbolic codes within rent boys' new (exaggerated) masculinity become unacceptable to the regime of hegemonic masculinity, or vice versa. The configuration of doing masculinity in a specific way, which is articulated with heterosexuality and class, is hybridised with new rules, requirements and negotiations within the gender order of that society. Rent boys' masculinities at home and among gay men at the city centre, despite their obvious discrepancies, start to become correlated with each other and make the two cultural milieus that rent boys act within more permeable.

I think we need a queer subject which places emphasis on inconsistency, indecisiveness (self-) contradiction, hesitation and liminality in order to revisit the productive framework of hegemonic masculinity that suggests a model of exemplary masculinity for modern societies.

The Poisonous Abject

Rent boys are unwanted, toxic, dangerous subjects in the 'erotic field of homosexuality.'[10] My self-identified gay interviewees talked about rent boys as 'improper' and 'approximate' gay men, men that cannot gradually become 'real' gays. Rent boys, according to this view, which was held by most of the gay men I talked to, are outside of a legitimate and acceptable field of (gay) subjectivity. In this sense, they determine the boundaries of legible gay identity by their presence and their queer erotic affiliations. They are the constitutive others, abjects in the sexual ideology of gay men in Istanbul. Gay men look at rent boys when they strive to define their own (dis-)belongings and domain of possibilities (i.e., what is wearable, doable, desirable, speakable or imaginable). They position themselves through immediate and tangible contrast to rent boys, who are 'outsiders within' when they are among gay men. In the absence of the absolute other, heterosexual men, who are careful not to interact with gays in sexual spaces, rent boys are the only available sexual (constitutive) others who can be related to and given meaning in the context of intimacy. However, contact with rent boys is also suspicious, immoral, disrespected, demurred, forbidden and rendered invisible in the middle-class gay men's moral universe in Istanbul. It is notable that most of my gay respondents told me that they think their language, anxieties, fears and aspirations are radically different than those of rent boys'. One of my gay informants sarcastically said that '[t]aking your chance with a rent boy may mean the beginning of a series of scandals that can end with your death, if you are lucky enough.' Such a presumption signifies a complicated matrix of sexuality, pleasure, danger, stigma and risk. The rent boy is desired not only because he embodies an exaggerated heterosexual masculinity, but also because his body implies the unknown, uncertainty, venture and rejection, as well as the possibility of scandal.

Homonormativity in Istanbul incites ideas and discourses about the rules for normal, decent, respected gay identity, as well as who will be included or denied access to globalised, modern gayness, embellished with signs of transnational cultural capital. According to this governing logic of homonormativity, rent boys are most definitely not gay, are not incorporated in the discourses on same-sex sexuality and their bodies are always marked as other due to class, gender, sexual and ethnic/racial differences. Furthermore, sexual contact with them is never seen as respectable. Istanbulite homonormativity stigmatises gay men who have sexual encounters with rent boys as promiscuous, wicked subjects who are enticed away from social concern and standards by their uncontrollable bodily and erotic urges. Other gay men disapprove of, warn and label the clients of rent boys as ignorant, uncontrollably horny or slutty, sometimes describing them as people who can only have sex if they pay for it. These clients are neither prominent community members nor legible subjects in the moral universe of respected gay men. The clients, on the other hand, when confronted, describe their interactions with rent boys as just another sexual possibility, an adventure or fantasy with which other people should not interfere. The critical point in this moral equation is the possibility of falling in love with a rent boy, which seems to happen quite often. In the discourses of homonormativity, having a crush to a rent boy is frequently equated with a sexual or emotional obsession with straight guys – the sexually preposterous. Only novice gays or nonsensical young boys are free to fall into this trap. An experienced, rational, realistic gay man, on the other hand, is expected to be seasoned enough to understand the denigrating nature of such unreciprocated and improbable love. By falling in love with a rent boy, the over-emotional and irrational gay man also positions himself outside of the legible field of modern gay identity. One of my respondents (Suleyman, aged 30) clarified this situation for me:

> A real homosexual, a modern gay must be together with other people who openly share his identity. We are not animals; we identify ourselves [as gay]. But if a gay man chases a heterosexual man or a rent boy, who says he was straight, then I can say that this guy could not understand the meaning of being gay. Or, I would rather say, he did not internalise the rules of modern homosexuality and he had internalised homophobia.

Hence, a gay man who falls in love with a rent boy or falls in love with a number of non-gay men continuously starts to be excluded from his social networks. His membership in his half-confidential community is being questioned, and he faces the risk of losing his (sexual) identity by his failure.

Being with a Rent Boy

Arif was one of my respondents who was in his mid-forties. In his words, he was a 'sexual activist' who had fought for the rights of sexual minorities for a long time. He was proud that he had always been connected with the rest of the world. When he told me that there was no such thing as a rent boy during an interview, I was surprised. He explained that what he really meant was the understudied relation between class and (queer) sexualities in Turkey.

Arif: For me, the rent boy is a sensational phenomenon. The term originated from outside [of homosexual circles]. Other people made it up.

Cenk: But there are a lot of people who call themselves 'rent boy.' I also talk to them for this research.

A: They may, you may. But this is just a label. They learn to say this. Look, for example, I tell you now, 'I have been with a rent boy.' What do you understand from this? It means I paid for sex, right? What if I tell you instead: 'I have been with a rent boy but I haven't paid for sex.' What does this mean? Without the money transaction, it means that two men have had sex, right? It is gay. Without money, we talk about two men here, two gays. That's it. But, in this scenario, has that guy turned gay? No, he hasn't; he is still a guy from the slums. He had always been a slum guy. He just made up this story of 'being a rent boy' in order to have sex with me, or any other gay person. A slum guy cannot become gay, how could he? Because he can't be gay, he calls himself rent boy. [It is] just a mask, this enables him to act and fuck like a gay man, fuck a gay man. He might also get some pocket money after the sex. Perfect story, right?

Later during the interview that day, I pushed him to expand his ideas on sexuality, prostitution and class.

Cenk: Before, you said that you think rent boys are actually gay. However, I have been observing that they develop tactics not to be seen as gay and strive to be differentiated from gay men.
Arif: Like what?
C: For example, they pay attention to what they wear, they have sex with transvestites, they are vigilant about drinking and they do not take the passive role in penetration.
A: All the others are about being a slum guy. I don't say they are not from the slums, though. What I am trying to say is they cannot be gay because they are from the slums. The issue of being in the top-only position is not unique to rent boys. There are plenty of gay men who are also top-only. For instance, my friend X works at an advertisement agency, and he lives in Nisantasi [a gentrified, upper-middle-class neighbourhood]. And he is top-only. What is the difference between my friend X and the poor, unemployed Y from Gaziosmanpasa [an informally built, lower-class slum] in sexual terms? Where is the sexual difference? The difference here is that one is a slum guy and the other is a rich gay.
C: But a gay man who wants to have sex with Y needs to pay?

A: He needs to, but what if he does not pay? Then, it is the same thing as with my friend X. You have sex with a guy who defines himself as top-only. So it is the same thing.

Other respondents interpreted Arif's bold comments and conclusions in different ways. While some interlocutors told me how they improved their techniques for having sex with rent boys without paying them, others emphasised that rent boys' claim of the top-only position was a marketing strategy and that everything had a price in the sexual economy, including penetrating a supposedly top-only rent boy. Accordingly, as rent boys are insistent on their top-only sexual roles, their real, authentic heterosexual identities are consolidated. Thus, they become more attractive in gay men's eyes. Gay men who are seen as smart are not fooled by these narratives and they know that the real and authentic heterosexualities are just normative facades. When the masks are down, they believe everything can happen between themselves and rent boys.

At this point, it was interesting to me to notice that, despite all the bodily, relational and discursive efforts of rent boys to highlight their heterosexual identities, almost all gay men I talked with approached these claims with cynical humour and disbelief. Hence, this is a double performance. On the one side, rent boys display exaggerated and stylised masculinity to prove that they have authentic, unspoiled Anatolian manhood, radically different from that of gay men. They do this even when they know they are acting in a performative and not necessarily convincing fashion. On the other side, there are gay men who are fairly sure that the constructed, learnt and perfected masculinities of rent boys are not authentic at all, and that their heterosexuality is a fiction. However, they still connive with rent boys' masculine self-presentation. Only when they encounter with a first-timer, an inexperienced newcomer who acts strange and distant to them, are they impressed by the realness of his heterosexual aura. A competent rent boy, however, inevitably loses his magnetism and turns into a kind of a gay man or a 'fake' heterosexual and becomes a part of an instantaneous identity position, a kind of queer disbelonging.

Strategies of Upward Mobility

The gay men who I spoke to over the years collectively imagined the rent boy as an opportunist, ambitious, calculating, rational and instrumental subject who strategically places himself based on upwardly mobile desires and strives to take his chance to rise in economic and social terms. For example, Cem, in his late forties at the time of the interview, said,

> [The rent boy] is a human type that even when he falls to the ground he can raise again with some earth on him [he can benefit from the worst situation]. [A rent boy] always thinks about how he can maximise his own good, how he can find a fool [to exploit]. Those are people that can do anything for the smallest benefit, or even for an insignificant object. That is their innate character. This is not about manhood-womanhood, or being top or bottom. This is a matter of personality, of character. It is a question of whether I exchange an old t-shirt, a small amount of money or a bottle of cologne for my pride. At that point of oblivion, [a rent boy] can do anything for that worthless thing. [He is] blinded because of his narrow mind and low character.

With the exception of a few popular accounts in the news media, the only discursive context in which one can talk about the existence and meaningful presence of rent boys is the queer (counter-) public. Only the participants in the queer public are aware of the presence of rent boys, only they have opinions about rent boys and only they are able to interact with them. There is a distinction between 'good' and 'bad' rent boys within this queer counter-public. This distinction stems from rent boys' desire for upward mobility and willingness to rise in social and symbolic hierarchies. In this framework, rent boys with smart tactics for improving themselves in the long run, who communicate with people in a mutually respectful way ('strategies of rising') are seen as good and decent. Rent boys without such desires or strategies are perceived as irrational, unstable, dangerous and overly ambitious for immediate and insignificant material gain. Abdullah (aged 30) says, 'It is like in the story: don't give me fish but teach me how to catch fish. Would it be better for me if this faggot gives me money or make me meet with other people that can open me a door, like a job opportunity in the future? If he were without a vision for the future, the rent boy would opt for the money. If he were smart, he would play the game thinking for his future.'

Those who know rent boys, who are familiar with the discourses about rent boys in the queer counter-public, are aware that rent boys are neoliberal subjects. In this sense, rent boys internalise neoliberal values, logic and rules (for instance, by being egotistical and devious) and act accordingly. They focus on opportunities and self-interest, and they reorient their bodies and sexual subjectivities towards these. Hence, they are flexible subjects whose abilities to invest in the strategies of rising are evaluated in moral terms. Good rent boys are described as those who want a decent life (getting out of the slums, having their own flat in the city, having a personal computer, a car and a well-paying job), and for this reason they take sex work seriously, consider it a resource, and prioritise people's trust and respect over cash or other direct benefits. They choose to learn from gay men, develop rapport, use their clients as intermediaries for future job opportunities or social networks, and thus increase their cultural and social capitals. In contrast, those seen as bad rent boys do not care about their lower class identity or its denigrating connotations (slum, poor, unemployed, ignorant, vulgar or Kurdish) and do not endeavour to alleviate by 'using their brains' or 'acting smart.' They perceive gay men as one-time-only fools from whom to get disposable income or, worse, may be overtly homophobic. Of course, the introverted, disconnected rent boys who act in otherising, hostile, threatening ways are *the* bad ones, who gay men ought to avoid for their own sake.

Those who are seen as bad rent boys might actually be queer subjects who have 'been bound epistemologically, to negativity, to nonsense, to anti-production, to unintelligibility and, instead of fighting this characterisation by dragging queerness into recognition.'[11] With his rational capacities and strategies of rising, the good rent boy is supposed to yearn for middle-class values. He wants to be included by the modern gay community and the middle-class so he can get rid of the slum culture. He produces a narrative of self-improvement and conceives of sex work as yet another step towards the bourgeoisie lifestyle. This narrative of upward mobility presents an understandable, legible, sympathetically absorbable trace for most of the gay men I talked with. Both heteronormativity and homonormativity emphasise economical or symbolic betterment, self-expansion and self-enhancement. Good rent boys are complicit in their middle-class longings while the bad ones seem to accept the fact that nothing can be done to change who they are. Gay men snub the bad rent boys, although they also develop a clandestine desire for them. This moral duality diffuses into the hierarchy that reigns in homosexuality as a 'sexual field.'[12]

At this intricate intersection, the good rent boy is devalued because he embodies the complicit self, not the dissident other. The bad rent boy, however, is chased after because he is mysterious, incomprehensible and ferocious; he is different from gay men and wannabe-gays, so he represents the 'real' man who is fetishised and pursued by gay men. My respondent Engin (in his early forties), for example, explains this dynamic:

> If I want to have sex with a gay man I can easily find one. I am able to find even the cutest one. What can a rent boy who tries to become gay offer me? I am fed up with gay men and their attitudes, their gayness. That's another story. [Rent boys] want to imitate [us] and I can understand that. They also want nicer homes, better jobs; they want to leave the rat holes in which they live. So, he wants to resemble me; he accepts that I am superior in terms of culture and manners. That's okay. It makes sense to me; I don't have any opposition. But he also departs from what I find sexually attractive. If I were ready to pay a rent boy I would choose the most masculine, most virile one. Not the one that tries to be like me.

Some of the rent boys have an alternative account of self-advancement. It includes components such as a decent job, getting married and having children, buying or constructing a new home, leaving their family house in the slums and moving to the city centre, and (for some of them) living gay lives. During my research, I was particularly curious about the jobs that they imagine. The jobs that rent boys dream of are not the typical lower-class occupations that their families require them to take as soon as possible. Instead, when asked, rent boys offer ambiguous descriptions of the jobs they would want to take such as 'working at an agency,' 'doing business on the web,' 'working at a bar' or 'working in music production as a DJ.'

As Laura Kipnis says, 'visibility is a complex system of permission and prohibition, of presence and absence, punctuated alternately by apparitions and hysterical blindness.'[13] Rent boys in Istanbul appear and disappear instantaneously, enter and leave the queer context through an alternative spatiality and temporality, quit male sex work and start it again by finding themselves in a rent boy bar in the early hours of the morning. They oscillate between absence and presence, between visibility and invisibility. They can become present or visible only through encounters between different masculinities, sexualities, classes and nationalities. They do not foster different or consistent selves through their times in the city centre and in the slum districts, across communities they pretend to belong to or avoid attaching to. On the contrary, they tell different stories in different ways, generate accents of embodiment in diverse situations, perform before multiple audiences and thus generate subjectivities in which intricacy and contradiction are inherent. It might not be possible to deem all rent boys to be hidden gays, but it is also impossible to see them entirely as pretending heterosexual youth who seek fun. Although some of them decide to become gay at the end of the road and some realise from the beginning that they are heterosexual to an extent that precludes queer sex, most rent boys I have come across feel queer sex work as fragmentation, duality, liminality and inconsistency, as I have recounted some aspects in this book. Rent boys, thus, are queer subjects who are members of the queer counter-public in Istanbul and participate in social discourses about queer sex work in certain places and at certain times.

Masculinity has an undeniable role in the states of the queer subjectivity of rent boys. As I have discussed in Chapter 3, rent boys animate, embody, examine, repeat and recalibrate an exaggerated form of masculinity. Exaggerated masculinity enables them to engage in compensated sex with local men and tourists and to continue their heteronormative lives at home despite their queer escapades. Can ritualised, controlled, repeated sexual acts produce sexual identity even when they are seen as anomalous? What type of social relations do rent boys establish in the two symbolic worlds between which they swing? How do they rearrange their identities, selves and bodies through this course of perverse mobility and liminality? All these questions are concerned with the bounds between gender and sexuality, between heterosexual masculinity and queer subjectivity. Rent boys' reflexively manipulated, transformed, malleable masculinity reveals that heteronormativity might not be as steady and unvarying as is commonly assumed. Rent boys also demonstrate that multiple counter-hegemonic masculinities can engender invisible, permeable and incongruous positions of gender identity.

CHAPTER 5

CONTEMPORARY MALE SEX WORK

The thought of sexual difference within homosexuality has yet to be theorised in its complexity.
Judith Butler, *Bodies That Matter: On the Discursive Limits of 'Sex'* (New York, 1993), p. 183

Previous chapters in this book have focused on different but related aspects of queer male sex work in Istanbul, Turkey. I need to underscore two additional points in the beginning of this final chapter. First, although there have always been sensational stories on the topic in the gossip columns of newspapers, in the course of a decade of research I have not come across a single young man who says he sold sex to women in exchange for money, gifts or other rewards.[1] Thus, my research has been restricted to male sex work involving male clients. Second, as I have explained throughout the book, from the late 1990s to the early 2010s, rent boys who were not supposed to be homosexual, and their clients, mostly self-identified 'out' gay men, were the two distinct and mutually exclusive sides of male prostitution in Istanbul. Recently, these categories have blurred to a certain extent. The vendors of the commercial male-on-male sex scene in the 2010s can be divided into two groups: The conventional, supposedly straight rent boys and a bevy of self-identified gay men who provide sexual services to other men. Both types of men have their place in queer life in Istanbul today.

In the wake of a long, convoluted and fluctuating history, homosexuality in Turkey has become more publicly visible since the late 1980s. This slight increase in visibility has been paralleled by an unpretentious sexual liberation in the country: the opening of newer and bigger gay bars and clubs; a small but growing academic interest in sexuality; a number of best-selling novels about same-sex love, both male and female; increasing transgender presence on the street and in media representations; an annual gay pride march in the centre of Istanbul and queer activist groups fighting for sexual rights and equality under the law.[2] Despite this progress, however, certain social groups remain excluded from the growing queer culture.[3] They include those from the lower social classes, those who are disabled and those of Kurdish ethnicity, as well as lesbians and 'bears'. Each of these groups has expressed discontent with the emergent queer lifestyle in urban Turkey and has striven to create space in which its members can express and realise themselves.[4]

In spite of a relatively liberal atmosphere in which minority gender and sexual identities can be enacted and displayed publicly, serious social issues continue to impact queer life as it is lived in Turkey. While citizens are not punished for consensual homosexual sex between adults, homosexuality has not been decriminalised by law. The surreptitious way in which the state continues to subjugate sexual minorities can be seen, for example, in the examinations conducted by the army in order to exclude and mark gay men as having 'advanced psycho-sexual disorders' via 'a rotten report,'[5] and by increasing police pressure on the bars and clubs that queers visit. At a societal level, homophobia is manifested in the seemingly innocuous but deeply marginalising humour featured in the mass media and popular movies. It is reinforced in the education system through silences within the curriculum and explicitly discriminatory hiring practices. In the course of everyday life, a normalised, naturalised homophobia comprises the major structure of feeling expressed towards lesbians, transgender people and gay men in Turkey. In terms of family, many gay men and lesbians have great difficulty coming out and opt instead for closeted, solitary lives involving occasional clandestine same-sex encounters.[6]

Gay men tend to perceive rent boys as 'real' men with an uncontaminated, authentic and naturalised sense of masculinity. Coming from the outlying areas of the city is translated in essentialist gender terms as being inevitably more masculine: only real (and straight) men can survive in the *varos* districts, and thus, men from the *varos* are real, untarnished men. This sense of cultural difference is articulated in a form of fetishism for working-class bodily and gender codes (i.e., *bona fide* masculinity) among gay men, and provides the symbolic background for the male sex work scene in Istanbul. The city centre, Taksim Square, which is simultaneously the most important transport hub and the main entertainment zone, is not especially close to *varos* regions, although it is not difficult to get there via the intersecting subway and bus lines. The area around Taksim also houses most of the gay bars, cafes and clubs and is well known as the heart of queer life. Rent boys come to Taksim Square on the weekends for sex with other men, and then return home to the *varos* areas to continue their family lives as decent straight young adults.

Although they have sex with other men, it is crucial for rent boys to reclaim and stabilise their straight identities. Being a rent boy in this context means becoming a 'nocturnal queer' without spoiling an assumed and vindicated heterosexual pretence. Offering same-sex sexual service only as tops, rent boys promise local and foreign gays a rigidly defined, limited and somehow purloined intimacy with the authentic, normal, presumably straight men. They straightforwardly ask for money or gifts in return for sex or, more infrequently, strategically use their relations with gay men to expand their social networks and increase their opportunities for future employment and self-betterment.

During the interviews I conducted with rent boys, they always told me that the only issue they really cared about was how much they received before or after sex. Not long after, though, I realised that most rent boys, especially in the early hours of the morning after a tiresome and unsuccessful night, are willing to go to gay men's apartments to spend the rest of the night and have breakfast. After spending many nights over the years in queer dance clubs, I was able to comprehend the strategies some rent boys developed during their interactions with gay men. Atakan (aged 25), for example, was a security guard at a department store, and for him being a rent boy meant an opportunity to transfer into an office job, which he was eventually able to get:

> I started to see this guy, the advertiser, on a regular basis and we became pretty close. I was going to his home not only in the

evenings but also on weekend afternoons when I do not work. I even thought that he fell in love with me at some point. Then, he, but not I, he told me that they were looking for somebody at the office where he works. It was an advertisement agency. [It was] a very posh place. He asked me if I wanted to try to get the job and he could help me [...] He left the job at the agency after a while, but I still work there. It will be two years next month.

Some rent boys will agree to have sex with another man and stay until morning simply because there is no public transportation to the far off neighbourhoods where they live, or they do not have the money for taxi fare. Some local gay men say they have advanced their negotiation skills and become experts at having sex with rent boys without payment. One gay man I talked to joked that he was 'a bed and breakfast only,' giving no cash to the rent boy he had sex with. Another informant, Kutay (in his mid-forties) told me:

> They [rent boys] have become quite professional now. You know twenty, thirty years ago there was nothing like this. Everybody was so amateur and they [rent boys] or we [gay men] did not really know what to do. They were really surprised when they came [into gay men's apartments]. You know people got killed, robbed, etc. But now, things seem to have an order. If you know the scene well, you can have a lot of fun with them without paying at all, or paying very small amounts [to rent boys], like tips [...] and, don't forget this, most of them are actually gay. Although they insistently say they aren't, they are into men. I do not even argue about this. So if you can stimulate their desire or promise a bright future, like a good job, they will come with you and please you. Not for money, but for pleasure, for themselves, for their future.

It is critical for rent boys to protect and promote their heterosexual public identities. In order to find gay patrons looking for 'real' straight men, and, in order to be safe at home and in their circle of friends if their same-sex escapades are exposed, rent boys develop and display a number of bodily, relational and discursive tactics, which I have described as 'exaggerated masculinity' in Chapter 2. They may, for example, look after their bodies to appear fit and healthy, wear clothes that are mildly stylish (not *varos*) but never effeminate (not gay) and wear cologne that they borrow or steal from gays while calculating carefully not to smell unmanly. Some may master styles of dancing to attract potential customers without looking like a belly dancer, befriend other rent boys but hide information from them, staying away from emotional and sexual engagements with similar men, have sex with transgender sex workers to demonstrate their manhood and virile performance and refuse to use condoms during penetration in order to show off.

One of my key informants, Deniz (aged 24) explained some of the rules for becoming a good and successful rent boy:

> Brother, do not be a faggot (*ibne*). This is the first thing. Faggots do not like faggots. Faggots like men, real men. So, do not act like a sissy, do not wear clothes they would wear. [...] You should always be careful with the other [rent] boys. Do not be close with them because people would talk about it. They would say you fucked each other; you were also faggots. [...] This job happens at night, right? All the bodies are relaxed, everybody's high, you are drunk. You should not give in and lose your control. Because you dance. And anything can happen when tired, drunk people dance together, touching each other. You can kiss somebody, another boy. Or somebody can grab your ass. You can accept an offer to participate in a group [orgy] with some big guys. Anything can happen, and then you cannot control it afterwards.

In their conduct, rent boys must remain vigilant to manage their self and public image as unquestionably heterosexual and insolent, thus serving gay men's fantasy of having sex with a real, straight man. Talking with gay men for too long and becoming too involved in gay things contradicts the mandates of exaggerated masculinity and harms the rent boy's sense of heterosexuality. Consequently, in communicating with gay men, rent boys try to be reserved and distant, which solidifies their heterosexual bravado and in return strengthens gay men's fantasies of enticing heterosexual men.

Rent boys dominated the male sex work scene in Istanbul in the mid-1990s and the late 2000s. Back then, no one thought of any other alternative personas in terms of compensated sex between men. One of my interviewees, Kemal (in his mid-sixties) said:

> In the beginning, in the late 1980s and 1990s, there were just a couple of small bars where gay men could hide from the public view and hang out together. You could see some very young, straight, poor boys there. We knew that *we were gay* but *they were not*; we did not even question the possibility because back then everything was much more obvious. We also knew that some of us [gays] gave them money either before or after sex. I mean, money for penetration. I remember I was always telling my friends that we should not have done that. It was no good to make them believe that it was a job and that they could make money out of it, from us. Because they were doing it for pleasure, right? But, of course, nobody listened to me. And the first rent boys in Istanbul became available then. Because they are not stupid; [they are] ignorant, but not stupid. They eventually learnt it. They learnt how to use us, exploit us. It is pretty normal now. We all know them.

As Kemal points out, rent boys are quite visible, knowable and, to a certain extent, negotiable for gay men in Turkey today. However, they are not alone in the queer sex scene of the city any more.

Recent Diversification of Male Sex Work

My research engagement with the subject of queer sex work in Istanbul has allowed me to recognise that rent boys are no longer the only figures (or even the predominant figures) on the transactional sex scene, as they gradually lose their privileged position among other options or forms of compensated sex between men. In other words, it is possible to witness a profound diversification of male sex work in Istanbul in the last decade. This heightened heterogeneity displays three key characteristics.

First, the class structure of the male sex worker pool is now much more varied. In the past, rent boys tended to come from lower-class families who had recently migrated to the city and did not have the economic and cultural capital to attain middle-class status. Rent boys' educational backgrounds were limited, they had not been able to travel abroad and their class habitus did not support knowledge about or consumption of global brand goods. As shown above, class differences were frequently recast as gender differences in sex, empowering rent boys and positioning them as the most desirable 'real' men, in contrast to their middle-class and more effete counterparts. Lower-working-class rent boys currently comprise only part of the male sex work market in Istanbul. Increasingly, a variety of mostly gay-identified young men have joined them in exchanging sex for money or other forms of compensation.

The increased variety of social classes that can be encountered in the sexual economy is paralleled by an enhanced diversification of gender norms and sexual practices. While the typical rent boy displayed an exaggerated sense of masculinity as a coherent style, now men in sex work can act in a variety of ways, adopting flexible forms of self-construction and communication in which they do not have to remain ruggedly masculine. Additionally, clients can negotiate over a repertoire of sexual acts, which may or may not include being the receptive partner in anal sex. In brief, the stereotypical working-class, distant, strictly top-only masculinity which denoted the imagined straightness of the rent boy has become blended, with increasing numbers of self-assured gay men and gender-bending queer individuals engaging in compensated sex.

Finally, there have been changes in the use of urban space. The two major venues that rent boys used to meet customers were a small, dimly lit park in the city centre near Taksim Square, Gezi Park and a few small bars on the side streets of Istiklal Avenue, which is adjacent to Taksim Square. After 2007, however, the municipality started renovating the park, making the area brighter and more amenable to regulation by the police. One of the implicit aims behind the rejuvenation was to stop homosexual encounters taking place in the park at night, including escapades with rent boys. Bientot, the most famous small bar for rent boys and their customers, was closed down around 2012 because of increasing pressure from the municipality and the police. Following these events, some long-avoided porn theatres throughout the city became more popular among men who were interested in public sex or sex for money. Recently, however, these theatres have also been raided by police, with many men being taken into custody and accused of (male) prostitution. As a result, the male sex work scene in Istanbul has, to a certain extent, been de-territorialised.

Nowadays, queer sex work interactions tend to take place mostly in the few regular gay bars and clubs, but the internet is also a prime setting for that purpose. Rent boys and other young men who are interested in compensated sex with men use gay websites, mobile applications or mainstream channels, such as Facebook and Instagram, to create profiles with pictures, presenting themselves as *escort* (escorts) or *masör* (masseurs) and negotiating online with potential customers. Some of these new-generation male sex workers or enthusiasts rent small, cheap apartments, using these spaces as homes but also as places in which to host customers to have sex. In many ways, this is a radical departure from the past, when rent boys used to live with their families and could never take a sexual partner home. Now it is possible to talk about *yeri olan* (a person who has his own place to have sex) men who live in male sex workhouses in Istanbul.

When Gays Sell Sex

As I have discussed in Chapter 4, rent boys are queer subjects in at least two ways. The first of these relates to the domain of sexuality itself. While engaging in sexual activities with other men (whether in exchange for money or not), rent boys stress that they are straight, normal guys, and refuse even to entertain the idea of a transformation from heterosexuality (or putative normalcy) to bisexuality or gayness. Hence their behaviour, to a degree, destabilises heteronormativity, making its boundaries about what is acceptable and what is not contradictorily flexible. What it means to be a gay or straight person (as continual personal identifications) changes through rent boys' discursive and bodily actions, as they neither fit with the rigid definition of heterosexuality, nor can they easily be tagged as gay or bisexual.[7]

The second aspect of rent boys' queerness comes from their play with the spatial and temporal fictions of normal, decent heterosexuality through the production of counter-normative queer space and time.[8] Rent boys subvert the presumed balance between sexual practices and identities, class, urban places and the use of time. They embody a queer subjectivity that hangs on this unsettled, liminal constellation. These men find themselves in places where normal people are not supposed to go, during time periods when straight people would not have the nerve to visit, mingling with people different from their own that they would not normally socialise with, doing things that they should absolutely not be doing as young, normal, straight men. Each non-compliant act, as understood within the spatial, temporal, sexual and relational regime of heteronormativity, puts rent boys at risk as they take up queer subject positions, repeatedly act and talk in conflicting ways and improvise an exaggerated masculinity as a disguise. In this sense, rent boys expose the conditions of the making of homo- and heterosexual identities in Istanbul through somatic intimacies and cultural references, while they undeniably disfigure the seemingly impervious boundary between these two mutually exclusive sexual identities.

Young, self-identified gay men in Istanbul, on the other hand, increasingly engage in sex work in its various forms. Despite their diversity, these men share a more conventional standpoint regarding identity-formation and identity politics. Since most identify as gay, it would not be confusing to find them in gay bars after midnight or having sex with other men. Thus, they do not actually queer the normative spatial and temporal regimes as rent boys do. (It can, however, be argued that they challenge the implicit homonormativity in Turkey through the exchange of queer sex for money, considering the fact that rent boys were seen by gay men largely as 'moral others').

Gay men who may engage in transactional sex defend their gay identification as a cultural marker and a symbol of middle-class class position highly unlike that of rent boys, who tend to eschew the notion of sexual identity entirely. As one of my interviewees, Tamer (aged 20), said:

Yes, I tell everybody that I am gay. I do not have a problem with that. I am out. I am 20 years old, always have been gay and will always be gay [...] It just occurred to me, what if I charged money for sex? It was an idea that came up instantaneously. I have searched for love for a long time and I have learned that nobody in Turkey actually looks for love. It is just about sex. So I thought if it was only sex and not love, I can make money out of it. That is how I started to ask for money when somebody approaches to me for sex through the internet or Grindr [...] Sometimes they agree and sometimes they don't. If I really like [the guy] then I can have sex without money, too. I do not have to do this as a job. It's just something I do to feeling better about myself. [I feel] I am not used for someone's own pleasure [by charging money].

It is noteworthy that Tamer said that by replacing his unsuccessful attempts to find love with money, his humiliation at the sense of being used is mitigated. This talk of emotion management is quite the opposite of what I have observed in rent boys' mostly quick, temporary and impersonal relationships. Rent boys rarely connect their desires and feelings with the money they can get out of sex. As Deniz explained above, they strive to avoid emotional intimacy with other men, and when intimacy does occur, they deny it fervently. Even simple forms of socialisation with gay men run the risk of rent boys' 'going gay.' More serious affective attachments are out of the question. It is interesting to note the transformation of male sex work in Istanbul from a rough, quick bodily encounter driven by economic motives, at least on the surface, to an option (or substitute) for missing same-sex feelings and a yearning for love.

It is unlikely that one will approach somebody who looks gay at one of the queer bars or dance clubs in Istanbul and hear that this person is involved in sex work. Most gay men in Istanbul still have a doxic belief that only rent boys, who are distinguishable through their clothes or straight-acting performances, can sell sex, and that people who pass as gay or exude an air of queerness can be approached for sex without thinking about money. Then how do gay men who are keen to practise compensated sex present themselves to other men who may be interested in sex? My informant Cihat (aged 24) explained:

> I have an 'escort' account on the website planetromeo.com. I also have a normal [gay] profile there. So a person who looks for normal gays as well as escorts can easily see me. If he sends a message to me through my normal profile, I evaluate him on the basis of his attractiveness. If he is my type, then I may meet him for sex or for fun. It is not about money. However, if somebody writes to me via the escort account, whether he is cute or not does not matter. I only check if he is clean, healthy and trustworthy at least on the surface. I also have a profile at gabile.com, which is

all local. No tourists visit that site because [it is in Turkish]. It is mostly useless for me because people look there for *varos* boys to tempt. They [gays] are willing to pay only very small amounts, for example 20 Turkish lira [$10], and call it the 'taxi fare.' So it does not really work for me. Finally, I have Grindr on my iPhone. I know almost everybody there; it has a limited number of profiles, but all the tourists use it. You are more likely to find a foreigner with money (*parali yabanci*) who is looking for a hot one-night-stand.

From recent interview data, it is clear that what Cihat does with his online profiles is a common strategy among Turkish gays. Some men use other websites, including mynet.com, and mobile applications like Hornet, but the principles that govern commercial and erotic involvement remain the same. There are also numerous Turkish Facebook pages, some directly related to male sex work, others directed towards more general audiences, all concerned with facilitating compensated or uncompensated queer encounters.

I asked Cihat how much he charged for sex and what he did and did not do sexually. He said, 'It depends on the type [of the client]. If he lives somewhere expensive, or looks rich, then I ask for 150 Turkish lira ($50). If he looks like he has an average income, then I say 75 Turkish lira ($25). And this is for one hour. I do not really like to be versatile with the same guy. So I ask if he wants to be active or passive. I can be both, but not with the same guy within an hour. Otherwise, I can do almost anything he wants'.

Cihat lives in the central Besiktas district with a roommate. They both are college students at a respected public university. His parents live in a small Anatolian town where he grew up and send him money on a monthly basis. He says he does not actually need the money from sex because the amount his parents send is enough. I asked him what his rationale was. He said, 'I do not know. Maybe just adventure or the pleasure that comes from having the extra money. I like to have sex; I am a sexual person. Nobody can have authority over my body, including my parents. So, I think it is just the extra excitement that I seek [through transactional sex].'

When I asked Cihat if his family, roommate or friends at college knew that he had sex for money, he said,

> No. My family does not even know that I am gay. I am not planning to tell them; they do not need to learn about this stuff. My roommate knows I am gay, but I do not tell him that sometimes I get money from men. Only a couple of close gay friends of mine know about this. Some of them also do it. But we do not advertise this. I am sure many gays would do that if they got the chance [...] I think it is not permanent in our lives. It is something we do for fun and to remember in the future. These things happen when you are young.

Cihat and Tamer's accidental, near discretionary, involvement does not tell us the whole story, however. Some young gay men (college students or not) endeavour to make money out of sex with other men because they are genuinely in need of it. Osman (aged 18) was one such informant. He explained the situation as follows:

> My father lives in Rize [a small provincial town] and my mother in Istanbul. They got a divorce a long time ago and now she is with someone else. My mother cannot help me financially, and I depend on the money my father might give me. However, he knows that I am gay, and he does not want me to live in Istanbul. He is against me taking the art school exams. He does not pay the tuition for the preparatory courses I have to take. He believes that if I cannot pass the exam, I will return to Trabzon and live with him, and he will have control over my actions. I mean he would stop me from being gay. I come to Istanbul whenever I have an opportunity and attend studios and workshops here to develop my drawing skills. Instructors at these places say I am really talented. When I am here [in Istanbul] I can stay at my cousin's place, but I do not have money for the courses [...] There was this guy I have been sleeping with for a while, when I was around, and almost a year ago I asked for money for having sex. He was surprised in the beginning but then accepted it because he has no money issues. I mean he is well off. So then I found a number of other men who pay me for sex. When it starts once you cannot help it. A person tells another that he pays you and fucks you. It is not much and it is not regular, but somehow it is enough to cover my expenses when I am in Istanbul, which is really an expensive city.

I asked Osman how he felt about his sex work experiences:

> I had serious problems at the beginning but I have self-confidence now. I am trying not to think about it very much. Instead, I focus on my goals. I do not care much [about commercial sex] and I show around that I do not care. I think this is the rule. You should not make it into something bigger than it actually is. Also, I play the ignorant boy most of the time. I act like I do not have much information on men or sex. This makes the men happier [...] It is not that they are bad people, or that I hate them, or that I do not get any pleasure from having sex with them [...] There was just one guy who fooled me, said that he knew some of the teachers at the art school, and they could help me through the interviews. So I went with him a few times. Although I did not really enjoy the sex, I did not take his money so as not to offend him. I was hoping that he would introduce me to his friends. Then he stopped talking to me. He did not help me. Other than this man, people have been okay so far. I do not have any sad memories.

Queer Sex Work Online

As the centre of male prostitution in Istanbul has shifted from Taksim Square, which has a number of public and semi-public, closeted spaces, to the virtual environments of computers and smart phone applications with geographical positioning systems, which I refer to as the deterritorialisation of queer sex work, I have surveyed the online profiles of gay men and rent boys on the most popular gay dating application, Atomic,[9] on 1 August–30 October 2015. I have scrutinised more than a thousand online profiles that got online in the greater Istanbul area during that period, and 231 among them were either related to male sex work or mentioned rent boys and male prostitutes in order to define who they were not.

I took a screenshot for each online profile and then classified them into four basic groups. These visual and textual self-depictions do not necessarily reflect the real nature of queer sex work or the true self-representations of sex providers, rent boys or gays. Instead, I approach this form of data as a visual and discursive language in which subjectivities are crystallised, and interpersonal relations (negotiations, conflicts and processes of misrecognition) are developed.

The first group consists of top-only male sex vendors, who seemingly follow the legacy of putatively straight rent boys, with a strong emphasis on their top role during penetration, youthful virility and penis size. For example, I saw three related profiles, seemingly three very young friends with facial photographs on each profile, which read, '3A: Tops, two 18 and one 19 years old. We have a car. For people who want us now, have a place and provide financial support.' Another profile with a smiling facial photograph reads, 'I am a top, into professional meetings only. One session is 200 [Turkish] liras. Let's communicate if it makes sense. If you like virtual sex, stay away [18 years old].' A moustached, traditional-looking man wearing a black shirt says on his profile, 'The Dark Kid: I am a top-only escort, yours respectfully [24 years old].' Other young men with fierce looks on their faces write things like 'Top Escort [22 years old]' and 'I am an escort $: Doing it for money, write to me if it suits you. Decide after seeing my private photos. I am a top [20 years old].' A full body-length photo of a man with clothes on reads, 'Emir the Top: I am an escort, write to me if interested. 6'3'. For money [20 years old].' A young guy posing with sunglasses and a swimming suit says, 'Athletic 20 years old, Top: Into professional meetings. Open for elite and decent people. My dick is big and thick.' Another one in a sunglasses and swimwear combo, which reveals his smooth torso, notes, 'Hi guys. 5'10'. I am 18, top and doing it for money. I am real, virtual people shall not write. One session is 200 [Turkish] liras.' Three more young men with casual full beards write, respectively, '21 cm Masseur: Don't send a request without talking about yourself. I don't have my own place. I am top only, doing this for money [24 years old];' 'Sex machine. 19 years old. For money. Full top. Unique taste;' and 'Top Masseur: I have my own place in Findikzade. Top Masseur. Serious, real people who want to meet can send me a message [25 years old].'

The second group of profiles show the men who advertise themselves as sex workers without specifying sexual roles as top or bottom; hence these are versatile male sex workers – a contrast to the idea of the straight-identified rent boys of the near past. The silence about active or passive sex roles also implies the possibility of further negotiation for a better price for the desired erotic acts. In general, a rent boy charges less for playing the top role during intercourse and more for playing the passive role, if he accepts that position at all. A small percentage of the escorts who do not specify their sex roles one their profiles may expect customers to take it for granted that if they sell sex, they play the top role. Overall, the apparently role-versatile rent boys are cute, and their photos seem to have been carefully selected to create a sense of effortlessness. Many of these profiles do not have textual content at all, except for US dollar signs. One role-agnostic profile which does have text (the profile lists a 24 year old man, and his photo shows him with his naked upper-body revealed) says, 'Rent Arda $$: I am in Kadikoy and I meet with special appointments. I have a transvestite friend for group sex.' Another profile, where the subject has posed lying down in the photo, reads 'Masseur: The purpose is obvious. Let us not chitchat. Whatsapp me [phone number] [24 years old]'. A profile which shows a masculine, hairy young man lying on his bed reads 'Kaan the Masseur: For those who are real and serious. The virtual types need not apply. I would block them otherwise [23 years old].' In one case, a naked photo appears on a profile which reads, 'Atasehir and vicinity. I don't have my own place. I can meet only with guys who have their own place or car. Professional meetings for elite gentlemen. I am versatile [24 years old].' There are also underage profiles, although this is not normally allowed. One of them says, 'I am 17. Have my own place in Beylikduzu. Sex for money. Available all the time. Can reach me by [phone number].'

The third group of profiles appears to belong to men who offer sex as bottom-only partners (receivers in anal or oral sex, as specified briefly in the texts). These are the most clearly different from the rugged and virile sex workers who perform exaggerated masculinity and contract an aura of authentic and unquestioned manhood. A profile showing a naked young man, 20 years old, with his face blurred, reads, 'Read my profile text. I am bottoming for money. My place is in Taksim. People without money should stay away. I am doing sex for money for a short time. If you are poor, don't push. It may start from 300 to 500 [Turkish liras].' Another two writers describe their specific expectations: 'For Money $: [I am] Here only for those looking for fellatio. I am only into giving head to top guys. 40 liras for half an hour and 60 liras for an hour. For security reasons I don't meet with guys who don't send their face pictures [28 years old],' and 'Only Fellatio. 60 liras for 30 minutes. I don't answer fake profiles without photos and information. Are you stupid, would anyone ever perform anal sex for 60 liras? Bottoms should not send a message. I don't have a place.'

The last online group consists of people who are not interested in compensated sex or male prostitution, but feel the need to say so explicitly in their profiles in order to avoid confusion. They use rent boys and gay sex workers as constitutive sexual and social others and distance themselves from that discourse by rejection and abjection. For example, 'Church: I am not rent, I will block if someone asks me such a question {20 years old}' and 'Arman: I am looking for a decent human. I am not an escort! [22 Years old].' One man, whose photo shows him posing in a hot tub, writes, 'Bottom slave: My name is Ertug. I am a bottom for free to those with penises larger than 21 cm. Available for group sex. Where are the tough guys? [26 years old].' Another man's photo reveals his back, and he writes that he is a top who does not charge money: 'My name is Arda, and I am doing sex for free. I am a hidden top. I am interested in smooth bottom CDs only. I don't have a place. I live in Kadikoy [24 years old].'

One day in September 2015, I received a message from the Atomic application. The message came from the account of a handsome young man with an easy smile. It read, 'Hello, I am urgently in need of money. I am a top.' In all the years I had investigated the queer male sexual economy in Turkey, this was the first time I saw a message sent from a not-explicitly-commercial online profile to the profile of someone who openly stated that he was an observer. It demonstrated to me once again how male sex work has become mainstreamed and normalised among the members of the Istanbulite queer community and how fast the new male sex workers are taking the initiative in starting an act of transactional sex.

Tim Dean[10] defines barebacking as 'anti-homonormative sex.' Following Dean, I discovered while talking to men who sell sex online that there is also a form of anti-heteronormative sex which prioritises oral sex, kissing, mutual masturbation, rimming, touching and making out without penetrative anal sex. As I have noted previously, in the context of AIDS in Turkey, where everybody acts as if everybody was negative, the rise of anti-heteronormative sexual practices within the queer sexual economy provides a safer environment.

Alet nasil? (how big it is?) is still the most common question asked online. It not only underlines the genuine curiosity about penis size but also communicates the questioner's interest in the passive (bottom) role, his interlocutor's possible interest in the active (top) role and the exact direction of a possible sexual interchange. In this sense, it was interesting to learn that when a male sex worker answers this question by saying that his penis is not that big, he is not necessarily rejected. On the contrary, his interlocutor may respond by saying something like '[d]icks that are too big hurt' or '[s]ize does not matter.'

Neoliberal Subjectivity and Male Sex Work

It is almost impossible not to detect a strong sense of self-consciousness and self-absorption in the narratives of rent boys and gay men who sell sex when the interviews I conducted with both are juxtaposed. Both parties are highly reflexive in their sense of identity, belonging and community, carefully calculating their decisions as to what they should do or tell, observing their own behaviour meticulously and taking the possible results of their actions into consideration all the time. In rather different ways, neither rent boys nor gay men who sell sex position themselves within the normative frameworks offered by tradition, culture, religion, the global political economy, their parents or other legal or moral authorities. They both project themselves as long-term investors, taking full responsibility for their bodily actions, developing different stories for multiple audiences and preserving their sense of self through various life-enhancing opportunities or disappointing encounters. In a sense, they all resist aspects of the social structure by engaging in dissident and hole-and-corner sexual activities that would be criticised and discredited by the dominant value systems of their own cultural milieu and by society more generally.

All these elements of self-constitution and agency (i.e., versatile egocentrism, playful renegotiation of the risk of exclusion and marginalisation, confrontation with normative undertows) imply that many men who sell sex to men assume a neoliberal subjectivity.[11] In this final section of this book, I will sketch out how the symptoms of neoliberal subjectivity inform the actions of male sex work scene in Istanbul in two fundamental ways.

The first of these symptoms can be seen in rent boys' and young gay men's desire to have a life of their own, to implicitly challenge existing moral and social rules and to manage their lives as they wish, not on the basis of communication and solidarity with others, but through their internal self-meditations. Virtually everything in their lives (their lifestyles, their homes, their bodies, their daily rhythms and their social interactions) becomes part of this rearrangement, as in the case of the emergence of *yeri olan* gays. Men simultaneously consider (and probably try) alternatives to sex work but leave them behind. The collective mind, which 'governs the soul'[12] as well as the body, is highly instrumental, pragmatist and privatised. The following description taken from a profile listed on the escorts' page of planetromeo.com exhibits a life and physical space that has been reordered in the pursuit of male sex work:

> Hi, I am Erdinc. I am a masseur who provides services in the clean and hygienic atmosphere of my own home. Being naughty is not a problem as long as it is compensated. Call me if this ad attracts you. I live alone in the Asian Side of Istanbul. 0 588 900 – –.

Male sex workers like Erdinc, who have intentionally reorganised their lives and homes, are not the only kinds of people in which the governing of desire and a business-like instrumentality can be observed. In the earlier phases of my research with rent boys, I often heard stories of a man who had sex with someone who promised to find him a job in the company he worked for, similar to Atakan's story above. Such an encounter cannot be framed straightforwardly as the exchange of sex for money, but rather is a sexual interaction undertaken in the hope of finding a steady job. Over the years, I began to hear similar tales from self-identified gay men, too. It seems that, for many people in the queer scene, whether they are 'straight' rent boys or not, it is more acceptable, if not quite normal, to have sex with someone for a specific purpose without the involvement of deeper emotions or bodily allure. Sex itself, detached from pleasure and bodily needs and somehow disenchanted, becomes an almost legitimate implementation of material desire, a part of a labour process outside the conventional meaning of prostitution, which too readily equates sex with immediate cash exchange. What I have observed in the field of male prostitution is paralleled by the transformation of the (masculine) neoliberal subject in terms of his increasing readiness and predilection to receive paid services to satisfy his bodily, sexual and even emotional needs.[13] Men who sell sex to men and their customers in Istanbul might be conceptualised as even more open to using their bodies, gender identities and sexual or erotic exchanges in a practical and entrepreneurial fashion to attain the desires and purposes they invest in, as an expansion or part of the prevailing neoliberal subjectivity.

The second illustration of the silhouette of a neoliberal subjectivity can be seen in specific fears and insecurities in circulation in the sexual economy in Istanbul. Ageing, among many other factors, seems the most decisive of these for both sellers and buyers of sexual services. In line with the neoliberal subject's constant self-examination and evaluation as the foundation for self-improvement, men in male sex work are highly preoccupied with the fact that they are getting old. Aytac is a self-identified gay man who works at a television studio [age 29] and is attracted to masculine *varos* boys. In our interview, he explained things this way:

> I used to take care of my body in the past, sometimes even obsessively, because it was really important for me to be liked by the boys that I fancy. You know they are young and tough with the attitude. So I went to the gym almost every day, careful of what I eat. Waxing, tanning and everything else one could do to improve his looks. But after a certain age, it started to be meaningless. Boys were not impressed by how I looked, it does not matter what I do to conserve myself, keeping up. Honestly, they did not even pay attention. If you are aged 22 or 23, at most, they may come and fuck you for their own pleasure. If you are older than this, they just ask for money. Or sometimes I tell them the company I work at is looking for security officers or office boys, just to lure them to come to me. I have accepted a long time ago that I am an old fag and boys are not interested in me anymore. Money is what attracts them, not gays. If you are rich, you can always find boys.

In contrast to the erroneous assumption that male sex work happens between two relatively equal parties (as opposed to the female seller and male buyer), there are certain discrepancies between the two parties involved here mediated though poly-directional intersubjective power relations. Rent boys confront similar realities about their bodies and sexual performance behind the semblance of exaggerated masculinity, amid tacit understandings and muted embarrassments. While implying that it would not be a problem for them personally, many of the rent boys I talked to described their concerns about how gay men desire younger men for sex work. Getting older without alternative strategies is the biggest worry they might have. Gay men who exchange sex for money, on the other hand, are still relatively young, and ageing is not yet an issue they talk about. But it is not hard to predict that they will share such an apprehension about their age and bodies in the future.

These points ought to be considered in relation to two key features of the social organisation of male sex work in Istanbul today. First, there are no fixed social groups called 'male sex workers;' instead, people with gay and straight identities (although these are also contested) may become involved in different forms of compensated sex at certain times and with different motivations. They may then take a break from this or quit for good. Second, unlike forms of male prostitution in other contexts, the activities that constitute the erotic economy in Istanbul are not survival strategies. Rent boys or gays exchange sex for money in order to empower themselves materially, symbolically and emotionally. It is therefore important to understand male sex work in contexts such as these in relation to broader neoliberalising tendencies whereby bodies, selves, relations and intimacies become progressively more flexible, commercialised and commodified. My research and observations in Istanbul simply demonstrate that male sex work here operates as an arena in which shifting definitions of masculinities and male sexualities meet one another and interact, in return transforming subjects as they continue their lives.

CONCLUSION

PERVERSE MOBILITIES AND DEVIANT CAREERS

> [W]alking over, [he] was not surprised to find the entrance populated by young chaps in age from seventeen to twenty. With a cursory glance he scanned their faces, which seemed to him partly worn-out and greedy, partly crude and common. He noticed that his glance immediately received an understanding response from some of them.
> John Henry Mackay, *The Hustler: The Story of a Nameless Love from Friedrichstrasse* (San Bernardino, 2002), p. 19

One evening in the summer of 2013, I was invited to the apartment where an unusual gay couple, Abidin and Genco, reside together in Kurtulus, a historical district in central Istanbul that had recently become a queer neighbourhood, in addition to its renowned multi-religious and diverse character. Abidin is 37 years old. He received his master's degree in literary and cultural studies, and he works simultaneously at two jobs: As an editor at a publishing house and as a screenwriter for popular TV shows. He also publishes mystery stories under a pseudonym every few years. He is an intellectually self-sustaining, energetic, talkative, optimistic, creative and industrious person who likes to tell and listen to stories. Abidin's family is affluent, and his mother had bought him this hundred-year-old, very spacious flat. In contrast, Genco, a 25-year-old, shy looking and attractive guy, comes from a disadvantaged family background. He had come to

Istanbul and started college to study industrial development and labour relations but 'felt suffocated' and left before he completed his sophomore year. Even before quitting college, he had started to work as a waiter at the most favoured modern gay café in town as and became hugely popular among customers due to his youth and cool looks. 'At that moment, intense work conditions at the café, gay men's persistent demands for sex, never-ending money issues and the idea that I could save my parents from sending me money every month in the midst of their impoverishment came together, and I decided to become a rent boy. Well, you know, I could not be a rent boy in the exact sense of the term, since I was not *varos*, I am from Izmir [allegedly the most European city in the country], I am a self-proclaimed gay and a college student. But [it was] just the idea [of sex work] ... [It was] like I can do what they [rent boys] do. Even more, even better [than them].' Thus, Genco began to work part-time at the café, where he was already famous and received most of his sex requests, in addition to his busy online profiles. He says he made a lot of money: 'I soon became the object of desire. Many men seemed to fall in love with me because, I guess, I was somehow the impossible one in their eyes. They could make love with me by paying me, but they could not be together with me in a boyfriend sense, permanently. This inaccessible man made them all crazy. And [it] made me rich for a time.'

Until he met Abidin three years ago. They started seeing each other in a 'romantic comedy' fashion as they say, after a mutual friend met and encouraged them to spend some time together. In this pre-relationship period they were 'culture buddies;' i.e., they went to exhibitions, museums and film festivals together. After a while, they had sex and enjoyed it. Abidin said, 'I know it sounds like a deadly cliché, but everything was illuminated when [they had sex] after the romantic friendship we had. I remember I thought that I might have never made love so beautifully. Everything was so beautiful.' I asked whether and how he was informed of his partner's involvement with male prostitution. Abidin said, 'I knew. Of course, I did. Everybody who used to know him, knew about the rent boyhood (*rent boy'luk tarafı*). Well, I was an open minded person. I am still an open minded person. I thought this was business or a sort of career. We start life from different positions. I have a socialist background. So I believe we are not equal when we are born. And, everybody does something in order to be equal with the 'more

Conclusion: Perverse Mobilities and Deviant Careers

equal' [enfranchised] classes. So this was the path he chose. Or this was what was available to him. And, I thought it was okay. I did not take it as a moral issue, as a problem of honour.'

Notwithstanding Abidin's flexible, amoral attitude towards his partner's experiences within the sexual economy, Genco soon quit being a rent boy and moved in with Abidin. Genco says his decision to stop being a rent boy was related to his emotional relation with Abidin, but that this was not the only factor:

> I was also tired. I felt disempowered. My libido was always high. I liked to get laid. I am not ashamed of it. Yet sex for money gets you tired and consumed somehow. Because, you know, although I had a chance to choose with whom I was going to make it, it still was a job. Something you do with both your body and your feelings. And it does not matter how much you enjoy sex, after a point it is not sex at all. I was tired of washing myself and brushing my teeth three times after each encounter [...] So I thought this chance of the relationship was great, Abidin was great, and he wanted to live with me. Maybe, I thought, this was the right time to change and try new things.

Now Genco works in the public relations unit of a company that organises cultural events and concerts. He also takes lessons in photography, which he believes he has a talent for (and I agree). His career as a kind of a rent boy is genuinely over; However, it is not a poignant story or a sad secret that nobody talks about it anymore. Instead, the couple has accepted it as a part of the long adventure they have committed to together and even invited me to talk about it, alongside other issues that they renegotiate in their harmonious and inspiring partnership.

****

Turkey is economically linked and politically aligned with Western democracies via powerful institutions of the Global North, such as the EU (via candidateship) and NATO (via membership). Today, within these transnational networks, Turkey is the only country that does not struggle at the level of policy, even cosmetically, to alleviate homophobia

Photograph 2 Three consecutive gay pride parades in Istanbul: Crowded and exuberant in 2014; the police intervening with water cannons and tear gas in 2015; and the government banning the whole pride parade with extreme sanctions, while queers responded by 'not gathering but dispersing around' in 2016. Source: kaosgl.org

CONCLUSION: PERVERSE MOBILITIES AND DEVIANT CAREERS 149

and discrimination based on sexual identity and gender nonconformity. According to many views, LGBT rights and queer visibilities are used today as a benchmark for evaluating and classifying a society's relative position on democracy, human rights, inclusive citizenship and social justice. As I mentioned earlier, homosexual acts and identities have never been a legal crime in the history of Turkey. However, there has always been a strong state policy against homosexuality (as well as forms of gender-bending, transgenderism, counter-normative erotic expressions and other dissident sexualities). All the state institutions, most of the mainstream political parties, economic giants, significant NGOs, and even the universities are either standing unapologetically against demonstrations of homosexuality or fostering homophobia inchoately. Whenever it is measurable, observable or decipherable, society in Turkey appears obviously homophobic, too. Politicians, journalists, opinion leaders and leading business people reiterate constantly that Turkish society is conservative, religious and traditional. Such an intensified conservative discourse signifies, for example, multidimensional blocks against women's equality with men at home and in the public sphere, mechanisms of reconfiguring the educational system as being rooted in Islam and not in the principles of modern science, a sacred emphasis on marriage and reproduction as expectations for youngsters to realise and, of course, an absolute rejection and abjection of homosexuality. Social scientists detect and document many social dynamics and cultural undertows that demonstrate clear patterns acting against the existence of sexual diversity and freedom of sexual expression.[1] Concepts like sexual citizenship, gender- and sexuality- based human rights, queer social justice, equality and enfranchisement in Turkey of the twenty-first century thus seem like unattainable figments of the imagination.

The rent boy identity in Istanbul emerged at the turn of the century under these circumstances. As I have recounted many times in this book, and in particular in relation to Genco's experiences as a male sex worker above, rent boys invest in 'pervert careers,' as Howard Becker defines them, 'The first step in most deviant careers is the commission of nonconforming act, an act that breaks some particular set of rules.'[2] Rent boys perform both intended and unintended acts of nonconformity, in the sense that it is almost impossible to be certain whether they are challenging heteronormativity and rendering their straight identities more flexible on purpose or are doing it naively, without necessarily giving queer sex such destabilising capacity and meaning, i.e., naturalising and trivialising it as an aspect of their unquestionably 'normal' virility. In both interpretations, it is clear that they eventually come across new social situations (real or imagined but always meditated and discussed) depending on their dissentient sexual relations with gay men: 'Being caught and branded as deviant has important consequences for one's further social participation and self-image. The most important consequence is a drastic change in the individual's public identity [...] He has been revealed as a different kind of person from the kind he was supposed to be.'[3] Turning into a different kind of person, in this context, designates loosening one's ties with his family, kinship and friends as well as his future social self as a respected individual within his community. Being caught and labelled queer or someone who sells sex, or worse, sells sex to men, may imply the social death of a heterosexual life and future expectations. It is amusing that one of the examples Becker uses in his mid-twentieth-century sociological analysis of deviant careers is indeed rent boys, with a deep discussion of leading themes that seem valid across history and geography: 'Juvenile delinquents who "hustle" homosexuals. These boys act as homosexual prostitutes to confirmed adult homosexuals. Yet they do not themselves become homosexual [...] They look on the homosexual acts they engage in simply as a means of making money that is safer and quicker than robbery or similar activities [...] Their peer group, while permitting homosexual prostitution, allow only one kind of activity, and forbid them to get any special pleasure out of it.'[4] Within this social trap, rent boys develop a number of peculiar discursive, bodily, relational tactics, which I call exaggerated masculinity, in order to become and remain legible subjects to different audiences in particular cultural milieus. Put differently, they form deviant careers as rent boys: they swim against the tide by surreptitiously participating in male prostitution, exercising 'perverse mobilities' within the city, shifting the directions and temporalities of 'normal' travel to the city centre, sharing space and spending time with abjected individuals, visiting queer people's homes in middle-class neighbourhoods, experiencing unanticipated transnational tastes, adding a unique joy and adventure in their lives and collecting stories that they may never tell. These deviant careers sometimes end with relinquishment, disappointment, frustration,

Conclusion: Perverse Mobilities and Deviant Careers 151

condemnation or repugnance. Sometimes, however, they mutate into parallel life projects and generate an entirely different palette of affective qualities, such as a sense of finding one's own position in the world or a reflexive turn in listening to oneself, connecting to others in different ways, revamping the self and developing a queer subjectivity.

The symbiosis of deviant careers and perverse mobilities which rent boys enact (and which, in return, enables them to become legible subjects of the erotic economy), once again shows us that understanding the cultural conditions, social situations and (semi-) material rationales behind male sex work requires us to take the working of heteronormativity, the construction of hegemonic and dissident masculinities in a culture, the reconfiguration of class in the midst of neoliberal globalisation and the effects of disempowerment in the context of migration to the city seriously into account. Following a cohort of fellow researchers who study male prostitution in diverse geographical settings, I have noted that this knowledge points out a shift from psychological and psychopathological explanations of the delinquent behaviour of juveniles to a perspective that stems from a critical sociology of men and masculinities as well as the anthropology of sexuality, which prioritises 'how' questions in order to understand and unravel socio-sexual contingencies, instead of solving social problems and correcting these transgressing, abnormal young adults. This epistemological turn in conceptualisation and knowledge production regarding male sex work brings in a new neoliberal, entrepreneurial subjectivity that finds no problem in the self-presentation and marketing of the male body, phallic virility and heterosexual(-ising) masculinity. As this subjectivity expands and becomes the new gendered norm for neoliberal citizens, the definitions (rent boys, male prostitute, hustler, etc.), the 'real' sexual identities (gay, straight, bisexual, etc.) and the hidden identities of male sex workers become insignificant. I argue that this shift emphasises the sociological importance of studying the practices and discourses of male sex work in different locations. Such an approach can (and does) tell us about the changing contours of masculinity as it is affected by gendered relations with women and other men, the global political economy and cultural trends through an extreme, if not outrageous, example of selling (or renting) virilities for money.

Middle- and upper-middle-class gay men's fetishisation of youthful, straight acting male bodies (sometimes also migrant, working class, or racialised bodies, or permutations of these) is a virtually global and transhistorical phenomenon.[5] In Istanbul, for more than a decade, this tendency expressed itself contradictorily in the stigmatisation and self-identity of the *varos* label. Slowly, in the 2010s, the distinction between the middle-class, middle-aged gay client and the young, heterosexual *varos* rent boys evaporated and paved the way, as I have described in Chapter 6, for a more diverse array of service vendors and buyers, including gay men of all ages, body types and gender attributes. Masculinity is marketable, and sexuality is commodified in the world of the new queer sexual entrepreneurs. As Peter Aggleton and Richard Parker[6] recently explained, male sex work has de-territorialised, individualised, and lost its connection with a particular sexual identity, community or subculture:

> The gradual shift from male sex work carried out by supposedly straight 'rent boys' to a predominantly gay economy in which sexual services are offered primarily by gay-identified men to other gay-identified men is perhaps the most common trajectory – unsurprisingly common perhaps in cities and countries where highly defined and developed gay communities and cultures are present, but nonetheless also present in many places where gay communities have emerged more recently, and even in some cases where little of what might be described as a gay world seems to exist.

In this sense, each and every gay, bisexual, heterosexual or queer person (or couple) is potentially a participant in the sexual economy, and this trend runs in accordance with the emergence of neoliberal masculinity, drawing novel boundaries around what is thinkable, acceptable, speakable and doable with masculinities and male bodies.

The primary emphasis of *Queering Sexualities in Turkey* is on the liminal and inherently fragile (queer) space within which rent boys embody exaggerated masculinity and perform their sexual roles without becoming (or publicly coming out as) gay men, while their clients and the larger queer community participate in and witness the sexual economy. Nicola Mai[7] spells out this incongruent set of (dis-)identification and discordant practices among Albanian and Romanian male sex workers via the concept of 'fractal'. 'The prevalence of embodied and tacit practices in the challenging of sexual restrictions

Conclusion: Perverse Mobilities and Deviant Careers 153

to mobility and forms of normativity highlights the 'fractal' quality of the queer subjectivities of male sex workers. The term 'fractal' here refers to the possibility of engaging in practices and lifestyles, such as migration and sex work, which challenge established life trajectories and sexual/gender roles, without having to take full public moral ownership and responsibility.' The construction and navigation of deviant careers and perverse mobilities by rent boys, as they are in fractal features indeed, is based on entrepreneurial decisions and calculations, in order to attain the status of enterprising young, full citizens. This approach may provide an answer to a question I have encountered many times: Why do they not just quit sex work and stop being rent boys if, as they say, they do not like having sex with men or gay culture? Most of the answers that other researchers and I had previously produced implied that rent boys do not quit because, in fact, they are closeted gay men. In the course of this research project, I came to another conclusion; that, while it is possible that some rent boys are closeted gay men, more generally rent boys do not leave the male sex work scene because they see the partying aspect of the work as an experience and an accumulation of small benefits presented to them by urban life. By performing male sex work, they believe they are taking their rightful share of what is available outside, and attaining the status, both symbolically and materially, of enjoying life. In addition to this accumulating yet ephemeral sense of experience and profit, rent boys enjoy the possibility of an additional, however small, income. To make some extra money, even in insubstantial amounts, is the right thing to be doing according to their neoliberalising moral views, which designate the imagination, planning, preparation and endeavour of moneymaking as the highest possible priority. Some rent boys perceive queer sex as an innocuous and tolerable practice of self-sacrifice that will eventually lead them towards a better life, one possible mode of inclusion into a middle-class society embellished by a dreamscape of hyper-consumerism, upward mobility and cursory respect.

****

In this book, I have tried to understand and explain how my respondents realise and make sense of the neoliberal masculine subjectivity, local and transnational social relations, the erotic economy and sexuality within the context of the aestheticisation of the male body and the social fetishisation of butch virilities and masculine demeanours as the masculine (as defined in bodily, social, sexual, and economical ways) loses its untouchable, unquestionable authority and privilege and turns into a marketable commodity with an exchange value in the erotic economy. The boundaries between sex and sex work or heterosexual and gay identities may become blurry as not only the older gay men, who search for more authentic, real and macho men and masculinity, but also the gay men who want to avoid the risk of rejection, emotional drama and affective charges, develop a predisposition to engage in the sexual economy by hiring rent boys and having sex with them.

In the early phases of this research, the gendered/gendering gap between rent boys and gay men was wider than it is now and even conversation with a 'real' *varos* man or rent boy was exciting to potential clients, as one respondent once told me, '[i]t is exciting even to negotiate about sex with such a young man who normally would not talk to me in everyday life. During the chat, which is always short and obstructed, the rent boy is always in this standoffish mood. He shows that he does not want to talk to you. Sometimes [they] just quit talking and walk away without saying anything. How dazzling'. More recently, however, this gap has dwindled, and the dialogue between the male sex worker (a straight rent boy or a gay man) and the client is more egalitarian, friendly and cooperative. Another interviewee explains this shift by saying, 'We used to purchase local masculinity. We do not find that any more. Rent boys became gay-like, modernised. Or we all became *varos*. I do not know really. Today, what we look for is youthful outlook, lean bodies and big endowments. That old provincial virility, or the *delikanli* (rugged, young masculinity) remain in the past, in the memory'.

In this book, my focus has not been on the formation of gay subjectivity in Turkey in the 2000s. The discourses and practices that intersect with and trigger this subject and the nature of the boundaries between the history of gay Turkish subjectivity formation and the same-sex sexual acts that were existent long before the emergence of this gay subject could fill another book. Instead, I have brought a focus on the dynamics behind the commodification of masculinity and organisation of queer sex work in Istanbul. Older gay men constantly mention that in the past, there was no money involved in their homoerotic sexual experiences. They say that if they were about to have

CONCLUSION: PERVERSE MOBILITIES AND DEVIANT CAREERS   155

sex with a (straight-seeming) man, it was either because of his desires and sexual arousal (to fuck a queer) or because they were able to persuade him without money. Money has come to permeate the queer intimate economy as Turkish society has re-stratified and experienced social decline since the late 1980s, while neoliberalism has become the sovereign logic in governing the state, ordering society and relocating cultural normativity.[8] Today queer public presence, gender nonconformity, forms of sex work and even the cultural manifestations and representations of (heteronormative) sexuality undermine the self-assured national presentation of the Islamist politics of piety and neoliberal developmentalism. Therefore, whether you are a queer, a sex worker or just a lay citizen who happens to enjoy talking about sexuality in front of other people, you are not only sinful and immoral; you are also working against professed national/conservative ideals. You are an enemy of the neoliberal, Islamist, traditional 'state of securitisation.'[9]

I argue that a radical democratic standpoint that favours queering sexualities in Turkey is translated in this cultural and political context into the intransigent acts of defining sexual citizenship, renegotiating moral values, respectability and individual dignity, pursuing and expanding erotic possibilities and discourses and emphasising gender and sexuality based human rights alongside deepening knowledge of the rise of the neoliberal, entrepreneurial sexual self and the cunning affective capacities that centre self-interestedness, renouncement for upward mobility and reckoning movements of contingency.

NOTES

Introduction: Queering Sexualities in Turkey

1. Gamma Hydroxybutyrate acid (GHB), which is known as 'liquid ecstasy' in the United States.
2. I later understood that this person used the word *temiz* (clean) in two senses. The first meaning is about completing the interaction without trouble, in a smooth and easy way. The second implies the acts of personal hygiene for both parties, including douching, taking a shower, shaving, and tooth brushing among other procedures. In the course of this study, I often heard stories and complaints from my respondents (both gays and rent boys, blaming each other) about how bodies were not clean in Turkey, and how people did not know how to take care of themselves or prepare themselves for interpersonal intimacy. People who had not showered recently, people with strange body odors and people who smelled excessively of tobacco were the most frequent subjects of these complaints. Interestingly, both gay men and male sex workers accused their sexual partners as well as other gays and rent boys of being *pis* (dirty or gross).
3. In this book, I prefer to use the term rent boys, following the self-definition of these men in the early 2000s. Today the terms 'rent boy' and 'rent' are used widely, in addition to the less frequent use of 'masseur' and 'escort,' especially on the internet. Throughout the text, I tend to use 'queer sex work,' 'male sex work,' 'male prostitution' and 'male-to-male transactional/commercial/compensated sex' interchangeably without referring to the genealogy of the distinction between sex worker and prostitute within feminist theory and grassroots politics because this difference was specifically derived for women and not men. Men do not engage in sex work in order to make a living in contemporary Turkey, as I demonstrate in this book.
4. Aylin Nazliaka's case constitutes a good example of the extent of the sex-negative culture in Turkey. A female member of the parliament, Mrs Nazliaka

said, 'The Prime Minister should quit watching the vaginas of women,' while she was criticising governmental discourses against abortion in 2012. A member of the cabinet, in response, told her that he was ashamed when a married lady talked about her sexual organ in public. Nazliaka said she would sue the minister for his misogynist inclinations ('Arinc'tan Vajina Monologlari', *Bianet*, 12 December 2012, http://bianet.org/bianet/siyaset/142743-arinc-tan-vajina-monologlari, accessed on 23 January 2016).

5. Saying this, I must confess that one can never be sure. Rent boys are young people; some continue their physical development and their appearances can change rapidly. Gaining several pounds, shaving his head, or growing a beard can make a rent boy a totally different person, especially in the dim and overcrowded social space of queer nightclubs.

6. Setha Low (ed.), *Theorizing the City* (New Brunswick, 1999).

7. Joel S. Migdal, 'Finding the Meeting Ground of Fact and Fiction: Some Reflections on Turkish Modernization', in Sibel Bozdogan and Resat Kasaba (eds), *Rethinking Modernity and National Identity in Turkey* (Seattle, 1997).

8. Carlos Ulises Decena, *Tacit Subjects: Belonging and Same-Sex Desire Among Dominican Immigrant Men* (Durham, NC, 2011), pp. 2–3.

9. For a review of such encounters in urban Turkey, see: Gul Ozyegin, *Untidy Gender: Domestic Work in Turkey* (Philadelphia, 2001); Gul Ozyegin, 'The Doorkeeper, The Maid and the Tenant: Troubling Encounters in the Turkish Urban Landscape', in Deniz Kandiyoti and Ayse Saktanber (eds), *Fragments of Culture: The Everyday of Modern Turkey* (London, 2002). For domestic cleaners: Aksu Bora, *Kadinlarin Sinifi: Ucretli Ev Emegi ve Kadin Oznelliginin Insaasi* (Istanbul, 2005). For highways: Berna Yazici, 'Towards an Anthropology of Traffic: A Ride Through Class Hierarchies on Istanbul's Roadways', *Ethnos* 78/4 (2013), pp. 515–42. For college campuses: Gul Ozyegin, *New Desires, New Selves: Sex, Love and Piety Among Turkish Youth* (New York, 2015a). For public urban spaces: Bengi Akbulut and Ayfer Bartu Candan, 'Bir Iki Agacin Otesinde: Istanbul'a Politik Ekoloji Cercevesinden Bakmak' in Ayfer Bartu Candan and Cenk Özbay (eds), *Yeni Istanbul Calismalari: Sinirlar, Mucadeleler, Acilimlar* (Istanbul 2014). For spaces of consumption: Esra Sarioglu, 'New Imaginaries of Gender in Turkey's Service Economy: Women Workers and Identity Making on the Sales Floor', *Women's Studies International Forum* 54 (2016), pp. 39–47; Cenk Özbay (2012b) 'Sexuality', in A. L. Stanton (eds), *Cultural sociology of the Middle East, Asia, and Africa* (London, 2015b).

10. Yildirim Turker, 'Bu Sehir Kimin?' *Radikal Iki*, 24 April 2005.

11. *Varos* was a term that dominated the Turkish urban studies scene as well as public debates on television starting from the 1990s for more than a decade. It is the hostile and denigrating name given both to informally and illegally built squatter neighbourhoods and the people who reside in these areas by the middle-class urbanites, or 'the established'. *Varos* neighbourhoods arose (or expanded) following the massive waves of economic and political (forced) migration from every corner of Anatolia to Istanbul, which took place and/or intensified during the 1990s, causing the population of the city to exceed ten million residents by

the year 2000 (Cenk Özbay, 'Neoliberal Erkekligin Sosyoljisine Dogru: Rent Boylar Ornegi', in Cenk Özbay, Aysecan Terzioglu and Yesim Yasin (eds), *Neoliberalizm ve Mahremiyet: Turkiye'de Beden, Saglik ve Cinsellik*, [Istanbul, 2011]). Most newcomers, both from Turkish and Kurdish ethnicities, settled in the *varos* neighbourhoods, utilising the informal housing, job opportunities and networks of communication and support they found there. The overwhelming majority of rent boys in Istanbul are from the *varos* areas. In contrast, the customers they serve tend to be upper-middle class, urbane, stylish gay men, living in more expensive, modern and gentrified areas of the city. As I write these lines in the beginning of 2016, Istanbul's population is estimated to be more than 15 million people after the latest inflow of Syrian refugees through informal channels.

12. For an early account of this, see: Ayse Oncu, 'Istanbulites and Others: The Cultural Cosmology of 'Middleness' in the Era of Neoliberalism', in Caglar Keyder (ed.), *Istanbul: Between the Local and the Global* (Boston, 1999).

    Ayse Oncu, 'Consumption, Gender and The Mapping of Istanbul in the 1990s', in Deniz Kandiyoti and Ayse Saktanber (eds), *Fragments of Culture: The Everyday of Modern Turkey* (London, 2002).

13. Alperen Atik, 'Neo-Delikanlilar', *Radikal Iki*, 9 May 2005.
14. Annick Prieur, *Mema's House, Mexico City: On Transvestites, Queens and Machos* (Chicago, 1997), p. 148.
15. John D'Emilio, *Sexual Politics, Sexual Communities* (Chicago, 1998); Peter M. Nardi and Beth E. Schneider (eds), *Social Perspectives in Lesbian and Gay Studies: A Reader* (New York, 1998); Ken Plummer (ed.), *Modern Homosexualities: Fragments of Lesbian and Gay Experiences* (London 1992); Steven Seidman, *The Social Construction of Sexuality* (New York, 2009); Jeffrey Weeks, *Sexuality and Its Discontents: Meanings, Myths and Modern Sexualities* (London, 1990).
16. Yesim Arat, 'The Project of Modernity and Women in Turkey', in Sibel Bozdogan and Resat Kasaba (eds), *Rethinking Modernity and National Identity in Turkey* (Seattle, 1997); Nukhet Sirman, 'The Making of Familial Citizenship in Turkey', in Ahmet Icduygu and Fuat Keyman (eds), *Citizenship in a Global World – European Questions and Turkish Experiences* (New York, 2005).
17. Resat Ekrem Kocu, *Istanbul Ansiklopedisi* (Istanbul, 1946)
18. Cenk Özbay, 'Queer Kral', *Radikal Iki*, 27 September 2009.
19. Murat Hocaoglu, *Escinsel Erkekler: Yirmi Bes Taniklik* (Istanbul, 2002).
20. Yasemin Oz, 'Ahlaksizlarin Merkansal Dislanmasi', in Ayten Alkan (ed.), *Cins Cins Mekan* (Istanbul, 2009); Aslan Yuzgun, *Turkiye'de Escinsellik: Dun ve Bugun* (Istanbul 1986); Aslan Yuzgun (1993) 'Homosexuality and police terror in Turkey', *Journal of Homosexuality* 24/3–4 (1993), pp. 159–69.
21. Yuzgun, *Turkiye'de Escinsellik*; Hocaoglu, *Escinsel Erkekler*.
22. Hocaoglu, *Escinsel Erkekler*; Huseyin Tapinc (1992) 'Masculinity, femininity and Turkish male homosexuality', in Ken Plummer (ed.), *Modern Homosexualities: Fragments of Lesbian and Gay Experiences* (London, 1992), pp. 39–50.
23. Aydin Oztek, 'Turk Sinemasinda Escinsellik', *Kaos GL* 52 (2007).
24. Ozbay et al., 2016.

25. Decena, *Tacit Subjects*.
26. Ibid., p. 19.
27. Hocaoglu, *Escinsel Erkekler*; Tarik Bereket and Barry D. Adam, 'The emergence of gay identities in contemporary Turkey', *Sexualities* 9 (2006), pp. 131–51.
28. Begum Basdas, Begum, 'Cosmopolitanism in the city: Contested claims to bodies and sexualities in Beyoglu, Istanbul.' Unpublished PhD dissertation, 2007, Department of Geography, University of California-Los Angeles; Cenk Özbay and Serdar Soydan, *Escinsel Kadinlar: Yirmi Dort Taniklik* (Istanbul, 2003); Savci 2011.
29. Oz, 'Ahlaksizlarin Merkansal Dislanmasi'; Yuzgun, 'Homosexuality and police terror in Turkey.'
30. Savci, 2011.
31. Hocaoglu, *Escinsel Erkekler*; Ozbay and Soydan *Escinsel Kadinlar*.
32. Oz, 'Ahlaksizlarin Merkansal Dislanmasi'; Savci, 2011.
33. Basdas, 'Cosmopolitanism in the city;' Bereket and Adam 'The emergence of gay identities in contemporary Turkey;' Tarik Bereket and Barry D. Adam, 'Navigating Islam and Same-Sex Liaisons Among Men in Turkey', *Journal of Homosexuality* 55 (2008), pp. 204–22; Ozbay 2010; Gul Ozyegin, 'Reading the closet through connectivity', *Social Identities* 18 (2012), pp. 201–22.
34. Ozbay, 2010.
35. Bereket and Adam 'The emergence of gay identities in contemporary Turkey;' Hocaoglu, *Escinsel Erkekler*; Ozbay and Soydan *Escinsel Kadinlar*; Ozyegin, 'Reading the closet through connectivity.'
36. Bereket and Adam, 'Navigating Islam and Same-Sex Liaisons.'
37. Hocaoglu, *Escinsel Erkekler*; Ozbay and Soydan *Escinsel Kadinlar*.
38. Thomas J. D. Armbrecht, 'The cucumber seller: Homosexuality and class in Turkey', *Gay Men's Fiction Quarterly* 3/4 (2001), pp. 51–9; Hocaoglu, *Escinsel Erkekler*; Ozbay, 2010.
39. Ozbay, 2010.
40. Peter Aggleton (ed.), *Men Who Sell Sex: International Perspectives on Male Prostitution and HIV/AIDS* (Philadelphia, 1999); Don C. Barrett and L. M. Pollack, 'Whose Gay Community? Social Class, Sexual Self-Expression, and Gay Community Involvement', *Sociological Quarterly* 46 (2005), pp. 437–56; Richard Parker, *Beneath the Equator: Cultures of Desire, Male Homosexuality and Emerging Gay Communities in Brazil* (New York, 1999).
41. Selin Berghan, *Lubunya: Transeksuel Beden ve Kimlik* (Istanbul, 2007).
42. Alp Biricik, 'Rotten report and reconstructing hegemonic masculinity in Turkey', in Ozgur Heval Cinar and Coskun Usterci (eds), *Conscientious Objection: Resisting Militarized Society* (London, 2009); Mehmet Tarhan (2008) 'Zorunlu Askerlik ve Sivil Alternatif Hizmete Direnis Olarak Vicdani Red', in Nil Mutluer (ed.), *Cinsiyet Halleri* (Istanbul, 2008).
43. Biricik, 'Rotten report.'
44. Cuneyt Cakirlar and Serkan Delice (eds), *Cinsellik Muammasi: Turkiye'de Queer Kultur ve Muhalefet* (Istanbul, 2012); Ozbay, 2010; Ozyegin, 'Reading the closet through connectivity;' Savci, 2011.

45. Perihan Magden, *Two Girls* (London, 2006); Perihan Magden, *Ali and Ramazan* (Las Vegas, 2012); Duygu Asena, *Paramparca* (Istanbul, 2006). Safak, 2007; Niyazi Zorlu, *Hergele Asiklar* (Istanbul, 2003); Mehmet Murat Somer, *The Prophet Murders: A Hop-Ciki-Yaya Thriller* (London, 2008); Mehmet Murat Somer, *The Jigolo Murder: A Turkish Delight Mystery* (London, 2009).
46. Aaron Betsky, *Queer Space: Architecture and Same-Sex Desire* (London, 1997), p. 5.
47. Ozbay, 2012.
48. Cenk Özbay (2010a) 'Nocturnal Queers: Rent Boys' Masculinity in Istanbul', *Sexualities* 13/5 (2010a), pp. 645–63; Ozbay, 'Neoliberal Erkekligin Sosyoljisine Dogru.'
49. As in most other qualitative studies of contemporary sex work, this research is not meant to be representative, or generalisable, to different social situations in other locations. Instead, it is an attempt to form and present knowledge for a specific time and context through *my* encounters with respondents and *my* interpretations of the stories that I heard. I have always been careful not to glamorise or stigmatise male sex work and the actors involved in it. I personally believe that adults should be able to freely engage in commercial sex as buyers and sellers, as long as they are aware of it and not forced, trafficked or blackmailed.
50. All private names, including bars' and clubs' and people's, are pseudonyms.
51. Lambevski (Alexander S. (1999) 'Suck My Nation: Masculinity, Ethnicity, and the Politics of (Homo)sex', *Sexualities* 2/4 (1999), p. 402) highlights the significance of being an insider and participating in the queer (sub)culture in order to have 'intimate, rich, and meaningful knowledge' of the gay scene of Skopje, Macedonia. Nicola Mai ((2015) 'Surfing Liquid Modernity: Albanian and Romanian Male Sex Workers in Europe', in Peter Aggleton and Richard Parker (eds), *Men Who Sell Sex: Global Perspectives*, [New York, 2015], 28) also underscores reflexive methodologies: 'Researching gendered and sexualised identities, subjectivities and mobilities requires a specific degree of self-reflexivity to bypass the normative self-representations emerging in interviews and during fieldwork.' Although I am well aware of the fact that an interviewer is also gendered, sexualised and classed before and during the conversation, that sex and work can merge in unpredictably queer ways, and that there are more flexible approaches to the dynamic relationality between the researcher and the informant, including hints of erotic intersubjectivity and possibilities of flirtation, I have always been on the more distanced side, and when I felt I encountered a sexual innuendo I pretended to be naïve and continued the conversation as it flowed. See Don Kulick and Margarey Wilson's classical work *Taboo: Sex, Identity and Erotic Subjectivity in Anthropological Fieldwork* (New York, 1995) as well as Fran Markovitz and Michael Askhenazi (eds), *Sex, Sexuality and the Anthropologist* (Urbana-Champaign, 1999) and Ellen Lewin and William Leap, *Out in the Field: Reflections of Lesbian and Gay Anthropologists* (Urbana-Champaign, 1996). For a classical account of methodology for the sociology of sexualities, see Ken Plummer, *Telling Sexual Stories: Power, Change and Social Worlds* (London, 1995) and for a recent contribution to issues of methodology in

critical masculinity studies, see Barbara Pini and Bob Pease (eds), *Men, Masculinities and Methodologies* (Hampshire, 2013).
52. Melissa Gira Grant (2014) *Playing the Whore: The Work of Sex Work* (London, 2014), p. 27.
53. Humphrey, *Tearoom Trade*, p. 29.
54. Ibid., pp. 32–3.
55. Frederic J. Desroches, 'Tearoom Trade: A Research Update', *Qualitative Sociology* 13/1(1990), pp. 39–61; John F. Gallier, Wayne Brekhus and David P. Keys, *Laud Humphreys: Prophet of Homosexuality and Sociology* (Madison, WI, 2004); Peter M. Nardi, 'The Breastplate of Righteousness: Twenty-Five Years After Laud Humphreys' Tearoom Trade: Impersonal Sex in Public Places', *Journal of Homosexuality* 30/2 (1995), pp. 1–10; Michael Lenza, 'Controversies Surrounding Laud Humphreys' Tearoom Trade: An unsettling example of politics and power in methodological critiques', *International Journal of Sociology and Social Policy* 24/3–4–5 (2004), pp. 20–31.
56. Katherine Irwin, 'Into the Dark Heart of Ethnography: The Lived Ethics and Inequality of Intimate Field Relationships,' *Qualitative Sociology* 29/2(2006), pp. 155–75; Kari Lerum (2001) 'Subjects of Desire: Academic Armor, Intimate Ethnography, and the Production of Critical Knowledge', *Qualitative Inquiry* 7/4(2001), pp. 466–83.
57. See Heidi Kaspar and Sara Landolt, 'Flirting in the Field: shifting positionalities and power relations in innocuous sexualisations of research encounters', *Gender, Place & Culture* 23/1(2016), pp. 107–19 for a recent discussion on the importance of sexuality in researchers' and their informants' positionality and the capacity for flirtation (in addition to aggression and anger) in social scientific research practices on intimacy.
58. Ayfer Bartu Candan and Cenk Özbay (eds), *Yeni IstanbulCalismalari: Sinirlar, Mucadeleler, Acilimlar* (Istanbul, 2014); Ozbay et al., 2016.

Chapter 1 Sexuality, Masculinity and Male Sex Work

1. The entry on www.eksisozluk.com (established as a part of sourtimes.org) about the topic 'Turkish Gay Community' (*turkiye gay camiasi*) by a nickname of 'el cancer del besiktas', https://eksisozluk.com/turkiye-gay-camiasi–4910808? p=2, accessed on 15 September 2015. For an extensive analysis of faggot (*ibne*) discourse and gay identities in Turkey, see Gul Ozyegin, *New Desires, New Selves: Sex, Love and Piety Among Turkish Youth* (New York, 2015a).
2. Teela Sanders, Maggie O'Neill and Jane Pitcher, *Prostitution: Sex Work, Policy and Politics* (London, 2009).
3. See, for example, Anne Allison, *Nightwork: Sexuality, Pleasure, and Corporate Masculinity in a Tokyo Hostess Club* (Chicago, 1994); Elizabeth Bernstein, *Temporarily Yours: Intimacy, Authenticity, and the Commerce of Sex* (Chicago, 2007); Denise Brennan, *What's Love Got to Do with It?: Transnational Desires and Sex Tourism in the Dominican Republic* (Durham, 2004); Christine B. N. Chin (2013)

Cosmopolitan Sex Workers: Women and Migration in a Global City (Oxford, 2013); Alexander Edmonds, *Pretty Modern: Beauty, Sex, and Plastic Surgery in Brazil* (Durham, 2010); Siddarth Kara (2010) *Sex Trafficking: Inside the Business of Modern Slavery* (New York, 2010); Kamala Kempadoo and Jo Doezema (eds) (1998) *Global Sex Workers: Rights, Resistance, and Redefinition* (New York, 1998); Jill Nagle (ed.), *Whores and Other Feminists* (New York, 1997); Elina Penttinen, *Globalization, Prostitution and Sex Trafficking: Corporeal Politics* (New York, 2007); Williams, Erica Lorraine Williams, *Sex Tourism in Bahia: Ambiguous Entanglements* (Urbana, 2013); Viviana A. Zelizer (2007) *The Purchase of Intimacy* (New Haven, 2007).

4. Marieke Ridder-Wiskerke and Peter Aggleton, 'Lifestyle, Work or Easy Money? Male Sex Work in the Netherlands Today', in Peter Aggleton and Richard Parker (eds), *Men Who Sell Sex: Global Perspectives* (New York, 2015), pp. 17–18.

5. Michel Dorais divides male prostitution in Canada in three groups: 'street hustling, the best known and most visible type; stripping, which takes place in specialised bars and often [...] involves an offering of 'extras'; and escorting, in which high-priced sexual services are offered indirectly through an agency or other organised channel,' (*Rent Boys: The World of Male Sex Workers* [Montreal, 2005], p. 4). A marginalised form of street prostitution was available at two or three specific locations in Istanbul during the early phases of this study. As the police increased control over streets and public squares under the current AKP government (since 2002), male prostitution on the street disappeared. The other two forms Dorais mentions are not present in the male sex work scene in Istanbul.

6. For a global and interdisciplinary collection of essays on the topic, see Peter Aggleton (ed.), *Men Who Sell Sex: International Perspectives on Male Prostitution and HIV/AIDS* (Philadelphia, 1999); Peter Aggleton and Richard Parker (eds), *Men Who Sell Sex: Global Perspectives* (New York, 2015); Victor Minichiello and John Scott (eds), *Male Sex Work and Society* (New York, 2014). See also Todd G. Morrison and Bruce W. Whitehead (eds), *Male Sex Work: A Business Doing Pleasure* (New York, 2007), which presents case studies from across different jobs in male-to-male sex work industry, including erotic dancing and pornography, mostly from the US; and Joseph Itiel, *A Consumer's Guide to Male Hustlers* (New York, 2014) for a seasoned client's comparative experiences.

7. See Samuel R. Delany, *Times Square Red, Times Square Blue* (New York, 1999); Dorais, *Rent Boys*; Robert P. McNamara, *The Times Square Hustler: Male Prostitution in New York City* (New York, 1994); Leon Pettiway, *Honey, Money, Miss Thang: Being Black, Gay and on the Streets* (Philadelphia, 1996); Michael D. Smith and Christian Grov, *In the Company of Men: Inside the Lives of Male Prostitutes* (New York, 2011); Sterry, David Henry Sterry, *Chicken: Self-Portrait of a Young Man for Rent* (New York, 2002); Sam Steward, *Understanding the Male Hustler* (New York, 2014); Kevin Walby, *Touching Encounters: Sex, Work and Male-to-Male Internet Escorting* (Chicago, 2012); Rick Whitaker, *Assuming the Position: A Memoir of Hustling* (New York and London, 1999).

8. See P. Fernandez-Davila et al., 'Compensated sex and sexual risk: Sexual, social, and economic interactions between homosexually and heterosexually identified

men of low income in two cities of Peru', *Sexualities* 11/3 (2008), pp. 352–74; Steven Gregory, *The Devil Behind the Mirror: Globalization and Politics in the Dominican Republic* (Berkeley and Los Angeles, 2007); Don Kulick, *Travesti: Sex, Gender and Culture among Brazilian Transgendered Prostitutes* (Chicago, 1998); Gregory Mitchell (2016) *Tourist Attractions: Performing Race & Masculinity in Brazil's Sexual Economy* (Chicago, 2016); Mark Padilla, *Caribbean Pleasure Industry: Tourism, Sexuality, and AIDS in the Dominican Republic* (Chicago, 2007); Richard Parker, *Beneath the Equator: Cultures of Desire, Male Homosexuality and Emerging Gay Communities in Brazil* (New York, 1999); Prieur (1998); Jacobo Schifter, *Lila's House: Male Prostitution in Latin America* (New York, 1998); and Noelle M. Stout, *After Love: Queer Intimacy and Erotic Economies in Post-Soviet Cuba* (Durham, 2014).

9. For research on other locations, see Donald West, *Male Prostitution* (New York, 2012) for the United Kingdom; Victor Minichiello et al., 'Male sex workers in three Australian cities: Socio-demographic and sex work characteristics', *Journal of Homosexuality* 42/1 (2001), pp. 29–51 for Australia; Timothy M. Hall, 'Rentboys, barflies, and kept men: Men involved in sex with men for compensation in Prague', *Sexualities* 10/4 (2007), pp. 457–72 for the Czech Republic; Peter Jackson and Gerard Sullivan (eds), *Lady Boys, Tom Boys, Rent Boys: Male and Female Homosexualities in Contemporary Thailand* (New York, 1999) for Thailand; Hasan Mujtaba, 'The other side of midnight: Pakistani male prostitutes', in Stephen O. Murray and Will Roscoe (eds), *Islamic Homosexualities: Culture, History, and Literature* (New York, 1997), pp. 267–74 for Pakistan; and Paul Alexander Bouanchaud, 'Male Sex Work in China: Understanding the HIV Risk Environments of Shenzhen's Migrant Money Boys,' unpublished PhD dissertation (London School of Economics and Political Science, 2014) for China.

10. The shift Aggleton and Parker (*Men Who Sell Sex*, p. 3) marked recently in studying male prostitution is significant in this regard: 'we want to call attention to an important distinction between much early research which tended to focus on male sex work as a kind of psychological pathology or a form of social deviance, and more recent work which has increasingly sought instead to develop a fuller understanding of the social forces that shape male sex work as a form of lived experience – a shift that we might describe as moving from viewing male sex work as a "social problem" in need of intervention to a social phenomenon in need of understanding.' I would like to call this shift the movement from psychology and other 'normalising' clinical disciplines, public health, medical sociology and the sociology of juvenile delinquency towards critical masculinity studies, the cultural anthropology of sex work and the sociology of sexualities. Unless otherwise noted, the literature I speak about here, and which the book contributes to, is the critical interpretive tradition in studying male prostitution and not the pathologising, moralising or policy-oriented lens about the subject.

11. Dennis Altman, 'Foreword', in Peter Aggleton and Richard Parker (eds), *Men Who Sell Sex: Global Perspectives* (New York, 2015), p. xvii.

12. Tarik Bereket and Barry D. Adam, 'Navigating Islam and Same-Sex Liaisons Among Men in Turkey', *Journal of Homosexuality* 55 (2008), pp. 204–22; Cenk

Özbay, 'Sexuality', in A. L. Stanton (ed.), *Cultural Sociology of the Middle East, Asia, and Africa* (London, 2012b); Huseyin Tapinc, 'Masculinity, femininity and Turkish male homosexuality', in Ken Plummer (ed.), *Modern Homosexualities: Fragments of Lesbian and Gay Experiences* (London, 1992), pp. 39–50.
13. For a review of queer urban historical and sociological analyses in these metropolitan centres, see David Higgs, *Queer Sites: Gay Urban Histories Since 1600* (London, 1999); George Chauncey, *Gay New York: Gender, Urban Culture, and the Making of the Gay Male World, 1890–1940* (New York, 1995); Lilian Faderman and Stuart Timmons, *Gay L.A.: A History of Sexual Outlaws, Power Politics, and Lipstick Lesbians* (Berkeley and Los Angeles, 2009); Susan Stryker and Jim Van Buskirk, *Gay by the Bay: A History of Queer Culture in the San Francisco Bay Area* (San Francisco, 1996); Robert Beachy, *Gay Berlin: Birthplace of a Modern Identity* (New York, 2015); Francois Buot, *Gay Paris: Une histoire du Paris interlope entre 1900 et 1940* (Paris, 2013) and Matt Houlbrook, *Queer London: Perils and Pleasures in the Sexual Metropolis, 1918–1957* (Chicago, 2006).
14. Tarik Bereket and Barry D. Adam, 'Navigating Islam and Same-Sex Liaisons Among Men in Turkey'; Gul Ozyegin, *New Desires, New Selves: Sex, Love and Piety Among Turkish Youth* (New York, 2015a).
15. Cenk Özbay, 'Same-sex Sexualities in Turkey', in J. D. Wright (ed.), *The International Encyclopedia of Social and Behavioral Sciences* (Amsterdam, 2015a). Tapinc, 'Masculinity, femininity and Turkish male homosexuality;' Aslan Yuzgun, *Turkiye'de Escinsellik: Dun ve Bugun* (Istanbul, 1986).
16. Stephen O. Murray (1997) 'The Will not to Know: Islamic Accommodations of Male Homosexuality', in Stephen O. Murray and Will Roscoe (eds), *Islamic Homosexualities: Culture, History, and Literature* (New York, 1997), pp. 14–54.
17. Svati P. Shah, *Street Corner Secrets: Sex, Work and Migration in the City of Mumbai* (Durham, 2014): p. 3.
18. Carlos Ulises Decena, *Tacit Subjects: Belonging and Same-Sex Desire Among Dominican Immigrant Men* (Durham, 2011), p. 31.
19. Adam Isaiah Green, 'Queer Theory and Sociology: Locating the Subject and the Self in Sexuality Studies', *Sociological Theory* 25/1 (2007), pp. 26–45.
20. Christine L. Williams and Catherine Connell, 'Looking Good and Sounding Right: Aesthetic Labor and Social Inequality in the Retail Industry,' *Work and Occupations* 37/3 (2010), pp. 349–77.
21. Mitchell 2016: 55. Rent boys in Istanbul are not necessarily 'tourist attractions' as are the *garotos* Mitchell studied. Some rent boys have sex with foreigners and some never do. Some rent boys only charge tourists for sexual exchange and some have unpaid sex only with tourists. In this regard, it is not entirely possible to distinguish and theorise the sexual and economic negotiations between local rent boys and visiting gays in Istanbul. In the context of recent Islamisation and accentuated homophobia, gay tourism in Turkey has not really developed and the country is not among the top destinations for queer tours and travel agencies.
22. There is a growing literature on the linguistic, social, political, cultural and spatial aspects of Kurdish identity in Turkey and other Middle Eastern

countries. See, for example, Gambetti and Jongerden 2015; Goral 2016; Orhan 2015; and Saracoglu 2010.
23. Gregory Mitchell, *Tourist Attractions: Performing Race & Masculinity in Brazil's Sexual Economy* (Chicago, 2016), p. 5.
24. Mitchell, *Tourist Attractions*, pp. 34–55.
25. Patricia Ticineto Clough and Jean Halley (eds), *The Affective Turn: Theorizing the Social* (Durham, 2007), p. 2.
26. Gregory Mitchell, *Tourist Attractions: Performing Race & Masculinity in Brazil's Sexual Economy* (Chicago, 2016), p. 64.
27. Jane Ward, *Not Gay: Sex Between Straight White Men* (New York, 2015), p. 5.
28. Ibid., p. 28.
29. Ibid., p. 33.
30. Carla Freeman, *Entrepreneurial Selves: Neoliberal Respectability and the Making of a Caribbean Middle Class* (Durham, 2014).
31. Cenk Özbay, 'Nocturnal Queers: Rent Boys' Masculinity in Istanbul', *Sexualities* 13/5(2010a), pp. 645–63; Ozyegin, 2011.
32. Gul Ozyegin, *New Desires, New Selves: Sex, Love and Piety Among Turkish Youth* (New York, 2015a), pp. 3–4.
33. Cenk Özbay, 'Neoliberalizm ve Erkekligin Halleri', in Armagan Ozturk, *Yeni Sag, Yeni Sol* (Ankara, 2010b); Gul Ozyegin, 'Arzunun Nesnesi Olmak: Romans, Kırılgan Erkeklik ve Neoliberal Ozne', in Cenk Özbay, Aysecan Terzioglu and Yesim Yasin (eds), *Neoliberalizm ve Mahremiyet: Turkiye'de Beden, Saglik ve Cinsellik* (Istanbul, 2011); Suad Joseph (ed.), *Intimate Selving in Arab Families: Gender, Self, and Identity* (Syracuse, 1999).
34. Ozyegin, *New Desires, New Selves*, pp. 2–3.
35. For a different group of young men (straight, gay and bisexual high school and college students, who are readers of critical satirical comic magazines in Turkey) I have used the concept 'defamilial citizenship' in order to highlight their 'self-vigilant and egotistic,' and at the same time deeply neoliberal, subjectivities(Cenk Özbay, 'Inarticulate, Self-Vigilant and Egotistical: Masculinity in Turkish Drawn Stories', in Cenk Özbay, Maral Erol, Aysecan Terizoglu and Umut Turem, *The Making of Neoliberal Turkey* [Aldershot, 2016], pp. 87–110).
36. Ozyegin, *New Desires, New*, p. 26.
37. Ibid., p. 119.
38. Sebnem Iyinam, 'Varos Cocuklari Daha Iyi Sevisir', *Hurriyet*, 29 December 2001.
39. Kevin, Walby, *Touching Encounters: Sex, Work and Male-to-Male Internet Escorting* (Chicago, 2012), pp. 2–3.
40. Cenk Özbay, 'Virilities for rent: Navigating masculinity, sexuality and class in Istanbul'. Unpublished MA thesis (Bogazici University, 2005).
41. The rock singer Pamela Spence's song *Istanbul Seni Hapsetmis* was very popular in the mid-2000s. Sony Music, 2004.
42. The Turkish saying '*is baska, ibadet baska.*' A maxim used to mark the difference between what is compulsory and what is done voluntarily.

43. Rent boys generally talk about gay men in a homophobic and dehumanising way, with frequent cursing and insults. As our conversations proceeded and the sense of rapport established, most of them had a tendency to soften their language and accept the positive and humane characteristics of gay men. 'Faggot' (*ibne*) was the term the rent boys most frequently used. Sometimes they also used 'fruity' (*top*) and 'homosexual' (*homoseksuel*). Nicola Mai ('Surfing Liquid Modernity: Albanian and Romanian Male Sex Workers in Europe', in Peter Aggleton and Richard Parker (eds), *Men Who Sell Sex: Global Perspectives* [New York, 2015], p. 31) shows that in different parts of Europe, rent boys refer to gay men through the disparaging notion of 'fucking queers.'

Chapter 2   Rent Boys and the Contours of Exaggerated Masculinity

1. Taksim Square has always been a political space to a certain extent from the viewpoints of the modernist early Republican regime, the oppressive military administrations following the three coups in the history of the country, and the revanchist Islamist politicians of the recent past. Some political wings tend to see the square as representative of the new, modern country with its large Atatürk statue and opera building (Atatürk Cultural Centre), while others wish to recreate this contested public space as a manifestation of an Islamic society by erecting a huge mosque in the middle of it. As of 2015, neither pole had won the spatial-political war over Taksim. The statue is still there, the cultural centre abandoned, there is no mosque, the park survives and the square itself looks like an ugly urban vacant lot full of concrete, undeserving of any popular or ideological attention except flinching divergent memories.
2. The Prime Minister Tayyip Erdogan, who turned out to be the responsible authority behind the plan that would demolish the park, said, 'I was born and I grew up around here. I know it very well', http://www.hurriyet.com.tr/basbakan-bu-tayyip-erdogan-degismez-23479966, accessed on 22 August 2015. Most people did not interpret these words as a homophobic statement because they did not have knowledge about what went on in the park. For the minority that is privileged to know the significance of the park to the counter-hegemonic sexual geography of Istanbul, it was very obvious that Erdogan intended to terminate the queer legacy of the space.
3. Corie J. Hammers, 'Making space for an agentic sexuality? The examination of a lesbian/queer bathhouse', *Sexualities* 11/5 (2008), pp. 547–72.
4. The last police raid that intercepted the routine club temporality was in 2004. Nevertheless, everybody knows that there are always undercover police in the bars, as in any other public spaces in Turkey, including the college campuses.
5. Andrew Hewitt, *Social Choreography: Ideology as Performance in Dance and Everyday Movement* (Durham, 2005).

6. SenGel was a relatively marginal gay dance club in the early 2000s and known as a 'truck-driver' place. It changed its location three times, and every move brought it to a larger and more public space. Its current place is on one of the busiest streets of the Taksim area, and after most of the other gay clubs were closed down, it appears to be *the* gay club of the city, with its most variegated clientele in terms of gender, class, 'race' and ethnicity. On weekend nights today, SenGel can host some 500 people.
7. This is a common policy at different kinds of entertainment places in Turkey. They do not let single men or groups of men enter if they don't have women with them. Working-class (*varos*) men and Kurdish men are more vulnerable to this gatekeeping policy. The same strategy can sometimes favour gay men against heterosexuals because they might look 'harmless' to the women inside, but some bars use this policy against gay men, by saying they cannot enter because they do not have female partners with them.
8. I prefer to describe the rent boys' stylised embodiment as 'exaggerated masculinity' in order to underline its theatrical, playful, performative and decontextualising characteristics; as Metin said, knowing to do the right thing in the right place, at the right time and in a repetitive fashion. It is a constellation of learnt, imitated, calculated and socially regulated displays of doing masculinity. There are other similar terms for such excessive masculine performances, such as hyper-masculinity (Murray Healey, *Gay Skins: Class, Masculinity, and Queer Appropriation* [London, 1996]) or machismo (Matthew C. Guttmann, *The Meanings of Macho: Being a Man in Mexico City* [Berkeley and Los Angeles, 1996]) that are conceptualised in different webs of relations.
9. Jeffrey Weeks, *Sexuality and Its Discontents: Meanings, Myths and Modern Sexualities* (London, 1990).
10. Albert J. Reiss Jr., 'The Social Integration of Queers and Peers', *Social Problems* 9/2(1961), pp. 102–20.
11. Godelier, Maurice, 'What is a sexual act?', *Anthropological Theory* 3/2 (2003), p. 180.
12. Timothy M. Hall, 'Rent-boys, barflies, and kept men: Men involved in sex with men for compensation in Prague', *Sexualities* 10/4 (2007), pp. 457–72.
13. Donna M. Goldstein, *Laughter Out of Place: Race, Class, Violence, and Sexuality in a Rio Shantytown* (Berkeley and Los Angeles, 2003).
14. Loic Wacquant, *Urban Outcasts: A Comparative Sociology of Advanced Marginality* (Cambridge, 2008).
15. Patricia Hill Collins, 'Learning from the outsider within', *Social Problems* 33/6 (1986), pp. 14–32.
16. There is a small distinction between what rent boys do and how others interpret these acts in the Goffmanesque sense of impression management, or between 'their intentional manipulation of their self-presentation and impressions that they unintentionally gave to others' (Decena, *Tacit Subjects*, p. 20).
17. Dennis Altman, *Global Sex* (Chicago, 2001); Jon Binnie, *The Globalization of Sexuality* (London, 2004); A. Cruz-Malave and Martin F. Manalansan (eds), *Queer Globalizations: Citizenship and the Afterlife of Colonialism* (New York, 2002);

Martin F. Manalansan, *Global Divas: Filipino Gay Men in the Diaspora* (Durham, 2003); Elizabeth A. Povinelli and Chauncey George, 'Thinking sexuality transnationally', *GLQ* 5/4 (1999), pp. 439–50.
18. Ayfer Bartu Candan and Cenk Özbay (eds), *Yeni IstanbulCalismalari: Sinirlar, Mucadeleler, Acilimlar* (Istanbul, 2014).
19. Zygmunt Bauman and Tim Lay, *Thinking Sociologically* (Oxford, 2001), p. 33.
20. Jenny White, *Money Makes Us Relatives* (New York, 2004).
21. Neslihan Demirtas and Sema Sen, 'Varos Identity: The Redefinition of Low Income Settlements in Turkey', *Middle Eastern Studies* 43/1 (2007), pp. 87–106; Tahire Erman, 'Gecekondu Calismalarinda Oteki Olarak Gecekondulu Kurgulari', *European Journal of Turkish Studies* 1 (2004), http://www.ejts.org/document85.html, accessed 15 June 2010.
22. Zehra Etoz, 'Varos: Bir Istila, bir tehdit', *Birikim* 132 (2000): 49–53.
23. In the 1980s, when the term *varos* was not yet invented, there were others terms used in a derogatory and excluding discourse, such as *maganda* and *kiro* (Ayse Oncu, 'Istanbulites and Others: The Cultural Cosmology of 'Middleness' in the Era of Neoliberalism', in Caglar Keyder (ed.), *Istanbul: Between the Local and the Global* [Boston, 1999]; 'Consumption, Gender and The Mapping of Istanbul in the 1990s', in Deniz Kandiyoti and Ayse Saktanber (eds), *Fragments of Culture: The Everyday of Modern Turkey* [London, 2002]). Kurds were more explicitly indicated in these usages: Turks named Kurds in this humiliating way. *Varos*, on the other hand, is more neutral in terms of ethnic and racial background.
24. '*Varos* is never homogeneous.' The social scientist Sema Erder told me this once; I must thank her for reminding me of this significant point. Consisting of millions of people with diverse backgrounds and multifarious living conditions, *varos* cannot be reduced to a single archetype. What I allude to here is the relative position of *varos* boys in relation to the middle-class, middle-aged gay men. *Varos* provides a vague-enough background embroidered by bodies and personal histories, and only upon this basis do rent boys navigate masculinity, sexuality and class through their homoerotic relations.
25. For a similar situation among Brazilian male prostitutes, see Richard Parker, *Beneath the Equator: Cultures of Desire, Male Homosexuality and Emerging Gay Communities in Brazil* (New York, 1999).
26. Judith Butler, *Bodies That Matter: On the Discursive Limits of 'Sex'* (New York, 1993).
27. Tarik Bereket and Barry. D. Adam, 'The emergence of gay identities in contemporary Turkey', *Sexualities* 9 (2006), pp. 131–51; Murat Hocaoglu, *Escinsel Erkekler: Yirmi Bes Taniklik* (Istanbul, 2002); Cenk Özbay and Serdar Soydan, *Escinsel Kadinlar: Yirmi Dort Taniklik* (Istanbul, 2003); Huseyin Tapinc, 'Masculinity, femininity and Turkish male homosexuality', in Ken Plummer (ed.), *Modern Homosexualities: Fragments of Lesbian and Gay Experiences* (London, 1992), pp. 39–50; Aslan Yuzgun, *Turkiye'de Escinsellik: Dun ve Bugun* (Istanbul, 1986).

28. Roger N. Lancaster, *Life is Hard: Machismo, Danger and the Power of Intimacy in Nicaragua* (Berkeley and Los Angeles, 1994).
29. Stephen O. Murray, 'The Will not to Know: Islamic Accommodations of Male Homosexuality', in Stephen O. Murray and Will Roscoe (eds), *Islamic Homosexualities: Culture, History, and Literature* (New York, 1997), pp. 14–54.
30. Jay Clarkson, 'Everyday Joe versus "pissy, bitchy, queens:" Gay masculinity on straightacting.com', *Journal of Men's Studies* 14/2 (2006), pp. 191–207.
31. Judith Butler, *Gender Trouble: Feminism and the Subversion of Identity* (New York, 1999), p. 25; Candace West and Don Zimmerman, 'Doing Gender', *Gender & Society* 1/1 (1987).
32. Butler, *Gender Trouble*, p. 33.
33. Decena *Tacit Subjects*, p. 3.
34. R. W. Connell, *Gender and Power: Society, the Person and Sexual Politics* (Stanford, 1987); R. W. Connell, *Masculinities* (Berkeley and Los Angeles, 1995).
35. R. W. Connell, *The Men and the Boys* (Berkeley and Los Angeles, 2000), p. 83.
36. Tarik Bereket and Barry. D. Adam, 'Navigating Islam and Same-Sex Liaisons Among Men in Turkey', *Journal of Homosexuality* 55 (2008), pp. 204–22; M. Ghoussoub and Emma Sinclair-Webb (eds), *Imagined Masculinities: Male Identity and Culture in the Modern Middle East* (London, 2000); Lahoucine Ouzgane (ed.), *Islamic Masculinities* (London, 2006).
37. Laura M. Agustin, 'The cultural study of commercial sex', *Sexualities* 8/5 (2005), p. 619.
38. Les Wright, 'Introduction to "queer" masculinities', *Men and Masculinities* 7/3 (2005), p. 243.
39. Jeffrey Weeks, 'R.W. Inverts, perverts, and Mary-Annes: Male prostitution and the regulation of homosexuality in the nineteenth and early twentieth centuries,' *Journal of Homosexuality* 6/1–2 (1981), p. 129.
40. For Connell, *Men and the Boys*; Eve Kosofsky Sedgwick, *Between Men: English Literature and Male Homosexual Desire* (New York, 1986).
41. I was not particularly insistent because Berk was a minor when I met him. I was waiting him to turn eighteen years old in order to request a formal interview.
42. P. Fernandez-Davila et al. the (2008) 'Compensated sex and sexual risk: Sexual, social, and economic interactions between homosexually- and heterosexually identified men of low income in two cities of Peru', *Sexualities* 11/3 (2008), pp. 352–74.
43. The Islamist-conservative government has been ruling the country since 2002 (Cenk Özbay, Maral Erol, Aysecan Terizoglu and Umut Turem (eds), *The Making of Neoliberal Turkey* [Aldershot, 2016]). The government's aggressive pro-natalist policy, oppression to critical public debates about forms of erotic sociability and threatening of the media has made it impossible to talk about sexuality, including safe sexual practices, contraception and abortion. There is no single active campaign to teach young people about the risks of unprotected sex in Turkey. It is also difficult, if not yet impossible, to access free condoms. Beyond this constructed anti-sex common sense and policy, there is an evident

silence about HIV/AIDS epidemic in Turkey. My colleague, the public health professor Yesim Yasin, told me that there is not sufficient research on AIDS in Turkey, and as medical doctors they have great difficulty in accessing data on the dimensions, specific cases and patterns of the diffusion (Personal communication with Dr Yasin, 12 December 2014).
44. Ken Plummer, (2005) 'Male Sexualities', in Michael Kimmel et al. (eds), *Handbook of Studies On Men and Masculinities* (Thousand Oaks and London, 2005), pp. 178–95.
45. R. W. Connell, *Masculinities* (Berkeley and Los Angeles, 1995).
46. Gary W. Dowsett, et al., 'Taking it like a man: Masculinity and barebacking online', *Sexualities* 11/1–2 (2008), p. 124.
47. Decena *Tacit Subjects*, p. 31.

Chapter 3   Rent Boys' Intimacies in Neoliberal Times

1. R. W. Connell, *Gender and Power: Society, the Person and Sexual Politics* (Stanford, 1987); Ibid., *Masculinities* (Berkeley and Los Angeles, 1995).
2. The article in which Connell answers some of her critics is significant in better understanding the usefulness and boundaries of the concept. See R. W. Connell and James W. Messerschmidt, 'Hegemonic Masculinity: Rethinking the Concept', *Gender & Society*, 19/6 (2005), pp. 829–59.
3. For example, the dark corners of Istiklal Street, Taksim Square or Gezi Park, a gay sauna, a gay bar or a 'rent boy bar' such as Bientot. Regarding the urban geography of sexualities in Istanbul, rent boy bars and dance clubs should be considered separately from gay venues, which are greater in number, more visible, more available and have more cosmopolitan patrons. Rent boy bars, on the other hand, are small places that cater exclusively to rent boys and men who are interested in having sex with rent boys. Rent boy bars differentiate themselves according to different criteria such as whether transgender sex workers are allowed. Rent boy bars in İstanbul generally do not have cover fee, and when they do, they are cheaper than the other queer bars and dance clubs.
4. See Leslie McCall, 'The Complexity of Intersectionality', *Signs* 30/3 (2005), pp. 1771–800; Patricia Hill Collins, *Black Feminist Thought: Knowledge, Consciousness and the Politics of Empowerment* (New York, 2008); Joan Z. Spade and Catherine G. Valentine (eds), *The Kaleidoscope of Gender: Prisms, Patterns, and Possibilities* (London, 2013); Patricia Hill Collins and Sirma Bilge, *Intersectionality* (Cambridge, 2016); Ange-Marie Hancock, *Intersectionality: An Intellectual History* (Oxford, 2016); Vivian M. May, *Pursuing Intersectionality, Unsettling Dominant Imaginaries* (London, 2015); Sarah Fenstermaker and Candace West (eds), *Doing Gender, Doing Difference: Inequality, Power, and Institutional Change* (New York, 2002). For the methodological implications of knowledge production regarding an intersectional analysis of differences, standpoints and situatedness, see Sandra Harding (ed.), *The Feminist Standpoint Theory Reader: Intellectual and Political*

Controversies (New York, 2003); Nancy Duncan (ed.), *BodySpace: Destabilising Geographies of Gender and Sexuality* (London, 1996).
5. Gary T. Barker, *Dying to Be Men: Youth, Masculinity and Social Exclusion* (London, 2005); David Byrne, *Social Exclusion* (Buckingham, 2005).
6. Peter Aggleton (ed.), *Men Who Sell Sex: International Perspectives on Male Prostitution and HIV/AIDS* (Philadelphia, 1999); Peter Aggleton and Richard Parker (eds), *Men Who Sell Sex: Global Perspectives* (New York, 2015).
7. David Harvey, *A Brief History of Neoliberalism* (Oxford, 2007).
8. Pierre Bourdieu, *Acts of Resistance: Against the Tyranny of the Market* (New York, 1999); Michael Burawoy, 'Public Sociology vs. the Market', *Socio-Economic Review* 5 (2007): pp. 356–67; Cenk Özbay, 'Neoliberalizm ve Erkekligin Halleri', in Armagan Ozturk, *Yeni Sag, Yeni Sol* (Ankara, 2010b); Gul Ozyegin, 'Arzunun Nesnesi Olmak: Romans, Kırılgan Erkeklik ve Neoliberal Ozne', in Cenk Özbay, Aysecan Terzioglu and Yesim Yasin (eds), *Neoliberalizm ve Mahremiyet: Turkiye'de Beden, Saglik ve Cinsellik* (Istanbul, 2011).
9. Deniz Kandiyoti, 'Introduction: Reading the fragments', in Deniz Kandiyoti and Ayse Saktanber (eds), *Fragments of Culture: The Everyday of Modern Turkey* (London, 2002); Cenk Özbay, Aysecan Terzioglu and Yesim Yasin (eds), *Neoliberalizm ve Mahremiyet: Turkiye'de Beden, Saglik ve Cinsellik* (Istanbul, 2011); Ozbay, Cenk, Maral Erol, Aysecan Terizoglu and Umut Turem (eds), *The Making of Neoliberal Turkey* (Aldershot, 2016).
10. Barry Hindess, 'Neo-liberal Citizenship', *Citizenship Studies*, 6/2 (2002), pp. 127–43; Aihwa Ong, *Flexible Citizenship: The Cultural Logics of Transnationality* (Durham, 1999); Ibid., *Neoliberalism as Exception: Mutations in Citizenship and Sovereignty* (Durham, 2006); Ahmed Kanna, 'Flexible Citizenship in Dubai: Neoliberal Subjectivity in the Emerging "City-Corporation"', *Cultural Anthropology*, 25/1 (2010), pp. 100–29.
11. R. W. Connell, 'Globalization, Imperialism and Masculinities', in Michael Kimmel, Jeff Hearn and R. W. Connell (eds), *Handbook of Studies of Men & Masculinities* (Thousand Oaks, 2005); R. W. Connell and Julian Wood, 'Globalization and Business Masculinities', *Men and Masculinities*, 7/4 (2005), pp. 347–64.
12. Public sayings in Turkish explain this stark gendered difference. For example, 'If he squeezes the stone, he can produce juice out if it,' or 'He can be a porter and carry stuff, if he has to' are the worst imaginable life options for men. On the other hand, there are 'street women', 'common women' and usages like 'Whoever has a vagina has no anxiety' are used for women. Women, hence, cannot starve; in the worst case they can realise that possibility – thinkable only for them and not for men.
13. Men can always be thieves, smugglers or pimps, if their moral boundaries let them. None of these illegal, immoral or informal jobs is as manifestly sexist and gendered as sex work. In the Turkish language, all the disparaging discourse around sex work targets female bodies only. The male gender and the culture of masculinity are excluded from this linguistic construction. It is unintelligible to think of a male subject in prostitution, either when swearing or joking. The

meaning of words attached to sex work become tangible only through the presence of an available female body. Men can only arrive at this point by becoming feminised, transforming into a woman, or being a transvestite. Perceiving the existence of rent boys as sex workers in their manliest, even *exaggeratedly* masculine stylisation, puts us outside of the sexist and gendered social imaginary about sex work.

14. In other words, rent boys are not from the Turkish urban underclass that is struggling with intense poverty such that they will do anything for money (see, for example, Necmi Erdogan (ed.), *Yoksulluk Halleri: Turkiye'de Kent Yoksullugun Toplumsal Gorunumleri* [Istanbul, 2007]). As I explain throughout the pages of this book, I have been able to observe that rent boys in Istanbul are from the lower and lower-middle classes and have certain self-entrepreneurial tendencies and desires for upward class mobility. Therefore, what the news coverage in popular media (i.e., 'Young Sex Worker Men in the Center of Istanbul', *Tempo* 2008) presents as the needy, broke, homeless youth without any chance to negotiate and choose (or reject) partners is definitely not true.
15. Carlos Ulises Decena, *Tacit Subjects: Belonging and Same-Sex Desire Among Dominican Immigrant Men* (Durham, 2011), p. 3.
16. Michael Warner, 'Publics and Counterpublics', *Public Culture*, 14/1 (2002), pp. 49-90.
17. Ozbay, Terzioglu and Yasin, *Neoliberalizm ve Mahremiyet*.
18. Barrie Thorne, *Gender Play: Boys and Girls in School* (New Brunswick, 1993).
19. See, for example, Frances Cleaver (ed.), *Masculinities Matter: Men, Gender and Development* (London, 2002); Andrea Cornwall, et al. (eds) *Men and Development: Politicizing Masculinities*, London Kale Bantigue Fajardo, *Filipino Crosscurrents: Oceanographies of Seafaring, Masculinities and Globalization* (Minneapolis, 2011); Linda McDowell, *Redundant Masculinities: Employment Change and White Working Class Youth* (Oxford, 2003); Kris Paap, *Working Construction: Why White Working-Class Men Put Themselves – and the Labor Movement- In Harm's Way* (Ithaca, 2006); Christine L. Williams, *Still a Man's World: Men Who Do Women's Work* (Berkeley and Los Angeles, 1995); Cecile Jackson, *Men at Work: Labour, Masculinities and Development* (London, 2001).
20. Victor J. Seidler, *Transforming Masculinities: Men, Cultures, Bodies, Power, Sex and Love* (London, 2006).
21. Tim Edwards, *Cultures of Masculinity* (London, 2006); James Farrer, *Opening Up: Youth Sex Culture and Market Reform in Shanghai* (Chicago, 2002); Lisa Rofel, *Desiring China: Experiments in Neoliberalism, Sexuality and Public Culture* (Durham, 2007); Pascoe 2007.

Chapter 4 Queer in the Spatial, Temporal and Social Margins

1. Judith Halberstam, *In a Queer Time and Place: Transgender Bodies, Subcultural Lives* (New York, 2005), p. 6. On queer temporality and spatiality, see also

David Bell, et al. *Pleasure Zones: Bodies, Cities, Spaces* (Syracuse, 2001); Diane Chisholm, *Queer Constellations: Subcultural Space In The Wake Of The City* (Minneapolis, 2004); Lee Edelman, *No Future: Queer Theory and the Death Drive* (Durham, 2005); Elizabeth Freeman, *Time Binds: Queer Temporalities, Queer Histories* (Durham, 2010); Gordon Brent Ingram et al. (eds) *Queers in Space: Communities, Public Spaces, Sites of Resistance* (San Francisco, 1997).
2. Halberstam, *In a Queer Time and* Place, p. 10.
3. Lee Edelman, *No Future: Queer Theory and the Death Drive* (Durham, 2005), p. 17, emphasis original.
4. David Halperin, *Saint Foucault: Towards a Gay Hagiography* (Oxford, 1995), pp. 61–2.
5. See, for example, Tarik Bereket and Barry. D. Adam, 'The emergence of gay identities in contemporary Turkey', *Sexualities* 9 (2006), pp. 131–51; Murat Hocaoglu, *Escinsel Erkekler: Yirmi Bes Taniklik* (Istanbul, 2002); Cenk Özbay and Serdar Soydan, *Escinsel Kadinlar: Yirmi Dort Taniklik* (Istanbul, 2003); Nuray Sakalli and Ozanser Ugurlu, 'The Effects of Social Contact with a Lesbian Person on the Attitude Change Toward Homosexuality in Turkey', *Journal of Homosexuality* 44/1 (2002), pp. 111–19; Huseyin Tapinc, 'Masculinity, femininity and Turkish male homosexuality', in Ken Plummer (ed.), *Modern Homosexualities: Fragments of Lesbian and Gay Experiences* (London, 1992), pp. 39–50; Aslan Yuzgun, *Turkiye'de Escinsellik: Dun ve Bugun* (Istanbul, 1986).
6. Adam Isaiah Green, 'Queer Theory and Sociology: Locating the Subject and the Self in Sexuality Studies', *Sociological Theory* 25/1(2007), pp. 26–45.
7. See Kathryn Babayan and Afsaneh Najmabadi (eds), *Islamicate Sexualities: Translations across Temporal Geographies of Desire* (Boston, 2008). Balderstone and Guy (1997); Roger N. Lancaster, *Life is Hard: Machismo, Danger and the Power of Intimacy in Nicaragua* (Berkeley and Los Angeles, 1994); Sofian Merabet, *Queer Beirut* (Austin, 2014); Stephen O. Murray, *Latin American Male Homosexualities* (Albuquerque, 1995); Gul Ozyegin, *Gender and Sexuality in Muslim Cultures* (Aldershot, 2015b).
8. Sara Ahmed, 'Orientations: Towards a Queer Phenomenology', *GLQ* 12 4 (2006).
9. Gary W. Dowsett, *Practicing Desire: Homosexual Sex in the Era of AIDS* (Stanford, 1996); Plummer 1997.
10. Adam Isaiah Green, 'The Social Organization of Desire: The Sexual Fields Approach', *Sociological Theory* 26/1 (2008), pp. 25–50.
11. Judith Halberstam, 'The Anti-Social Turn in Queer Studies', *Graduate Journal of Social Science* 5/2 (2008), p. 141.
12. Green, 'The Social Organization of Desire.'
13. Kipnis, Laura, 'Feminism: The Political Conscience of Post-modernism?', in Andrew Ross (ed.), *Universal Abandon? The Politics of Post-modernism* (Minneapolis, 1988), p. 158.

Chapter 5 Contemporary Male Sex Work

1. This is probably about the profile of the typical rent boy: very young and coming from a migrant working-class background with a low degree of education and a kind of self-investment in terms of bodily and cultural symbols that precipitate social distinction. What I have heard, though, reinforces the common impression that men who cater to wealthy older women's sexual appetites, the *gigolo* (who may include unsuccessful actors or models), are slightly older, more refined in symbolic tastes, and better built. Therefore, it is possible to state that male sex workers in Turkey consist of two distinct groups based, not only on the gender of their clients, but also on the positions they occupy in the social hierarchy. Further research on male sex workers is needed to further illuminate this dichotomy.
2. Tarik Bereket and Barry. D. Adam, 'The emergence of gay identities in contemporary Turkey', *Sexualities* 9 (2006), pp. 131–51; Murat Hocaoglu, *Escinsel Erkekler: Yirmi Bes Taniklik* (Istanbul, 2002); Ozbay 2015; Huseyin Tapinc, 'Masculinity, femininity and Turkish male homosexuality', in Ken Plummer (ed.), *Modern Homosexualities: Fragments of Lesbian and Gay Experiences* (London, 1992), pp. 39–50.
3. I was attending a queer activist meeting in 2004. Two young college students from a nearby city showed up as guests. They were slightly effeminate men, a quality no one seemed to care about. Different topics were discussed in a relaxed manner, as is the custom in these meetings. At one point, the usual distinction between *gay ya da escinsel* (gay versus homosexual) was mentioned. The two guests said that they preferred to refer to themselves as homosexual because they did not think that they were masculine enough to be called gay. Everyone in the meeting was surprised. Nobody had thought of such a differentiation before this iteration. I was also surprised to see (once again) how many unacknowledged exclusions and classifications operate in gay culture.
4. Cenk Özbay and Serdar Soydan, *Escinsel Kadinlar: Yirmi Dort Taniklik* (Istanbul, 2003); Evren Savci, 'Queer in Translation: Paradoxes of Westernisation and Sexual Others in the Turkish Nation.' Unpublished PhD thesis, Department of Sociology (University of Southern California, 2011); Birkan Tas, 'Adam gibi adam olamamak: Ayi hareketi ve maskulenlik uzerine', in Cuneyt Cakirlar and Serkan Delice (eds), *Cinsellik Muammasi: Turkiye'de Queer Kultur ve Muhalefet* (Istanbul, 2012).
5. Oyman Basaran, 'You are Like a Virus: Dangerous Bodies and Military Medical Authority in Turkey', *Gender & Society* 28/4 (2014), pp. 562–82; Alp Biricik, 'Rotten report and reconstructing hegemonic masculinity in Turkey', in Ozgur Heval Cinar and Coskun Usterci (eds), *Conscientious Objection: Resisting Militarized Society* (London, 2009); Nurseli Yesim Sunbuloglu (ed.), *Erkek Millet, Asker Millet: Turkiyede Militarism, Milliyetcilik ve Erkeklikler* (Istanbul, 2013).
6. Murat Hocaoglu, *Escinsel Erkekler: Yirmi Bes Taniklik* (Istanbul, 2002); Ozbay and Soydan, *Escinsel Kadinlar*; Gul Ozyegin, 'Reading the closet through connectivity', *Social Identities* 18 (2012), pp. 201–22.

7. Rent boys never use the term bisexual to express or analyse their sexual orientation or identification. Instead they always think and speak through the duality of homo- and heterosexuality. A few gay men, however, have said that rent boys might have been bisexuals – an option that they were not entirely aware of. In the end, I have decided to dismiss bisexuality as a conceptual tool that might illustrate sexual relations between rent boys and gay men.
8. Judith Halberstam, *In a Queer Time and Place: Transgender Bodies, Subcultural Lives* (New York, 2005).
9. Not the real name of the application. I asked Atomic their permission to use screenshots from my phone if I covered the eyes on the profiles to make them unrecognisable, but they decided they would not allow me to do so. Therefore, I only use translations of the textual data on the profiles here.
10. Tim Dean, *Unlimited Intimacy: Reflections on the Subculture of Barebacking* (Chicago, 2009).
11. See Peter S. Cahn, 'Consuming Class: multilevel marketers in neoliberal Mexico', *Cultural Anthropology* 23/3 (2008), pp. 429–52; R. W. Connell, *Confronting Equality: Gender, Knowledge and Global Change* (Cambridge, 2011); Ahmed Kanna, 'Flexible Citizenship in Dubai: Neoliberal Subjectivity in the Emerging "City-Corporation"', *Cultural Anthropology*, 25/1 (2010), pp. 100–29; Cenk Özbay, 'Neoliberal Erkekligin Sosyoljisine Dogru: Rent Boylar Ornegi', in Cenk Özbay, Aysecan Terzioglu and Yesim Yasin (eds), *Neoliberalizm ve Mahremiyet: Turkiye'de Beden, Saglik ve Cinsellik* (Istanbul, 2011); Gul Ozyegin, *New Desires, New Selves: Sex, Love and Piety Among Turkish Youth* (New York, 2015a); Lisa Rofel, *Desiring China: Experiments in Neoliberalism, Sexuality and Public Culture* (Durham, 2007); Ava Wilson, *The Intimate Economies of Bangkok: Tomboys, Tycoons and Avon Ladies in the Global City* (Los Angeles and Berkeley, 2004).
12. Nikolas Rose, *Governing the Soul: The Shaping of the Private Self* (New York, 1999).
13. R. W. Connell and Julian Wood, 'Globalization and Business Masculinities', *Men and Masculinities*, 7/4 (2005), pp. 347–64.

Conclusion   Perverse Mobilities and Deviant Careers

1. See, for example, Basaran, 'You are Like a Virus'; Volkan Yilmaz and Ipek Gocmen, 'Denied Citizens of Turkey: Experiences of Discrimination Among LGBT Individuals in Employment, Housing, and Health Care', *Gender, Work & Occupation* 23 (2016); Deniz Kandiyoti, 'Introduction: Reading the fragments', in Deniz Kandiyoti and Ayse Saktanber (eds), *Fragments of Culture: The Everyday of Modern Turkey* (London, 2002); Burcu Karakas and Bawer Cakir, *Erkeklik Ofsayta Dusunce: Futbol, Escinsellik ve Halil Ibrahim Dincdag'in Hikayesi* (Istanbul, 2013); Cenk Özbay 'Men Are Less Manly, Women Are More Feminine: Shopping Mall as a Site for Gender Crisis in Istanbul', in Gul Ozyegin (ed.), *Gender and Sexuality in Muslim Cultures* (Surrey, 2015b),

pp. 73–94; Gul Ozyegin, *New Desires, New Selves: Sex, Love and Piety Among Turkish Youth* (New York, 2015a).
2. Howard Becker, *Outsiders: Studies in the Sociology of Deviance* (New York, 1963), p. 25.
3. Ibid., pp. 31–2.
4. Ibid., pp. 36–7.
5. Peter Aggleton (ed.), *Men Who Sell Sex: International Perspectives on Male Prostitution and HIV/AIDS* (Philadelphia, 1999); Peter Aggleton and Richard Parker (eds), *Men Who Sell Sex: Global Perspectives* (New York, 2015); James E. Elias et al. (eds), *Prostitution: On Whores, Hustlers, and Johns* (New York, 1998); Kerwin Kaye, 'Male Prostitution in the Twentieth Century: Pseudohomosexuals, Hoodlum Homosexuals, and Exploited Teens', *Journal of Homosexuality* 46(2003), pp. 1–77; Victor Minichiello and John Scott (eds), *Male Sex Work and Society* (New York, 2014). Smith and Grov (*In the Company of Men: Inside the Lives of Male Prostitutes* [New York, 2011], p. 8) make a similar point: 'Typically, more mature and older men seek the social and erotic company of attractive younger men, exchanging their experience and money for youth and sexual virility.'
6. Ibid., p. 11.
7. Ibid., p. 33.
8. Cenk Özbay, Maral Erol, Aysecan Terizoglu and Umut Turem (eds), *The Making of Neoliberal Turkey* (Aldershot, 2016).
9. Paul Amar, *The Security Archipelago: Human-Security States, Sexuality Politics, and the End of Neoliberalism* (Durham, 2013).

BIBLIOGRAPHY

Aggleton, Peter (ed.), *Men Who Sell Sex: International Perspectives on Male Prostitution and HIV/AIDS* (Philadelphia, 1999).
—— and Richard Parker (eds), *Men Who Sell Sex: Global Perspectives* (New York, 2015).
Agustin, Laura M., 'The cultural study of commercial sex', *Sexualities* 8/5 (2005), pp. 618–31.
Ahmed, Sara, 'Orientations: Towards a Queer Phenomenology', *GLQ* 12/4 (2006).
Akbulut, Bengi and Ayfer Bartu Candan, 'Bir Iki Agacin Otesinde: Istanbul'a Politik Ekoloji Cercevesinden Bakmak', in Ayfer Bartu Candan and Cenk Ozbay (eds), *Yeni Istanbul Calismalari: Sinirlar, Mucadeleler, Acilimlar* (Istanbul, 2014).
Allison, Anne, *Nightwork: Sexuality, Pleasure, and Corporate Masculinity in a Tokyo Hostess Club* (Chicago, 1994).
Altman, Dennis, *Global Sex* (Chicago, 2001).
—— 'Foreword', in Peter Aggleton and Richard Parker (eds), *Men Who Sell Sex: Global Perspectives* (New York, 2015), pp. xiv–xx.
Amar, Paul, *The Security Archipelago: Human-Security States, Sexuality Politics, and the End of Neoliberalism* (Durham, 2013).
Arat, Yesim, 'The Project of Modernity and Women in Turkey', in Sibel Bozdogan and Resat Kasaba (eds), *Rethinking Modernity and National Identity in Turkey* (Seattle, 1997).
Arenas, Reinaldo, *Before Night Falls: A Memoir*, translated by Dolores M. Koch (London, 1994).
Armbrecht, Thomas J. D., 'The cucumber seller: Homosexuality and class in Turkey', *Gay Men's Fiction Quarterly* 3/4 (2001), pp. 51–9.
Asena, Duygu, *Paramparca* (Istanbul, 2006).
Atik, Alperen, 'Neo-Delikanlilar', *Radikal Iki*, 9 May 2005.
Babayan, Kathryn and Afsaneh Najmabadi (eds), *Islamicate Sexualities: Translations across Temporal Geographies of Desire* (Boston, 2008).
Balderstone, Daniel and Donna J. Guy (eds), *Sex and Sexuality in Latin America* (New York, 1997).
Barker, Gary T., *Dying to Be Men: Youth, Masculinity and Social Exclusion* (London, 2005).

Barrett, Don C. and L. M. Pollack, 'Whose Gay Community? Social Class, Sexual Self-Expression, and Gay Community Involvement', *Sociological Quarterly* 46 (2005), pp. 437–56.
Bartu Candan, Ayfer and Cenk Ozbay (eds), *Yeni IstanbulCalismalari: Sinirlar, Mucadeleler, Acilimlar* (Istanbul, 2014).
Basaran, Oyman, 'You are Like a Virus: Dangerous Bodies and Military Medical Authority in Turkey', *Gender & Society* 28/4 (2014), pp. 562–82.
Basdas, Begum, 'Cosmopolitanism in the city: Contested claims to bodies and sexualities in Beyoglu, Istanbul'. Unpublished PhD dissertation, Department of Geography (University of California Los Angeles, 2007).
Bauman, Zygmunt and Tim Lay, *Thinking Sociologically* (Oxford, 2001).
Beachy, Robert, *Gay Berlin: Birthplace of a Modern Identity* (New York, 2015).
Bech, Henning, *When Men Meet: Homosexuality and Modernity* (Chicago, 1997).
Becker, Howard, *Outsiders: Studies in the Sociology of Deviance* (New York, 1963).
Bell, David, Jon Binnie, Ruth Holliday, Robyn Longhurst and Robin Peace, *Pleasure Zones: Bodies, Cities, Spaces* (Syracuse, 2001).
Bereket, Tarik and Barry D. Adam, 'The emergence of gay identities in contemporary Turkey', *Sexualities* 9 (2006), pp. 131–51.
——— 'Navigating Islam and Same-Sex Liaisons Among Men in Turkey', *Journal of Homosexuality* 55 (2008), pp. 204–22.
Berghan, Selin, *Lubunya: Transeksuel Beden ve Kimlik* (Istanbul, 2007).
Bernstein, Elizabeth, *Temporarily Yours: Intimacy, Authenticity, and the Commerce of Sex* (Chicago, 2007).
Betsky, Aaron, *Queer Space: Architecture and Same-Sex Desire* (London, 1997).
Bianet, 'Arinc'tan Vajina Monologlari', 12 December 2012, http://bianet.org/bianet/siyaset/142743-arinc-tan-vajina-monologlari, accessed on 12 January 2016.
Binnie, Jon, *The Globalization of Sexuality* (London, 2004).
Biricik, Alp, 'Rotten report and reconstructing hegemonic masculinity in Turkey', in Ozgur Heval Cinar and Coskun Usterci (eds), *Conscientious Objection: Resisting Militarized Society* (London, 2009).
Bora, Aksu, *Kadinlarin Sinifi: Ucretli Ev Emegi ve Kadin Oznelliginin Insaasi* (Istanbul, 2005).
Bouanchaud, Paul Alexander, 'Male Sex Work in China: Understanding the HIV Risk Environments of Shenzhen's Migrant Money Boys,' unpublished PhD dissertation (London School of Economics and Political Science, 2014).
Bourdieu, Pierre, *Acts of Resistance: Against the Tyranny of the Market* (New York, 1999).
——— 'The Forms of Capital', in Mark Granovetter and Richard Swedberg (eds), *The Sociology of Economic Life* (New York, 2001).
Brennan, Denise, *What's Love Got to Do with It?: Transnational Desires and Sex Tourism in the Dominican Republic* (Durham, 2004).
Buot, Francois, *Gay Paris: Une histoire du Paris interlope entre 1900 et 1940* (Paris, 2013).
Burawoy, Michael, 'Public Sociology vs. the Market', *Socio-Economic Review* 5 (2007), pp. 356–67.
Butler, Judith, *Bodies That Matter: On the Discursive Limits of 'Sex'* (New York, 1993).
——— *Gender Trouble: Feminism and the Subversion of Identity* (New York, 1999).
——— *Undoing Gender* (New York, 2004).
Byrne, David, *Social Exclusion* (Buckingham, 2005).

Cahn, Peter S., 'Consuming Class: multilevel marketers in neoliberal Mexico', *Cultural Anthropology* 23/3 (2008), pp. 429–52.
Cakirlar, Cuneyt and Serkan Delice (eds), *Cinsellik Muammasi: Turkiye'de Queer Kultur ve Muhalefet* (Istanbul, 2012).
Carrigan, Tim, Bob Connell and John Lee, 'Toward a New Sociology of Masculinity', *Theory and Society* 14/5 (1985), pp. 551–604.
Chauncey, George, *Gay New York: Gender, Urban Culture, and the Making of the Gay Male World, 1890–1940* (New York, 1995).
Chin, Christine B. N., *Cosmopolitan Sex Workers: Women and Migration in a Global City* (Oxford, 2013).
Chisholm, Diane, *Queer Constellations: Subcultural Space In The Wake Of The City* (Minneapolis, 2004).
Clarkson, Jay, 'Everyday Joe versus "pissy, bitchy, queens": Gay masculinity on straightacting.com', *Journal of Men's Studies* 14/2 (2006), pp. 191–207.
Cleaver, Frances (ed.), *Masculinities Matter: Men, Gender and Development* (London, 2002).
Clough, Patricia Ticineto and Jean Halley (eds), *The Affective Turn: Theorizing the Social* (Durham, 2007).
Collins, Patricia Hill, 'Learning from the outsider within', *Social Problems* 33/6 (1986), pp. 14–32.
——— *Black Feminist Thought: Knowledge, Consciousness and the Politics of Empowerment* (New York, 2008).
——— and Sirma Bilge, *Intersectionality* (Cambridge, 2016).
Collinson, David, *Managing the Shop Floor: Subjectivity, Masculinity and Workplace Culture* (Berlin, 1992).
Connell, R. W., *Gender and Power: Society, the Person and Sexual Politics* (Stanford, 1987).
——— *Masculinities* (Berkeley and Los Angeles, 1995).
——— 'Globalization and Masculinities', *Men and Masculinities* 1/1 (1998).
——— *The Men and the Boys* (Berkeley and Los Angeles, 2000).
——— 'Globalization, Imperialism and Masculinities', in Michael Kimmel, Jeff Hearn and R. W. Connell (eds), *Handbook of Studies of Men & Masculinities* (Thousand Oaks, 2005).
——— 'Two Cans of Paint: A Transsexual Life Story, with Reflections on Gender Change and History', *Sexualities* 13 (2010), p. 3.
——— *Confronting Equality: Gender, Knowledge and Global Change* (Cambridge, 2011).
——— and James W. Messerschmidt, 'Hegemonic Masculinity: Rethinking the Concept', *Gender & Society* 19/6 (2005), pp. 829–59.
——— and Julian Wood, 'Globalization and Business Masculinities', *Men and Masculinities* 7/4 (2005), pp. 347–64.
Cooper, Marianne, 'Being the "Go-To Guy": Fatherhood, Masculinity and the Organization of Work in Silicon Valley', *Qualitative Sociology* 23/4 (2000), pp. 379–405.
Cornwall, Andrea, Jerker Edstrom and Alan Graig (eds), *Men and Development: Politicizing Masculinities* (London, 2012).
Cruz-Malave, A. and Martin F. Manalansan (eds), *Queer Globalizations: Citizenship and the Afterlife of Colonialism* (New York, 2002).
Dean, Tim, *Unlimited Intimacy: Reflections on the Subculture of Barebacking* (Chicago, 2009).

Decena, Carlos Ulises, *Tacit Subjects: Belonging and Same-Sex Desire Among Dominican Immigrant Men* (Durham, 2011).
Delany, Samuel R., *Times Square Red, Times Square Blue* (New York, 1999).
D'Emilio, John, *Sexual Politics, Sexual Communities* (Chicago, 1998).
Demirtas, Neslihan and Sema Sen, 'Varos Identity: The Redefinition of Low Income Settlements in Turkey', *Middle Eastern Studies* 43/1 (2007), pp. 87–106.
Desroches, Frederic J., 'Tearoom Trade: A Research Update', *Qualitative Sociology* 13/1 (1990), pp. 39–61.
Dorais, Michel, *Rent Boys: The World of Male Sex Workers* (Montreal, 2005).
Dowsett, Gary W., *Practicing Desire: Homosexual Sex in the Era of AIDS* (Stanford, 1996).
———, H. Sharif Williams, Ana Ventuneac and Alec Carballo-Dieguez, 'Taking it like a man: Masculinity and barebacking online', *Sexualities* 11/1–2 (2008), pp. 121–41.
Duncan, Nancy (ed.), *BodySpace: Destabilising Geographies of Gender and Sexuality* (London, 1996).
Edelman, Lee, *No Future: Queer theory and the Death Drive* (Durham, 2005).
Edmonds, Alexander, *Pretty Modern: Beauty, Sex, and Plastic Surgery in Brazil* (Durham, 2010).
Edwards, Tim, *Cultures of Masculinity* (London, 2006).
Elias, James E., Vern L. Bullough, Veronica Elias and Gwen Brewer (eds), *Prostitution: On Whores, Hustlers, and Johns* (New York, 1998).
Erdogan, Necmi (ed.), *Yoksulluk Halleri: 'Turkiye'de Kent Yoksullugun Toplumsal Gorunumleri* (Istanbul, 2007).
Erman, Tahire, 'Gecekondu Calismalarinda Oteki Olarak Gecekondulu Kurgulari', *European Journal of Turkish Studies* 1 (2004), http://www.ejts.org/document85.html, accessed 15 June 2010.
Etoz, Zehra, 'Varos: Bir Istila, bir tehdit', *Birikim* 132 (2000): pp. 49–53.
Faderman, Lilian and Stuart Timmons, *Gay L. A.: A History of Sexual Outlaws, Power Politics, and Lipstick Lesbians* (Berkeley and Los Angeles, 2009).
Fajardo, Kale Bantigue, *Filipino Crosscurrents: Oceanographies of Seafaring, Masculinities and Globalization* (Minneapolis, 2011).
Farrer, James, *Opening Up: Youth Sex Culture and Market Reform in Shanghai* (Chicago, 2002).
Fenstermaker, Sarah and Candace West (eds), *Doing Gender, Doing Difference: Inequality, Power, and Institutional Change* (New York, 2002).
Fernandez-Davila, P., Ximena Salazar, Carlos F. Cáceres, Andre Maiorana, Susan Kegeles, Thomas J. Coates and Josefa Martinez, 'Compensated sex and sexual risk: Sexual, social, and economic interactions between homosexually- and heterosexually-identified men of low income in two cities of Peru', *Sexualities* 11/3 (2008), pp. 352–74.
Freeman, Carla, *Entrepreneurial Selves: Neoliberal Respectability and the Making of a Caribbean Middle Class* (Durham, 2014).
Freeman, Elizabeth, *Time Binds: Queer Temporalities, Queer Histories* (Durham, 2010).
Gallier, John F., Wayne Brekhus and David P. Keys, *Laud Humphreys: Prophet of Homosexuality and Sociology* (Madison, 2004).
Gambetti, Zeynep and Joost Jongerden (eds), *The Kurdish Issue in Turkey: A Spatial Perspective* (London, 2015).
Ghoussoub, M. and Emma Sinclair-Webb (eds), *Imagined Masculinities: Male Identity and Culture in the Modern Middle East* (London, 2000).

Godelier, Maurice, 'What is a sexual act?', *Anthropological Theory* 3/2 (2003), pp. 179–98.
Goldstein, Donna M., *Laughter Out of Place: Race, Class, Violence, and Sexuality in a Rio Shantytown* (Berkeley and Los Angeles, 2003).
Goral, Ozgur Sevgi, 'Urban Anxieties and Kurdish Migrants: Urbanity, Belonging, and Resistance in Istanbul', in Cenk Ozbay et al. (eds), *The Making of Neoliberal Turkey* (Aldershot, 2016)
Gordon, Avery F., *Ghostly Matters: Haunting and the Sociological Imagination* (Minneapolis, 1997).
Gould, Deborah, *Moving Politics: Emotion and the ACT UP's Fight against AIDS* (Durham, 2009).
Grant, Melissa Gira, *Playing the Whore: The Work of Sex Work* (London, 2014).
Green, Adam Isaiah, 'Queer theory and Sociology: Locating the Subject and the Self in Sexuality Studies', *Sociological Theory* 25/1 (2007), pp. 26–45.
—— 'The Social Organization of Desire: The Sexual Fields Approach', *Sociological Theory* 26/1 (2008), pp. 25–50.
—— (ed.) *Sexual Fields: Toward a Sociology of Collective Sexual Life* (Chicago, 2013).
Gregory, Steven, *The Devil Behind the Mirror: Globalization and Politics in the Dominican Republic* (Berkeley and Los Angeles, 2007).
Guttmann, Matthew C., *The Meanings of Macho: Being a Man in Mexico City* (Berkeley and Los Angeles, 1996).
Halberstam, Judith, *Female Masculinity* (Durham, 1998).
—— *In a Queer Time and Place: Transgender Bodies, Subcultural Lives* (New York, 2005).
—— 'The Anti-Social Turn in Queer Studies', *Graduate Journal of Social Science* 5/2 (2008).
Hall, Timothy M., 'Rent-boys, barflies, and kept men: Men involved in sex with men for compensation in Prague', *Sexualities* 10/4 (2007), pp. 457–72.
Halperin, David, *Saint Foucault: Towards a Gay Hagiography* (Oxford, 1995).
Hammers, Corie J., 'Making space for an agentic sexuality? The examination of a lesbian/queer bathhouse', *Sexualities* 11/5 (2008), pp. 547–72.
Hancock, Ange-Marie, *Intersectionality: An Intellectual History* (Oxford, 2016).
Harding, Sandra (ed.), *The Feminist Standpoint Theory Reader: Intellectual and Political Controversies* (New York, 2003).
Harvey, David, *A Brief History of Neoliberalism* (Oxford, 2007).
Healey, Murray, *Gay Skins: Class, Masculinity, and Queer Appropriation* (London, 1996).
Hewitt, Andrew, *Social Choreography: Ideology as Performance in Dance and Everyday Movement* (Durham, 2005).
Higgs, David, *Queer Sites: Gay Urban Histories Since 1600* (London, 1999).
Hindess, Barry, 'Neo-liberal Citizenship', *Citizenship Studies* 6/2 (2002), pp. 127–43.
Hocaoglu, Murat, *Escinsel Erkekler: Yirmi Bes Taniklik* (Istanbul, 2002).
Houlbrook, Matt, *Queer London: Perils and Pleasures in the Sexual Metropolis, 1918–1957* (Chicago, 2006).
Humphreys, Laud, *Tearoom Trade: Impersonal Sex in Public Places* (London, 1970).
Ingraham, Chrys, *Thinking Straight: The Power, Promise and Paradox of Heterosexuality* (New York, 2004).
Ingram, Gordon Brent, Anne-Marie Bouthillette and Yolanda Retter (eds), *Queers in Space: Communities, Public Spaces, Sites of Resistance* (San Francisco, 1997).

Irwin, Katherine, 'Into the Dark Heart of Ethnography: The Lived Ethics and Inequality of Intimate Field Relationships', *Qualitative Sociology* 29/2 (2006), pp. 155–75.
Itiel, Joseph, *A Consumer's Guide to Male Hustlers* (New York, 2014).
Iyinam, Sebnem, 'Varos Cocuklari Daha Iyi Sevisir', *Hurriyet*, 29 December 2001.
Jackson, Cecile, *Men at Work: Labour, Masculinities and Development* (London, 2001).
Jackson, Peter and Gerard Sullivan (eds), *Lady Boys, Tom Boys. Rent Boys: Male and Female Homosexualities in Contemporary Thailand* (New York, 1999).
Joseph, Suad (ed.), *Intimate Selving in Arab Families: Gender, Self, and Identity* (Syracuse, 1999).
Kandiyoti, Deniz, 'Introduction: Reading the fragments', in Deniz Kandiyoti and Ayse Saktanber (eds), *Fragments of Culture: The Everyday of Modern Turkey* (London, 2002).
——— 'Pink Card Blues: Trouble and Strife at the Crossroads of Gender', in Deniz Kandiyoti and Ayse Saktanber (eds), *Fragments of Culture: The Everyday of Modern Turkey* (London, 2002).
Kanna, Ahmed, 'Flexible Citizenship in Dubai: Neoliberal Subjectivity in the Emerging 'City-Corporation'', *Cultural Anthropology* 25/1 (2010), pp. 100–29.
Kara, Siddarth, *Sex Trafficking: Inside the Business of Modern Slavery* (New York, 2010).
Karakas, Burcu and Bawer Cakir, *Erkeklik Ofsayta Dusunce: Futbol, Escinsellik ve Halil Ibrahim Dincdag'in Hikayesi* (Istanbul, 2013).
Kaspar, Heidi & Sara Landolt, 'Flirting in the Field: shifting positionalities and power relations in innocuous sexualisations of research encounters', *Gender, Place & Culture* 23/1 (2016), pp. 107–19.
Katz, Jonathan Ned, *The Invention of Heterosexuality* (Chicago, 2007).
Kaye, Kerwin, 'Male Prostitution in the Twentieth Century: Pseudohomosexuals, Hoodlum Homosexuals, and Exploited Teens', *Journal of Homosexuality* 46 (2003), pp. 1–77.
Kempadoo, Kamala and Jo Doezema (eds), *Global Sex Workers: Rights, Resistance, and Redefinition* (New York, 1998).
Kessler, Suzanne J., *Lessons from the Intersexed* (New Brunswick, 2002).
Keyder, Caglar, 'Globalization and social exclusion in Istanbul', *International Journal of Urban and Regional Research* 29/1 (2005), pp. 124–34.
——— (ed.), *Istanbul: Between the Global and the Local* (Boston, 1999).
Kipnis, Laura, 'Feminism: The Political Conscience of Postmodernism?', in Andrew Ross (ed.), *Universal Abandon? The Politics of Postmodernism* (Minneapolis, 1988).
Kocu, Resat Ekrem, *Istanbul Ansiklopedisi* (Istanbul, 1946).
Kulick, Don, *Travesti: Sex, Gender and Culture among Brazilian Transgendered Prostitutes* (Chicago, 1998).
——— and Margaret Wilson (eds), *Taboo: Sex, Identity and Erotic Subjectivity in Anthropological Fieldwork* (New York, 1995).
Lambevski, Alexander S., 'Suck My Nation: Masculinity, Ethnicity, and the Politics of (Homo)sex', *Sexualities* 2/4 (1999), pp. 397–419.
Lancaster, Roger N., *Life is Hard: Machismo, Danger and the Power of Intimacy in Nicaragua* (Berkeley and Los Angeles, 1994).
Lenza, Michael, 'Controversies Surrounding Laud Humphreys' Tearoom Trade: An unsettling example of politics and power in methodological critiques', *International Journal of Sociology and Social Policy* 24/3–4–5 (2004), pp. 20–31.

Lerum, Kari, 'Subjects of Desire: Academic Armor, Intimate Ethnography, and the Production of Critical Knowledge', *Qualitative Inquiry* 7/4 (2001), pp. 466–83.
Lewin, Ellen and William L. Leap (eds), *Out in the Field: Reflections of Lesbian and Gay Anthropologists* (Urbana-Champaign, 1996).
Linde, Charlotte, *Life Stories: The Creation of Coherence* (Oxford, 1993).
Low, Setha (ed.), *Theorizing the City* (New Brunswick, 1999).
Mackay, John Henry, *The Hustler: The Story of a Nameless Love from Friedrichstrasse* (San Bernardino, 2002).
Magden, Perihan, *Two Girls* (London, 2006).
—— *Ali and Ramazan* (Las Vegas, 2012).
Mai, Nicola, 'Surfing Liquid Modernity: Albanian and Romanian Male Sex Workers in Europe', in Peter Aggleton and Richard Parker (eds), *Men Who Sell Sex: Global Perspectives* (New York, 2015).
Manalansan, Martin F., *Global Divas: Filipino Gay Men in the Diaspora* (Durham, 2003).
Markovitz, Fran and Michael Askhenazi (eds), *Sex, Sexuality and the Anthropologist* (Urbana-Champaign, 1999).
Mater, Nadire, *Mehmedin Kitabi: Guneydogu'da Savasmis Askerler Anlatiyor* (Istanbul, 1998).
May, Vivian M., *Pursuing Intersectionality, Unsettling Dominant Imaginaries* (London, 2015).
McCall, Leslie, 'The Complexity of Intersectionality', *Signs* 30/3 (2005), pp. 1771–800.
McDowell, Linda, *Redundant Masculinities: Employment Change and White Working Class Youth* (Oxford, 2003).
McNamara, Robert P., *The Times Square Hustler: Male Prostitution in New York City* (New York, 1994).
Merabet, Sofian, *Queer Beirut* (Austin, 2014).
Migdal, Joel S. 'Finding the Meeting Ground of Fact and Fiction: Some Reflections on Turkish Modernization', in Sibel Bozdogan and Resat Kasaba (eds), *Rethinking Modernity and National Identity in Turkey* (Seattle, 1997).
Minichiello, Victor, Rodrigo Marino, Jan Browne, Maggie Jamieson, Krik Peterson, Brad Reuter and Kenn Robinson, 'Male sex workers in three Australian cities: Socio-demographic and sex work characteristics', *Journal of Homosexuality* 42/1 (2001), pp. 29–51.
—— and John Scott (eds), *Male Sex Work and Society* (New York, 2014).
Mitchell, Gregory, *Tourist Attractions: Performing Race & Masculinity in Brazil's Sexual Economy* (Chicago, 2016).
Morrison, Todd G. and Bruce W. Whitehad (eds), *Male Sex Work: A Business Doing Pleasure* (New York, 2007).
Mujtaba, Hasan,'The other side of midnight: Pakistani male prostitutes', in Stephen O. Murray and Will Roscoe (eds), *Islamic Homosexualities: Culture, History, and Literature* (New York, 1997), pp. 267–74.
Murray, Stephen O., *Latin American Male Homosexualities* (Albuquerque, 1995).
—— 'The Will not to Know: Islamic Accommodations of Male Homosexuality', in Stephen O. Murray and Will Roscoe (eds), *Islamic Homosexualities: Culture, History, and Literature* (New York, 1997), pp. 14–54.
Nagle, Jill (ed.), *Whores and Other Feminists* (New York, 1997).

Nardi, Peter M. 'The Breastplate of Righteousness: Twenty-Five Years After Laud Humphreys' Tearoom Trade: Impersonal Sex in Public Places', *Journal of Homosexuality* 30/2 (1995), pp. 1–10.

———— and Beth E. Schneider (eds), *Social Perspectives in Lesbian and Gay Studies: A Reader* (New York, 1998).

Oncu, Ayse, 'Istanbulites and Others: The Cultural Cosmology of 'Middleness' in the Era of Neoliberalism', in Caglar Keyder (ed.), *Istanbul: Between the Local and the Global* (Boston, 1999).

———— 'Consumption, Gender and The Mapping of Istanbul in the 1990s', in Deniz Kandiyoti and Ayse Saktanber (eds), *Fragments of Culture: The Everyday of Modern Turkey* (London, 2002).

Ong, Aihwa, *Flexible Citizenship: The Cultural Logics of Transnationality* (Durham, 1999).

———— *Neoliberalism as Exception: Mutations in Citizenship and Sovereignty* (Durham, 2006).

Orhan, Mehmet, *Political Violence and Kurds in Turkey: Fragmentations, Mobilizations, Participations & Repertoires* (London, 2015).

Ouzgane, Lahoucine (ed.), *Islamic Masculinities* (London, 2006).

Oz, Yasemin, 'Ahlaksizlarin Merkansal Dislanmasi', in Ayten Alkan (ed.), *Cins Cins Mekan* (Istanbul, 2009).

Ozbay, Cenk, 'Virilities for rent: Navigating masculinity, sexuality and class in Istanbul'. Unpublished MA thesis (Bogazici University, 2005).

———— 'Queer Kral', *Radikal Iki*, 27 September 2009.

———— 'Nocturnal Queers: Rent Boys' Masculinity in Istanbul', *Sexualities* 13/5 (2010a), pp. 645–63.

———— 'Neoliberalizm ve Erkekligin Halleri', in Armagan Ozturk, *Yeni Sag, Yeni Sol* (Ankara, 2010b).

———— 'Neoliberal Erkekligin Sosyoljisine Dogru: Rent Boylar Ornegi', in Cenk Ozbay, Aysecan Terzioglu and Yesim Yasin (eds), *Neoliberalizm ve Mahremiyet: Turkiye'de Beden, Saglik ve Cinsellik* (Istanbul, 2011).

———— 'Rent Boylarin Queer Oznelligi: Istanbul'da Norm Karsiti Zaman, Mekan, Cinsellik ve Sinifsallik', in Cuneyt Cakirlar and Serkan Delice (eds), *Cinsellik Muammasi: Turkiye'de Queer Kultur ve Muhalefet* (Istanbul, 2012a).

———— 'Sexuality', in A. L. Stanton (ed.), *Cultural sociology of the Middle East, Asia, and Africa* (London, 2012b).

———— 'Same-sex Sexualities in Turkey', in J. D. Wright (ed.), *The International Encyclopedia of Social and Behavioral Sciences* (Amsterdam, 2015a).

———— 'Men Are Less Manly, Women Are More Feminine: Shopping Mall as a Site for Gender Crisis in Istanbul', in Gul Ozyegin (ed.), *Gender and Sexuality in Muslim Cultures* (Surrey, 2015b), pp. 73–94.

———— 'Hızlı, Ofkeli, Demokratik: Erkeklik ve Direnisin Yeni Grameri', in Efsun Sertoglu, *Cinselligi ve Rolleri ile Guclu Erkeklik* (Istanbul, 2015c), pp. 27–41.

———— 'Inarticulate, Self-Vigilant and Egotistical: Masculinity in Turkish Drawn Stories', in Cenk Ozbay, Maral Erol, Aysecan Terizoglu and Umut Turem (eds), *The Making of Neoliberal Turkey* (Aldershot, 2016), pp. 87–110.

———— and Serdar Soydan, *Escinsel Kadinlar: Yirmi Dort Taniklik* (Istanbul, 2003).

———— Aysecan Terzioglu and Yesim Yasin (eds), *Neoliberalizm ve Mahremiyet: Turkiye'de Beden, Saglik ve Cinsellik* (Istanbul, 2011).

―――― Maral Erol, Aysecan Terizoglu and Umut Turem (eds), *The Making of Neoliberal Turkey* (Aldershot, 2016).

Ozbay, Ferhunde (2011) 'Istanbulun Nufusu', in Murat Guvenc (ed.), *Eski Istanbullular & Yeni Istanbullular* (Istanbul, 2011), pp. 54–77.

Oztek, Aydin, 'Turk Sinemasinda Escinsellik', *Kaos GL* 52 (2007).

Ozyegin, Gul, *Untidy Gender: Domestic Work in Turkey* (Philadelphia, 2001).

―――― 'The Doorkeeper, The Maid and the Tenant: Troubling Encounters in the Turkish Urban Landscape', in Deniz Kandiyoti and Ayse Saktanber (eds), *Fragments of Culture: The Everyday of Modern Turkey* (London, 2002).

―――― 'Arzunun Nesnesi Olmak: Romans, Kırılgan Erkeklik ve Neoliberal Ozne', in Cenk Ozbay, Aysecan Terizoglu and Yesim Yasin (eds), *Neoliberalizm ve Mahremiyet: Turkiye'de Beden, Saglik ve Cinsellik* (Istanbul, 2011).

―――― 'Reading the closet through connectivity', *Social Identities* 18 (2012), pp. 201–22.

―――― *New Desires, New Selves: Sex, Love and Piety Among Turkish Youth* (New York, 2015a).

―――― *Gender and Sexuality in Muslim Cultures* (Aldershot, 2015b).

Paap, Kris, *Working Construction: Why White Working-Class Men Put Themselves – and the Labor Movement – In Harm's Way* (Ithaca, 2006).

Padilla, Mark, *Caribbean Pleasure Industry: Tourism, Sexuality, and AIDS in the Dominican Republic* (Chicago, 2007).

Parker, Richard, *Beneath the Equator: Cultures of Desire, Male Homosexuality and Emerging Gay Communities in Brazil* (New York, 1999).

Penttinen, Elina, *Globalization, Prostitution and Sex Trafficking: Corporeal Politics* (New York, 2007).

Pettiway, Leon, *Honey, Money, Miss Thang: Being Black, Gay and on the Streets* (Philadelphia, 1996).

Pini, Barbara and Bob Pease (eds), *Men, Masculinities and Methodologies* (Hampshire, 2013).

Plummer, Ken, (ed.), *Modern Homosexualities: Fragments of Lesbian and Gay Experiences* (London, 1992).

―――― *Telling Sexual Stories: Power, Change and Social Worlds* (London, 1995).

―――― 'Male Sexualities', in Michael Kimmel, Jeff Hearn and R. W. Connell (eds), *Handbook of Studies On Men and Masculinities* (Thousand Oaks and London, 2005), pp. 178–95.

Povinelli, Elizabeth A. and Chauncey George, 'Thinking sexuality transnationally', *GLQ* 5/4 (1999), pp. 439–50.

Reiss, Albert J. Jr., 'The Social Integration of Queers and Peers', *Social Problems* 9/2 (1961), pp. 102–20.

Ridder-Wiskerke, Marieke and Peter Aggleton, 'Lifestyle, Work or Easy Money? Male Sex Work in the Netherlands Today', in Peter Aggleton and Richard Parker (eds), *Men Who Sell Sex: Global Perspectives* (New York, 2015).

Rofel, Lisa, *Desiring China: Experiments in Neoliberalism, Sexuality and Public Culture* (Durham, 2007).

Rose, Nikolas, *Governing the Soul: The Shaping of the Private Self* (New York, 1999).

Safak, Elif, *Pinhan* (Istanbul, 2007).

Sakalli, Nuray and Ozanser Ugurlu, 'The Effects of Social Contact with a Lesbian Person on the Attitude Change Toward Homosexuality in Turkey', *Journal of Homosexuality* 44/1 (2002), pp. 111–9.

Sancar, Serpil, *Erkeklik: Imkansiz Iktidar* (Istanbul, 2009).
Sanders, Teela, Maggie O'Neill and Jane Pitcher, *Prostitution: Sex Work, Policy and Politics* (London, 2009).
Saracoglu, Cenk, *Kurds of Modern Turkey: Migration, Neoliberalism and Exclusion in Turkish Society* (London, 2010).
Sarioglu, Esra, 'New Imaginaries of Gender in Turkey's Service Economy: Women Workers and Identity Making on the Sales Floor', *Women's Studies International Forum* 54 (2016), pp. 39–47.
Savci, Evren, 'Queer in Translation: Paradoxes of Westernization and Sexual Others in the Turkish Nation.' Unpublished PhD thesis (Department of Sociology, University of Southern California, 2011).
Schifter, Jacobo, *Lila's House: Male Prostitution in Latin America* (New York, 1998).
Sedgwick, Eve Kosofsky, *Between Men: English Literature and Male Homosexual Desire* (New York, 1986).
Seidler, Victor J., *Transforming Masculinities: Men, Cultures, Bodies, Power, Sex and Love* (London, 2006).
Seidman, Steven, *The Social Construction of Sexuality* (New York, 2009).
Shah, Svati P., *Street Corner Secrets: Sex, Work and Migration in the City of Mumbai* (Durham, 2014).
Sirman, Nukhet, 'The Making of Familial Citizenship in Turkey', in Ahmet Icduygu and Fuat Keyman (eds), *Citizenship in a Global World – European Questions and Turkish Experiences* (New York, 2005).
Smith, Michael D. and Christian Grov, *In the Company of Men: Inside the Lives of Male Prostitutes* (New York, 2011).
Somer, Mehmet Murat, *The Prophet Murders: A Hop-Ciki-Yaya Thriller* (London, 2008).
——— *The Jigolo Murder: A Turkish Delight Mystery* (London, 2009).
Spade, Joan Z. and Catherine G. Valentine (eds), *The Kaleidoscope of Gender: Prisms, Patterns, and Possibilities* (London, 2013).
Sterry, David Henry, *Chicken: Self-Portrait of a Young Man for Rent* (New York, 2002).
Steward, Sam, *Understanding the Male Hustler* (New York, 2014).
Stout, Noelle M., *After Love: Queer Intimacy and Erotic Economies in Post-Soviet Cuba* (Durham, 2014).
Stryker, Susan and Jim Van Buskirk, *Gay by the Bay: A History of Queer Culture in the San Francisco Bay Area* (San Francisco, 1996).
——— and Stephen Whittle (eds), *The Transgender Studies Reader* (New York, 2006).
Sunbuloglu, Nurseli Yesim (ed.), *Erkek Millet, Asker Millet: Turkiyede Militarism, Milliyetcilik ve Erkeklikler* (Istanbul, 2013).
Tapinc, Huseyin, 'Masculinity, femininity and Turkish male homosexuality', in Ken Plummer (ed.), *Modern Homosexualities: Fragments of Lesbian and Gay Experiences* (London, 1992), pp. 39–50.
Tarhan, Mehmet, 'Zorunlu Askerlik ve Sivil Alternatif Hizmete Direnis Olarak Vicdani Red', in Nil Mutluer (ed.), *Cinsiyet Halleri* (Istanbul, 2008).
Tas, Birkan, 'Adam gibi adam olamamak: Ayi hareketi ve maskulenlik uzerine', in Cuneyt Cakirlar and Serkan Delice (eds), *Cinsellik Muammasi: Turkiye'de Queer Kultur ve Muhalefet* (Istanbul, 2012).
Thorne, Barrie, *Gender Play: Boys and Girls in School* (New Brunswick, 1993).
'Toplum ve Bilim' in *Erkeklik*, edited by Semih Sokmen, No: 101 (Istanbul: Birikim).

Turker, Yildirim, 'Bu Sehir Kimin?', *Radikal Iki*, 24 April 2005.
Van Hoven, Bettina and Louise Meijering, 'Transient Masculinities: Indian IT Workers in Germany', in Kathrin Hörschelmann and Bettina van Hoven (eds), *Spaces of Masculinities* (London, 2004).
Wacquant, Loic, *Urban Outcasts: A Comparative Sociology of Advanced Marginality* (Cambridge, 2008).
Walby, Kevin, *Touching Encounters: Sex, Work and Male-to-Male Internet Escorting* (Chicago, 2012).
Ward, Jane, *Not Gay: Sex Between Straight White Men* (New York, 2015).
Warner, Michael, 'Publics and Counterpublics', *Public Culture* 14/1 (2002), pp. 49–90.
Weeks, Jeffrey, 'Inverts, perverts, and Mary-Annes: Male prostitution and the regulation of homosexuality in the nineteenth and early twentieth centuries,' *Journal of Homosexuality* 6/1–2 (1981), pp. 113–34.
———, *Sexuality and Its Discontents: Meanings, Myths and Modern Sexualities* (London, 1990).
West, Candace and Don Zimmerman, 'Doing Gender', *Gender & Society* 1/1 (1987).
West, Donald, *Male Prostitution* (New York, 2012).
Whitaker, Rick, *Assuming the Position: A Memoir of Hustling* (New York and London, 1999).
White, Edmund, *The Flaneur: A Stroll Through the Paradoxes of Paris* (New York, 2001).
White, Jenny, *Money Makes Us Relatives* (New York, 2004).
Williams, Christine L. *Still a Man's World: Men Who Do Women's Work* (Berkeley and Los Angeles, 1995).
——— and Catherine Connell, 'Looking Good and Sounding Right: Aesthetic Labor and Social Inequality in the Retail Industry,' *Work and Occupations* 37/3 (2010), pp. 349–77.
Williams, Erica Lorraine, *Sex Tourism in Bahia: Ambiguous Entanglements* (Urbana, 2013).
Wilson, Ava, *The Intimate Economies of Bangkok: Tomboys, Tycoons and Avon Ladies in the Global City* (Los Angeles and Berkeley, 2004).
Wright, Les, 'Introduction to 'queer' masculinities', *Men and Masculinities* 7/3 (2005), pp. 243–7.
Yazici, Berna, 'Towards an Anthropology of Traffic: A Ride Through Class Hierarchies on Istanbul's Roadways', *Ethnos* 78/4 (2013), pp. 515–42.
Yilmaz, Volkan and Ipek Gocmen, 'Denied Citizens of Turkey: Experiences of Discrimination Among LGBT Individuals in Employment, Housing, and Health Care', *Gender, Work & Occupation* 23 (2016).
Yuzgun, Aslan, *Turkiye'de Escinsellik: Dun ve Bugun* (Istanbul, 1986).
——— 'Homosexuality and police terror in Turkey', *Journal of Homosexuality* 24/3–4 (1993), pp. 159–69.
Zelizer, Viviana A., *The Purchase of Intimacy* (New Haven, 2007).
Zinn, Maxine Baca, Pierrette Hondagneu-Sotelo and Michael Messner (eds), *Gender Through the Prism of Difference* (Oxford, 2010).
Zorlu, Niyazi, *Hergele Asiklar* (Istanbul, 2003).

INDEX

Affect, 16, 18, 36–7, 78, 92, 104
Alcohol, 2, 60, 71
  alcoholic beverages, 53, 59, 79
Ankara, 20,
Army, 18–19, 42, 79, 126
Asena, Duygu, 20
Ataman, Kutlug, 21
Atomic, 137, 140, 176

Besiktas (district), 135, 162
Beyoglu (district), 13, 21, 106, 160
Bientot, 5, 24, 59–60, 71, 131, 171
Boogie (bar), 59
Bosnian (men), 36
Bourdieu, Pierre, 10
Brothel, 32
Bulgarian (men), 36
Butler, Judith, 49, 109, 125, 169, 170

Candan, Can, 21
Capital, 37, 69, 108
  cultural, 17, 65, 67, 117, 122, 130
  forms of, 34, 115
  gendered, 96
  human, 100, 102
  symbolic, 112
City, the, 1, 5–9, 17, 21, 25, 28, 33–4, 46–7, 57–60, 65–7, 96–8, 100, 107, 111–12, 116, 122–4, 126–7, 130–1, 136, 146, 150–1, 158–9
Cologne, 45, 53, 60, 74–6, 121, 129
Connell, Raewyn, 70, 87–90, 92–3, 115
Consumerism, 17, 153
Consumption, 131
  spaces of, 158

Dating websites, 2, 15
Deindustrialisation, 8
Delikanli, 55, 154
Delikanlilik, 8–10
Deterritorrialisation, 137
Drugs, 2, 62, 79–80

Economy
  erotic, 56, 80, 90, 99, 112, 144, 151, 153–4
  intimate, 6, 28, 136
Embodiment, 10, 66, 80, 82, 102, 107, 124, 168,
Eroticism, 4, 16, 78, 86, 92, 100, 103
Eroticisation, 35
Ersoy, Bulent, 13
Escort, 23, 50, 107, 132, 134, 138–40, 142, 157, 163
Ethnography, 27

Foucault, Michel, 12

Gay culture
  global, 83
  homonormative, 65–6
  in Turkey, 43, 72, 153, 175
  urban, 14
  western, 33, 64, 69
Gentrification, 1, 59, 119, 159
Gifts, 45, 74–5, 125, 127
Globalisation, 14, 23, 27, 34, 66, 70, 83, 93, 151

Heteronormativity, 20, 25, 39, 41, 83, 95, 103, 107, 109, 114, 122, 124, 132–3, 149, 151
Heterosexuality, 16, 38–9, 41, 68, 71–2, 78, 83, 89–90, 95, 99, 103, 107, 109, 110, 113, 115–16, 120, 129, 132, 176
HIV/AIDS, 13, 19, 81, 140, 171
Homosexuality, 4, 11–19, 32, 38, 66, 95, 99–100, 103, 110, 116, 118, 122, 125, 149
Homonormativity, 117, 122, 133
Homophobia, 5, 14, 20–1, 68, 118, 126, 147, 149, 165
Humphrey, Laud, 26–7

Identity, 9, 16, 56, 65, 71, 90, 141
  categories of, 26
  class, 102, 122
  construction, 28, 89, 108–9
  formation, 114, 133
  gay, 66, 72, 98, 116–18
  gender, 7, 10, 36, 83, 87–8, 92, 94, 102, 124
  heteronormative, 36
  homosexual, 12, 64
  Kurdish, 9, 35, 165
  public, 150
  queer, 110
  self-, 27, 107, 152
  sexual, 17, 33, 39, 42, 102, 107, 114, 118, 124, 149, 152
  slum, 101
  social, 15, 39, 66
  urban, 9
Immigration, 12
Intimacy, 17, 24, 27, 39–40, 50, 54, 60, 77–8, 86, 92, 100, 102–4, 117, 127, 134, 157, 162
Islam, 16–17, 19, 149
Istanbul, 2–8, 10, 12–13, 15, 20–1, 24–5, 27–8, 31, 33–4, 40, 42, 48, 50, 53, 56–61, 64–7, 69, 71–2, 74, 76, 81–3, 89, 91, 93, 97, 99, 101–4, 107–8, 110–17, 123–7, 129–34, 136–7, 140–6, 149, 152, 154
Istiklal Street, 21, 58–9, 75, 131, 171
Izmir, 12, 146

Kadikoy (district), 59, 139, 140
Kurdishness, 35
Kurds, 67, 169

Labour
  aesthetic, 34
  affective, 31, 34, 36–8
  deskilled, 6
  performative, 38
  process, 142
  relations of, 102, 146
  sexual, 98
Lesbians, 4, 15–17, 19–21, 60, 126
Lubunya, 18–19

Magden, Perihan, 20–21
Market, free, 93
Masculinity, 3, 8–9, 11–12, 17–18, 34, 36–41, 46–49, 55, 60, 62–3, 67–8, 74, 92, 97–8, 127, 151, 154, 169, 172
  exaggerated, 10, 27, 56, 64–5, 69, 71–2, 75, 77–8, 80–83, 90, 94, 102, 116, 120, 124, 128, 129, 131, 133, 139, 143, 150, 152, 168
  gay, 14, 91

hegemonic, 70, 82, 87–90, 93, 104, 115, 116
heterosexual (straight), 35–6, 38, 66, 69, 113–15, 117, 124
neoliberal, 28, 39, 91, 93–96, 152
Masculinity Studies, 32, 101, 103, 162, 164
Mass media, 24, 65, 86, 126
Men
heterosexual, 6, 42, 66, 116, 129,
Middle class, 18, 66–7, 71, 81, 85, 88, 99, 111, 113, 117, 122, 130–1, 133, 150–3, 169
Minority, 26, 98, 126
Alevi, 16
ethnic, 35
Mungan, Murathan, 14, 45–7
Murders, gay, 86
Muren, Zeki, 12, 13

NATO, 147
Neoliberalism, 91, 93, 102, 155
Neoliberalisation, 9, 27, 86, 92–94, 96,
Network
intimate, 77
kinship, 71, 83
queer, 81
social, 38, 89, 97, 118, 122, 127, 159
transnational, 147
urban, 58

Orientation
affective, 3
sexual, 7, 19, 39, 114, 176
Ozpetek, Ferzan, 14
Ozyegin, Gul, 40–1, 158

Planetromeo.com, 134, 142
Profit, 5, 8–9, 85, 153,
Prostitution
female, 30–1
homosexual, 64, 71, 150

male, 4, 24, 28–32, 38, 42, 44, 53, 56, 64–5, 69–71, 76–78, 100, 115, 125, 131, 137, 140, 142, 144, 146, 150–1, 157, 163–4, 172
queer, 32, 98
same-sex, 4
Power
relations of, 7, 32, 85, 87, 103, 113, 143
social, 54, 87, 92
Public
heterosexual, 16, 21, 100

Queer Studies, 110–11
Queer Theory, 50, 110

Race, 8, 48, 90–1, 168
Racialisation, 35–6
Rotten report, 18–19, 126

Safak, Elif, 21
Sariyer (district), 60, 62
Segregation
gender, 89
social, 10,
spatial, 7, 35
urban, 7, 67
SenGel, 5, 25, 59, 60, 62, 168
Sex
anal, 50, 131, 139–40
anonymous, 26
commercial, 6, 23–4, 27, 36, 137, 161
compensated, 31–2, 49, 64, 71, 82, 91, 98, 101, 113, 115, 124, 130–2, 134, 140, 144, 157
group, 139–40
oral, 5, 50, 52, 85, 139, 140
transactional, 4–6, 11, 24, 32, 34, 54, 58, 83–4, 91, 98, 104, 133, 135, 140
unprotected, 81, 82, 170
virtual, 138

Sex work
  female, 31–3, 58
  male, 3–5, 7, 25, 28, 31–2, 34, 36, 42–3, 46–7, 49, 52, 56–7, 61, 63, 66, 72–3, 86, 91, 93–4, 97–8, 106, 110, 114, 123, 125, 127, 129–33, 137–8, 140–4, 151–4, 157, 161, 163
  transgender, 28, 33, 80, 129, 171
Slums, 8, 85, 99, 102, 114, 119, 122–3
Smart phone applications, 2, 137
Somer, Mehmet Murat, 21
Sociology, 7, 27, 30, 71, 101, 110–11, 151, 164
  of sexualities, 110, 161, 164
Space
  domestic, 111
  gay, 66
  intimate, 100
  political, 167
  public, 8, 13, 22, 26, 57, 167–8
  quasi-public, 3, 24
  queer, 4, 20–1, 25, 64, 107, 112, 132, 152
  sexual, 116
  social, 7, 14, 16, 64, 158
  urban, 3, 21, 58, 96, 110, 131, 158
Subjectivity
  erotic, 17, 68, 161

neoliberal, 9, 28, 86–7, 91, 94, 102, 122, 141–3, 151, 153, 166

Taksim Square, 1, 25, 57–8, 63, 78, 82, 97, 99, 105–6, 112–13, 127, 131, 137, 139, 167–68, 171
Top-only, 42–3, 50, 62, 66, 68, 82, 114, 119–20, 131, 138
Transgenderism, 13, 15, 149
Transnational flows, 23
Transsexuality, 18
Transvestites, 13, 18, 47, 52, 58, 59, 71, 80, 95, 119, 139, 173

Varos, 8–11, 17–19, 28, 43–4, 46–8, 56, 59, 65–8, 70–2, 74, 82–3, 85, 89, 91, 93, 99, 104, 112, 127, 129, 135, 143, 146, 152, 154, 158–9, 168–9

Whiteness, 35, 38
Working class, 88, 127, 131,
  background, 175
  bodies, 151
  neighbourhood, 5–6
  masculinity, 18
  men, 168
  people, 17

Zorlu, Niyazi, 21